GW01090289

When All This Is Over

JEAN MCLELLAN

 FriesenPress

One Printers Way
Altona, MB R0G0B0
Canada

www.friesenpress.com

Copyright © 2022 by Jean Mclellan
First Edition — 2022

Erin Wiebe & Lesley Wiebe, Editors
Megan Wiebe, Cover Artist

All places named are actual. Only first names, other than family, have been used to protect identity.

All rights reserved.

No part of this publication may be reproduced in any form, or by any means, electronic or mechanical, including photocopying, recording, or any information browsing, storage, or retrieval system, without permission in writing from FriesenPress.

ISBN
978-1-03-911105-9 (Hardcover)
978-1-03-911104-2 (Paperback)
978-1-03-911106-6 (eBook)

1. BIOGRAPHY & AUTOBIOGRAPHY, PERSONAL MEMOIRS

Distributed to the trade by The Ingram Book Company

Dedicated to my mother and father, my brother Roy, and to my best friend and confidant, my late husband, John.

All have now hung up their travelling boots, but were my companions at some stage of the journey.

Every child deserves to be taught by a teacher who truly cares about them, someone who ignites their imagination, someone who supports their life-long love of learning, someone who they will remember for the rest of their lives, and for me that teacher was Mrs. McLellan.

Mrs. McLellan taught me so much more than to read and write, she taught me to believe in myself, to be the person I am today. It is rare to find someone who has such a positive influence on your whole life. She ignited a spark within me that still burns- a passion to teach. From my first year in school, with her as my teacher, to my present position as deputy head teacher, Mrs. McLellan's influence has been key. I have always aspired to be the "Mrs. McLellan" to the children that I now teach and to have a positive impact on their lives like she has had on mine.

Karen Edwards
Deputy Head Teacher

Jean McLellan's account of her life, growing up in Mow Cop, marrying and growing a family, and training and working as a teacher, is illustrated by some very evocative photographs. Yet these pictorial images are nothing compared to the mental images which her writing conjures up. With an extraordinary and assured recall, she tells a story of childhood in a small cottage on the border of Staffordshire and Cheshire, in the shadow of the remarkable landmark which saw the birthplace of Primitive Methodism. From the outset, a down to earth, trusting and practical Christianity is the air which she breathes in, and which guides her throughout her life. The memories are always vivid, often entertaining, and sometimes terrifying – not least the annual visit of the school dentist. Occasionally a great sadness falls across her life: beginning at an early age, when she describes with evident pain the forcible removal to the workhouse of an elderly man, her next-door neighbour, all his few possessions unceremoniously carted out of the house. But the deepest lesson learned from that simple yet intense childhood is summed up in these words: 'We had very few treats and no luxuries, but the things we did have, we really appreciated'.

That sense of appreciation rings through clearly as the dominant note of Jean McLellan's life. Here is the autobiography of somebody who has lived life to the full, in close-knit community and in extended family, and who at the same time has explored with great freedom the inner life of the imagination and the spirit. And through it all is a full and persuasive assurance of faith. When Jean describes with great sadness her mother's death following an horrific car accident, she turns to the words of the Apostle Paul to write, simply: 'I thank God for every memory of you'. Just so, any reader of this wonderfully engaging narrative will want to thank God for every memory of its author.

Rt Revd Dr. Michael Ipgrave
Bishop of Lichfield, UK

I first met Jean back in 1987, just a few years before this book concludes. Beautifully written in a way that leaves you feeling that you are "right there" alongside Jean as she recounts her journey from being a small child on Mow Cop. Jean's evocative recollections, and heart-warming stories give insight, not only telling us of a time now gone, but how her husband-John, family, friends and faith formed and shaped the person who would go on to "change the nations", and also countless lives including mine. Enjoy this warm blanket of a book. I can't wait for its follow up!

David J Gotts
Founder, International China Concern

Contents

CHAPTER ONE

Early Days

Memory, like some old, forgotten masterpiece, becomes hazy with time—corners knocked off, edges ragged, and colours indistinct. Nevertheless, some things remain indelibly printed on the mind, memories of yesteryear that make up the fabric of who I am today. As I gaze at the landscape of my childhood, the overwhelming impression is one of security and safety: a carefree time of ease and freedom, of innocent friendships and sound family relationships. Warm summer days that stretched endlessly ahead, and cold winters that froze the windowpanes and clouded the breath.

My family—my haven of security—was made up of Dad, a traffic foreman at Shelton Iron & Steel Works, Mum, a housewife who occasionally cleaned for a neighbouring farmer and his wife, and my brother, Roy, who was four years older than me.

We lived in a small, semi-detached stone cottage. There was no electricity, no mod cons or luxurious trappings, but it was a place of comfort and familiarity. It comprised a living room and back kitchen on the first floor, while upstairs there were two small bedrooms. The only means of heating and cooking was a large, coal-burning black kitchen range, made up of a central fireplace, a side oven, hobs, and a mantlepiece. The ashes needed shovelling out daily, while the rest of the range was treated to an energetic black leading every Saturday morning. A large oil lamp—which had pride of place on the sturdy, wooden table in the middle of the living room—provided the light for the whole of the bottom floor, while candles were used to light the way up the wooden stairs at the end of the day.

Quarry tiles covered the floor downstairs, terracotta in colour and cold to the touch. It was one of my mother's weekly tasks to kneel and scrub those tiles, a scrubbing brush and cloth and a bucket of hot, soapy water by her side. As I became old enough to help with household chores, I would be allotted a few tiles to clean, which gradually became a few more, and a few more, until I was considered capable enough to tackle the whole job.

To bring a little warmth and colour to the tiled floor, there was a large rug in front of the range and a small one by the door. These were handmade with a hessian sack (an old bag that had once contained potatoes, procured from the local grocers), which was "pegged." Pegging was an occupation that filled many a winter evening. Old coats, skirts, jackets, and trousers were painstakingly cut into small pieces, which were then pegged into the hessian with a small tool called a "pegger." The result was extremely colourful and warm on the toes, and it was a favourite game for us children to identify which piece had come from which garment: "Oh look, that's a bit of my green coat!" "Oh, Roy, there's a piece of your short trousers!"

The three most important things in the living room were the range, the organ, and the central wooden table. The range, which functioned as the cooker, the heater, and the dryer, was the heart of the home. My mother cooked and boiled kettles and pans on the open fire, dried clothes on the rack, and baked in the oven. There was no thermostat or heat regulator, yet she produced amazing apple pies, custard tarts, and homemade lemon cheese. The family sat around it in the evenings. We would talk, read, learn our tables, and memorise our spellings. Mum might sew, peg, or darn our socks, while Dad would often read the newspaper or listen to the wireless.

"Don't put your feet too close to the fire or you'll get chilblains," my mother would warn. But we loved to huddle as close as possible and watch the flames burning yellow and red and orange at the heart of the blaze. We'd put our feet on the fender and daydream, going back over the day and wondering what excitement tomorrow would bring.

Our meals were eaten round the big table. They were basic but wholesome, and oftentimes delicious: new potatoes, peas, and beans from Dad's garden; heart-warming bowls of lobby stew; thick bread, toasted in front of the range on long toasting forks. Sometimes, we would each have a mushroom baked in the oven with a knob of butter and covered in milk or fresh, sliced tomatoes, sprinkled with salt and pepper, and served with a side of bread and butter. I can taste them now!

The table had several roles apart from mealtimes. It was the place we often gathered to play board games—draughts, dominos, snakes and ladders, ludo, or cards. Many a competition took place on the red chenille tablecloth in the light from the oil lamp.

The heavy chenille cloth itself had an important part to play when the table was used as a shelter, or a secret hiding place. Because it was so sturdy and strong, the table was the first port of call if the air raid sirens blared out. On such occasions, we would scramble underneath and take refuge there, feeling comparatively safe with the cloth nearly reaching the floor. It was a dark, deliciously secret place that was sometimes lit by Roy's small pocket torch, which flung shadows about the little space. We children would make our faces into scary masks as we put the light under our chins and grimaced at each other to see how scared we could get.

I sometimes used the table space for my own private purposes. On occasion, my mum would have a friend pop by to chat and catch up on the news. If I happened to be under the table—playing with my dolls and lining them up by the chair legs—I discovered that if I stayed perfectly still and quiet, my mum would forget I was there. I heard many a tale and snippet of gossip that were never intended for my tender ears!

Apart from the table shelter, many improvisations had to be made in those days. I was born in 1937, and the National Health Service wasn't brought into being until July 5, 1948. Before that, doctors had to be paid by the patients, and medications also had to be paid for directly. Consequently, there were many homemade and over-the-counter remedies employed instead. Syrup of figs (the memory makes my eyes water) for constipation; ipecac and phenol for bad coughs; castor oil and liquid paraffin for stomach problems; kaolin poultices for boils and swelling; a hot baked potato put on the cheek for toothaches; the smoke from my dad's cigarette blown into the ear for earaches; and—the remedy for *all* things—Vicks VapoRub. My mum believed that it cured virtually all ills.

If sickness struck a family, the whole village community rallied round to help. Death and sickness, misfortune and grieving—they were all experienced by everyone. Everyone went out of their way to support, help, and grieve together.

My Uncle Lloyd, a farm labourer, was badly gored by a bull one time. While attending to it in the cow shippen, the bull tossed him by its horns and threw him across the yard. He became very, very ill and nearly died. He didn't go to the hospital but was cared for by his wife, Auntie Doris, at home in his own bed. There were neighbours in and out of the house for weeks—sitting with him, changing dressings, bringing in food, and supporting the family. At such times, a hush descended over the village, and even we children played a little less boisterously and remembered to be quiet as we passed the house. The relief when he began to recover was almost tangible. Everybody seemed to heave a sigh of relief: "Lloyd is on the mend!"

I do remember one other thing that was brought in when I was small. Children were allowed a ration of cod liver oil and malt, a thick, gooey substance that was doled out every morning in our house. I loved it; Roy hated it. As I rolled it around my mouth and licked the spoon clean, I could hear Roy gagging and heaving in the kitchen, accompanied by threats from my mother.

If after a dose or two of fig syrup, our constipation was remedied and we needed to make a hasty retreat to the loo, there was no convenient flushing toilet; our toilet was outside, at the bottom of the garden, alongside Dad's vegetables! It was a "one-holer"—a piece of sturdy wood, with a round hole in the middle, that was laid on top of a large metal drum. I was always envious of my friend Esther, who lived further down the hollow, because her family had a two-seater. When I visited her, we did everything together—including going to the toilet. There was no toilet paper in the outside toilets, but rather a nail on the wall on which hung a wad of newspaper squares, carefully cut to the right size. If I needed to go when it was dark, and I was scared, my mum would say, "Go on, Roy, take the torch and go wait outside in the yard." We'd make our way down the garden path, Roy grumbling loudly all the way.

Once a week, a cart would go round the village. We children called it "the muck cart," and we didn't need to be told it was on the rounds, because the stink pervaded the whole of the area for miles. We would smell it as we came out of school, and it would follow us all the way home—about a mile-and-a-half to two miles away. We would also see evidence of the loo contents on the garden paths where the drums had been slopped a little by the two men who were carrying it from the lavatory to the muck cart.

But we were country children, used to country smells. Cows, with their distinctive "moist" smell, contentedly pulling clumps of green grass with their long, pink tongues, while filling the fields with dozens of cowpatches. Sweaty horses gazing over stable doors, and piglets skittering across the cobbles at nearby farms, while the pig-sties sent their pungent odours far and wide.

Neighbouring fields and lanes held far more delightful scents: lush green grass; thick hedgerows with the early hawthorn and black-thorn blossoms; sweet William and wallflowers after an early evening shower; pea pods freshly pulled, the delicate green peas stripped out of pods before being greedily consumed; Uncle Jack's garden, full of raspberry canes and row after row of multicoloured polyanthas that filled the nostrils with the scent of spring. The delicate smell of an early summer morning—before anyone else had stirred, with only the birdsong to break the silence—and the world seemed redolent with rose and orange blossom perfume.

Inside our house there were more homey smells. Monday was washing day, when the kitchen was full of steam and carbolic soap, and Mother was slaving over the dolly tub and whizzing the dolly peg round and round in the soap water and boiling pan after pan of water on the fire. Tuesday was ironing day, with the flat irons (held with a thick cloth to prevent burning) heated on the range as near to the fire as possible and then dashed over the freshly laundered clothes and starched collars of my dad's shirts.

But then there were also smells to make the mouth water and the stomach grumble: lobby stew, meat and potato pie, freshly cooked apples from a nearby farm, Mum's baking and zingy lemon curd, and baked potatoes rescued from the ashes under the open fire. I can be whisked through the years by a particular scent that brings memories tumbling back, and I pause and savour the moment—a hiatus that brings calm to my busy world.

In my mind, those summers were hotter than today's— long, endless, sun-filled days. Winters were colder, with snow-packed days when sledges were hauled out of sheds, and wellies retrieved from the bottoms of cupboards. Each day seemed long, filled to the brim with the activity and interest of school days or the leisure and fun and adventure of holidays. We went out with friends and enjoyed days filled with discovery. We knew so much about nature: fat, stripy honey bees that died if they stung you; wasps that stung indiscriminately and were to be avoided at all costs (a theory we didn't always manage successfully); birds and their nests and the colour of their eggs; flowers and where the violets and primroses hid beneath the hedges; how to entice jacksharps and tiddlers from the canal and streams; where we could find the bilberries and blackberries, while avoiding the berries that were poisonous.

We were knowledgeable about nature and how it worked, and we filled our days with it. But at the end of the day, hungry and thirsty and bone-tired, we would wind our way back to our place of safety—home.

After a meal, when the table had been cleared and the dishes washed, we children had time (if we'd finished our homework) to pursue our pastimes. While Roy would usually be sorting his cigarette cards with pictures of football teams and players on them (a popular pastime for boys, which involved swapping and haggling with friends), I would usually get my dolls out. There was Beryl, a much-loved rubber doll who ended up with an enormous split across her middle because I'd played with her so often. I can remember now the horror and disbelief on coming home from school one day to find her in the dustbin. My mother had been clearing out and obviously thought she was past her best. I retrieved her immediately, and after a good wash she was reinstated with the rest of her doll companions. I also had a large pitcher doll with a painted face that lost all its features because I'd washed her so often with a flannel, as I'd seen mums do with their babies.

Even from a very young age, I loved reading. I can remember phonically spelling words out, and the magic moment when it "clicked" and books became the doors into new worlds of discovery. I was already able to read when I went to school at four-and-a-half and was mystified when the teacher tried to explain basic phonics: "C-a-t says 'cat.'" Why was she breaking the words up when I'd already learned to put them together?

We had several wonderful books at home. There was an enormous Bible with amazing black and white ink illustrations. I'd look so carefully at the drawings that I'd virtually enter their world. I'd imagine drawing water at the well with Jacob, surrounded by camels in the middle of the desert, when he met Rebekah for the first time. Or gaze with horror at Abraham as he prepared to sacrifice his son, Isaac, on the stone altar he'd built, with the twigs at the side, ready to complete the sacrifice. On a lighter note, there were also books of fairy stories and nursery rhymes, and Enid Blyton adventures, where I could let my imagination run wild and go sailing on boats with the Famous 5 and Timmy the dog.

Another popular pastime was to create shadows on the wall by the light of the oil lamp or the flickering candles. Weird and wonderful rabbits, birds, and even giraffes and elephants appeared on the distempered walls, much to our delight.

"Time for bed," Mum would eventually warn. That would usually mean a wash in the brown stone sink in the cold kitchen, or, once a week, a bath in front of the coal fire. That was a lengthy task! The tin bath would be hauled in and put on the pegged rug, and the slow process of heating kettles and pans of water on the range would begin. We would (one at a time) be soundly soaped with the same block of carbolic soap Mum had used to do her washing. Hair underwent the same treatment before jugs of water from the bath would be poured over us until the bubbles had been washed away. We would be hauled out (splashing the rug in the process) and wrapped in a towel to be dried in front of the fire. I was usually bathed first because I was generally (though not always) cleaner than Roy.

Once bathed and snuggled into pyjamas, which had been warmed on the rack over the range, it was time for Mum or Dad to read us a story. This was often from the Bible, and we listened, fascinated as we gazed into the fire and enjoyed the last few moments of the day.

As there was no central heating, upstairs would be ice cold in winter. Mum would heat a brick in the oven, which she wrapped in a small blanket to put at the bottom of the bed. These bricks were wonderfully comforting when first put in, but I had many a rude awakening in the middle of the night when the blanket had come away from the brick, and the sharp corners had cut my toes.

We'd climb the stairs with our candles—Roy often going first because I was scared of the dark—and we'd both climb into the bed in the smaller of the two bedrooms. A motley collection of assorted blankets would be on top of the bed to keep us warm, while the essential chamber pot was underneath for use in the night. Mum would sit on the edge of the bed while we said our prayers, praying for everybody in the family (Christopher Robin prayers!) and for anything that might be worrying us. We'd finish with the Lord's Prayer, or another one we used to sing:

"Gentle Jesus, meek and mild,
Look upon a little child,
Pity my simplicity,
Suffer me to come to thee."

And so, our days would pass, and as I look with my long-distance, rose-coloured spectacles at a snapshot of my childhood, all seems well.

But not everything in the world outside our stone cottage was as peaceful. Outside, dark shadows loomed, which could not be dispelled with the light of a candle.

CHAPTER TWO

War Years

Although Roy had only just passed his fourth birthday by a month, he clearly remembers me being born.

Mum was upstairs in the bedroom with the person who was going to assist at the birth, while the downstairs living room was full of aunts and uncles, close neighbours, and trusted friends. Pan after pan of water was boiled on the range, and endless pots of tea were brewed, while most of the menfolk (especially my dad) calmed their nerves by smoking their cigarettes.

Suddenly, a shout rang out down the stairs: "It's a girl! It's a healthy little girl!"

Tensions disappeared and congratulations flew around the room as another safe delivery and birth were celebrated.

And so I made my first appearance in the world on September 23, 1937. That decade was ushered in by the Great Depression, a time of unemployment, deprivation, and poverty brought about as a consequence of the Great War. Stanley Baldwin had been the Prime Minister until 1937 but was replaced by Neville Chamberlain, who gained notoriety for his foreign policy of appeasement, especially toward Germany. He resigned and stepped aside to make room for Winston Churchill to lead Britain victoriously through the war with Germany, which took place from 1939, when I was two, until 1945, when I was eight years old.

My parents must have lived through those years in a state of near poverty and almost constant fear, yet they managed to shield us children in such a way that the circumstances scarcely seemed to impinge upon our lives at all. I don't remember ever living in a state of fear, nor did I think we really lacked anything. I do remember certain things with great clarity, though! A big air raid shelter made its appearance in the village, and gasmasks in their square boxes were slung over our shoulders and taken backwards and forwards to school on a daily basis. There were tales of bombs that had dropped a little too close for comfort, and the chilling sound of air raid sirens followed by the welcome sound of the "all clear."

Thick black-out curtains were hung at each window, which had to be very carefully closed so that no crack of light was seen from the outside. If, perchance, any glimmer escaped, there could be a knock on the door and a warning from a member of the Home Guard: "Close your curtains, Missus; I can see your light."

Ration books were issued, which put a limit on many things— sugar, butter, meat, and, most importantly in my mind, sweets. Our lack of sweets was substituted by sticks of rhubarb dipped into small quantities of sugar, or quaker oats or cocoa mixed with sugar and dipped into with a wet finger.

I distinctly remember the day sweets came off ration and appeared in three of the shops in the village: Hall's, Farmer's, and my grandma's shop. There were queues of children that squeezed into the shops and trailed along the streets, all wriggling with anticipation and shouting with excitement. The shopkeepers wisely limited each child's allowance to two quarter-pound bags each, and I clearly remember the ecstasy that gripped me as I waited by the counter, realising that I was the next one to be served. Mmmmm ... BLISS.

We had very few treats and no luxuries, but the things we did have, we really appreciated. Things seemed to taste better then, and we made everything last as long as possible to drag out the delight: a Dainty Dinah caramel; a stick of liquorice that we dipped into a small bag of kali, which was zingy and zesty and made the mouth fizz; an apple that we ate slowly and worked our way round the core till even the pips disappeared and only the stalk was left. In the school playground, an apple core passed on by a friend was a real treat, and a common plea was often heard at playtime: "Will you save me your apple core, and I'll be your best friend?"

There are several vivid memories that stand out in my mind from those early war years. Roy and I would often lie in our little bed, chatting quietly so as not to incur a reprimand from downstairs, and many nights we would hear the air raid siren begin its distant wail, followed by the heavy drone of aircraft in the sky. We would listen for a while before one of us would shout, "Is that the siren, Dad?" If the danger didn't seem too imminent, Mum or Dad would shout up, "No, it's only the kettle singing on the hob. Pull the covers up over your ears and go to sleep." And we would do just that and quickly fall asleep.

But one night, I remember Dad racing up the stairs.

"Quick, get out of bed and get some clothes on. We need to go to the shelter."

Roy jumped up and scrambled into some clothes, and Mum helped him into his coat. Dad snatched me out from under the covers and grabbed a blanket to wrap around me. The shelter lay across the fields in a neighbouring farm. There we made our way down into their stone cellar—bitterly cold, but safe, and lit by the glow of a storm lantern. On the way, Roy ran ahead, while Dad picked me up and carried me, wrapped in the blanket, with Mum running alongside us. In my eyes, my dad was a superhero, and as he held me close to his chest and made his way along the track, I remember looking at the surrounding darkness and feeling totally safe in his arms. All I remember of the time spent in the cellar was how icy cold the stone ledge was on my little bottom, and how good it was to be carried back home to our snug little beds when the danger was over.

One wartime memory is so indistinct that it hardly leaves an impression on my mind at all, and that's the one to do with the refugee children. During the war, children were sent from the larger cities, where the risk of danger was higher, to live with families in the smaller country towns. I know that at one point, Mum went to register her interest in homing a refugee child named Joyce, from Manchester. But she never came to live with us, and I assume she must have been taken in by another family.

Some things that happened in those war years affected not only our little family, but they changed the lives of our extended family forever. My dad was one of eight siblings born to Albert (Bertie) and Hannah Ecclestone. Dad was the eldest, and Uncle Raymond was the youngest, and they lived in a small cottage-cum-shop at the corner of the village of Mount Pleasant, which lay on the slopes of Mow Cop. Just two narrow, winding roads led from the village up to the summit, which was a well-known landmark, capped by a half-finished castle of sorts—a folly built as a summerhouse by Randle Wilbraham in the eighteenth century. The ridge on which the castle sits forms the boundary between the counties of Staffordshire and Cheshire, and stone was quarried from the slope leading up to the folly in the later nineteenth century. Many decades later, my brother, Roy, built a bungalow on those very slopes, within striking distance of the castle itself.

My dad, being the oldest of the siblings, worked extremely hard from an early age and told us many stories of the hardship and difficulty they all had to endure. We children did not live lives of plenty, but I remember listening, round-eyed with wonder, as he described how he and one of his brothers walked all the way from Mount Pleasant to Kidsgrove—a distance of six miles or so—with a donkey and cart to fetch fresh fish to sell in the shop. His mum took in washing to try and make ends meet, and I suppose the kitchen was full of steam and wet clothes on most days, accompanied by the hiss of boiling water, the banging of the dolly tub, and the whirr of the wooden mangle as Granny turned the handle and fed the wet clothes through the rollers.

Food and clothes were scarce, and Dad said it was a case of "first up, best dressed." He used to smile as he told of going to school with one sock on and a clog and a shoe. Most children wore clogs, and I can imagine it must have been a noisy affair when the children went to and from school, and the sound of dozens of metal-tipped clogs rang around the village.

The Ecclestone family was made up of six boys and two girls: Jack, Winston, Sidney, Jim, Lloyd, Raymond, and the girls, Winnie and Ruth. I never knew Winnie because she died of consumption long before I was born. Similarly, I never met my grandad, but I heard many tales of him and the wonderful person he was, and how well respected he was throughout the area. He was a preacher, admired not only for his preaching and writing of poetry but also for his kindness and generosity, and for the highly principled way he lived his life. Apparently, when he died the whole village went into mourning and lined the streets for the funeral, the men doffing their caps as the coffin was carried along from his house to the chapel.

The chapel featured largely in the lives of all the family, something that continued to be true in my little family too, as my dad continued in the same tradition and beliefs. Sunday was truly a Sabbath day in his childhood, with morning and afternoon Sunday school followed by an evening service. During the rest of the day, both work and play of any kind was frowned upon. Bibles and Bible storybooks were read, but no sewing, knitting, or games of any kind were allowed.

Dad raised us in the same way. He always took us to Sunday school and often to evening church, and the day passed uneventfully until the evening, when it seemed to be a common practice for many families to go for long walks together. Down to the Bank, up through the Big Wood, along the Sludge to the canal, and even climbing the quarried slopes of the Castle, while Mum would watch anxiously that we didn't go too near the edge of rocky inclines.

Right up until the time I went to high school at the age of eleven, most of my social activities (outside of school and the great outdoors) took place in Mount Pleasant Chapel. Apart from every Sunday, there were also Sunday school treats (probably involving an afternoon of games in a local farmers' field), socials, prize-giving for attendance, choirs, pantomimes, and children's anniversaries. My dad was a musician and choir master and trained the Sunday School children to sing on the stage at the anniversaries, as well as rehearsed and conducted the adult choir. Auntie Ruth, Dad's sister, was a well-known soprano soloist, while Dad had a lovely tenor voice, and they often sang duets in the nearby churches.

The Ecclestones were a close-knit family who spent lots of time together visiting each other's homes, having large family get-togethers, and sharing lots of things in common. But the war brought heartbreak and left those strong ties in tatters.

Conscription—the calling up of men to fight in the armed forces—was viewed with mixed emotions. The women dreaded the call-up papers dropping through the letterbox, as did many of the older men. But some of the young men who had never been outside the parameters of their rural villages must have thought that the prospect of travelling to a foreign country like France was a great adventure. Some people were exempt from call-up because of the jobs they did. Dad worked at the Steel Works, which produced metal for the production of bullets, tanks, and ammunition, so he was allowed to continue in his job.

His younger brother, Sidney, however, received his orders to go for a medical exam before joining up. He passed his medical, but because of an old injury to one of his arms, he was not classed as fit and was drafted to the Pioneer Corps. I never realised until I was talking to my brother recently what a horrific job that was. The Pioneers didn't go to the front lines to fight; they followed behind the battalions and retrieved the bodies of the wounded and the dead. They took the wounded soldiers back to base and carried the dead bodies elsewhere, searching among the bits and pieces of human debris for identity discs to place with the bodies. The smoke, the ear-splitting noise, and the stench of decay and death, as well as the horrific sights of dismembered bodies, would have seared into their minds and tortured their memories for the rest of their lives. Many returned home shell-shocked (PTSD), broken men. As did Uncle

Sid. He was never the same again. He never talked about his experiences, but he obviously relieved them frequently. He, Auntie Nellie, and my cousin Dorothy lived across the fields from us, next door to Leese's farm, and I was shocked when he died a year or so after being demobilised.

Death came even closer than the threat of the droning bombers and the air raids. It had stalked its way from the poppy fields of France to *my* field, next to *my* house, and it brought with it a previously unknown sense of fear and unease that broke into the shell of my safe little world.

Some years after Sidney was drafted, Raymond, the baby of the family, joined the army. He was the only one still living at home in the shop with Grandma, and she adored him. At that time, our little family had moved from the stone cottage in the Hollow to 116 the Flat, which was a stone's throw from the shop in Mount Pleasant. I remember Raymond coming to our house and singing around the organ while Dad played, often choosing the same hymn: "The Lord's my Shepherd" to the tune of "Crimond," which was his favourite.

Apparently, Raymond didn't wait to be called up—he volunteered! Because he didn't want to be thought a coward who shirked his responsibilities, he lied about his age and said he was eighteen when he was still only seventeen. He was assigned to the Highland Light Infantry and sent to Germany. Sadly, he was killed just two weeks before the war ended, and his war grave is in Soltau, Germany. A memorial was placed in St. Lucas Church, opposite our school, to commemorate his life, along with three others from our village.

Times and lengths of times are not clear in my memory because my life was lived far removed from wars and rumours of wars. My days were filled with school and friends, hunting for newts in the canal, and searching for owl pellets under the trees in Big Wood. Until reality came crashing into my daily routines and sent them spinning. That's what happened the day we learned of Raymond's death.

It was just a regular day at school. Nothing out of the ordinary through the morning, and then dinnertime arrived with the little oil cloth covers over the desks and the smell of cooking that would pervade the classrooms for the rest of the day. After a short playtime, I was almost ready to go to my classroom to begin afternoon lessons when a fellow classmate came running into the schoolyard, bursting with the importance of the momentous news she was privy to, which she was about to hurl into my world.

"I've just been into your grandma's shop," she declared. "Your gran was screaming and crying in the back room. I think your Uncle Raymond has been killed!"

I remember nothing else of the day.

Once again, the family was devastated. Raymond, the darling of the family and the apple of his mother's eye, lost. So young, as many of the boy soldiers were, so vital and full of life and energy. Gone— and too far away for anyone to say their last goodbyes.

Grandma had his framed photograph, in his uniform and beret with a pompom on the top, sitting on the sideboard, and she kissed it every night before she went to bed. A broken-hearted woman until the day she died.

It was some time later that a soldier, in his civilian clothes, came to visit her with the most remarkable news. He had actually been with Raymond when he died, and he reassured her that he had died peacefully and looked as though he had just gone to sleep. I think his news must have brought her a measure of comfort, which was then immediately shattered when she received a package from the war office. It contained Raymond's leather wallet, together with one or two personal possessions. The corner had been blown off the

wallet, and the letters inside had a jagged, star-shaped hole punctur-
ing them—clearly showing the passage of the bullet that had entered
his chest and killed him.

Raymond was the family's last war casualty. The other brothers
were farmers or farm labourers and were exempt from conscription.
The war had exacted its final toll on the Ecclestone family.

It's strange to look so far back across the years. It's like looking
at a graph—the base line showing the pleasant, largely uneventful
passage of time, when the route of life carried us gently through our
days. But then there are the occasional soaring peaks, when shocking happenings rocked our world, and time seemed to stand still. We
were used to the gentle rhythms of life, the human cycles of birth
and death, and the inevitable turn of the seasons.

I loved how spring seemed to watch for the lengthening of days
and the slight rise in temperature before unfurling the violets and
primroses, celandines and snowdrops beneath the hedges. How
she imperceptibly greened up the hawthorn and, seemingly overnight, covered trees with blossoms. Then, in turn, she ushered in
the summer, who filled the world with sunshine and warmth. Long
days that stretched endlessly, full of flowers and birdsong, when I
climbed rocks and shimmied up trees, fished in pools, and made
dens in the woods. At a more leisurely pace, autumn followed,
heavy in fruitfulness and abundance. Children helped farmers pick
potatoes from their fields, and whole families helped in getting the
harvest in. Tractors threshed the grain, and the stooks of hay stood
upright in the field before being baled and loaded onto the horse and
cart and trundled noisily back to the barns. I remember those hot,
sweaty days that finished in a host of children scrambling for a place
between the bales on the hay cart and riding triumphantly home:
hot, tired, and hugely proud of the part we'd played in gathering

the harvest safely in. I liked to sit on the front row of the chapel at Harvest Thanksgiving, and I'd look at all the apples, cabbages, potatoes, carrots, and flowers, and gaze at the stooks of corn at the front of the display, wondering if it was the one we'd helped to bale and load on the cart.

We never welcomed the advent of winter—short days, long nights, cold washes in the morning, and cold bedrooms at night, but once the snow came, we were delighted. One year it snowed so much and for so long that the Hollow was completely filled, and we could walk on the compacted snow from one farmer's field across the road to the neighbouring farm on the other side. The drifts were six to ten feet deep, and the roads were totally impassable. But when evening came and the dark fell at about four o'clock, and the curtains were drawn and the fire stoked up the chimney … how wonderful. Hats, gloves, scarves, and socks drying on the rack after getting soaked while sledging down the slopes of the fields; toes stretched out toward the warmth of the range; full tummies and a brick already in the oven, ready for bedtime. Yes, these were the rhythms of life we were familiar with, and when an unexpected turn of events happened, it would completely stumble us.

Like when a schoolmate of Roy's died after a long, drawn out illness. It was rumoured around the school classrooms that he had died of sleeping sickness. Whether that was so or not, I don't know. None of us knew what sleeping sickness was (we had never heard of the tsetse fly in Africa), but it sounded pretty awful.

And then there was Harold, the son of one of my mother's friends who dropped in for a chat on occasion. He died of liver disease. I listened with horror (probably while hiding under the kitchen table) as she described his demise: "His liver was just like a sponge," she declared as she recounted what the doctor had said after Harold died.

It was only on occasions like this that reality dawned and I realised that life didn't always follow regular patterns and cycles. There was always the unexpected blip—and, yes, the Grim Reaper did sometimes come and reap his macabre harvest far too soon. Even children were not exempt from his swinging scythe. At such times, we would say our prayers a little more earnestly: "God bless Mum and Dad, and Roy, and everybody… and "—said in a whisper under the bedclothes—"please don't let me die just yet."

CHAPTER THREE

Boy Meets Girl
(Two Worlds Come Together)

Dad was generally reckoned to be "punching above his weight" when his eye fell on the dark-haired, dark-eyed Nellie Dale from Mossley, Congleton. I wonder if they met at a choir practice in Biddulph Road Chapel when Dad was their young conductor, or whether he was one of the choristers. However they met, the court-ship began, and they would often be seen sitting together on the wall outside the corner house of Biddulph Street. The man who lived in the house must have watched them as they sat and chatted, for he called them "the two lovebirds." It turns out that he owned a pottery in a neighbouring town, and he had a beautiful tea set made for them in white porcelain, decorated with motifs of two little bluebirds sitting on a leafy branch. I still have a couple of the plates tucked away in my cabinet.

Mum was the youngest of the Dale family, who lived in quite a large stone cottage nestled at the foot of Congleton Edge. Peter and Emma Dale were the parents, and there were nine siblings: Ruth, Ginny, and Alice married and moved away, while Sarah, Fanny, and Jessie stayed in Mossley. I never knew the boys, Peter and Edward, and, as far as I know, I never even met them—although I do believe at least one of them only lived in Congleton. I was never close to the families who moved out of the area, and only knew (though was never at ease with) the Mossley aunties.

Let me give you a limited snapshot of the things I knew. I think Auntie Alice was the oldest girl, and she married Ted Pickford. They had two children, both boys. They were very proud of Frank, who was a civil servant in London (I only remember meeting him once) and Ted, married to Nancy. Ted worked in the grocery or supermarket trade. Mum used to take us for an occasional holiday to stay with Uncle Ted and Auntie Alice in Bulwell, Nottingham. Ted by that time was in a wheelchair and severely disabled. Auntie Alice had to do everything for him, including feeding him and interpreting what he was trying to say. I was a bit scared of him and avoided being alone with him because I couldn't understand him.

While there, we sometimes went to Ted and Nancy's for a meal, which we really loved because she was a brilliant cook. The other thing I enjoyed was being allowed to take Auntie Alice's dog for a walk around a nearby cricket field.

Auntie Ginny married Will Miushull and they moved to Blackpool to run a boarding house. They had two children: Mary, who later married Fred Brown, and Harry, who was in the Air Force and was another young war casualty.

Auntie Ruth married Henry Brown, and they had three daughters: Ruth, Hilda, and Beryl. They lived in Shifnal and were heavily involved with the Methodist Church.

I think Auntie Sarah married Peter Cotterill, and she had Winnie. Auntie Fanny married Ted Brough, and they had no children. They lived in a fine red brick property at the foot of Congleton Edge. After Auntie Fanny died, her husband, Ted, committed suicide by hanging in that very house.

Because Auntie Jessie never married, she never left the family home (now called Dexter Dale). Although I was never comfortable with Auntie Jessie, I loved her garden. She was a wonderful gardener and worked tirelessly in it. Whenever we visited, she would invariably be found there, kneeling on a mat to do the weeding, tending to the raspberry canes, or hauling heavy wheelbarrows full of rocks and stones when she was making a new plot. She allowed me to pick snowdrops from under the trees at the top of her sloping garden, or collect ripe, juicy raspberries from the canes if they were in season.

A model family one would think, but ah … there was a skeleton hiding in a dark cupboard that we were never told about until we were in our late teens.

Auntie Alice, when she was a young girl, became involved with a young man before she met Ted, and she had a child with him. That child—born "out of wedlock"— was my mum, Nellie. Because it was such a terrible disgrace in those days, she was brought up as one of the Dale daughters. It seems terribly cruel and unjust to me, but the disgrace never fell on Alice but rather on the baby. My mother was always looked down on by the other sisters, and I remember her crying many times because she hadn't been invited to weddings or family gatherings. But as a child, I was never privy to such things; I lived my childhood at Mount Pleasant, oblivious to the undercover secrets of the seemingly respectable Dale relations.

Apart from family in Mossley, there was one home we children were always delighted to visit. It was the home of my mother's life-long best friend, Auntie Dorrie, who lived with Uncle George in a pebble dashed, detached house in Whitemoor, just down the road from Mossley. Mum and Dad had lived with them for a while when Roy was small, but my memories come later. For several years we spent Christmas with them, and those Christmas times were wonderful. The food, the fun, the beautiful house, and the celebrations were highlights of our year. Lying in bed on Christmas Eve and listening to the grandfather clock in the hall downstairs, with its sonorous tick-tock-tick-tock, and the musical chime that heralded the slow count of the hours stretching endlessly through the night, when we were so longing for Christmas morning, with stockings and presents and excitement ... I can feel it now!

The joy of Auntie Dorrie and Uncle George's family was complete when John was born, and our Christmases became even more magical. As well as everything else that we enjoyed, I now had a delightful, curly-haired, chubby-cheeked baby to cuddle—I could wish for nothing more.

Over the years, I have often thought of the circumstances around my mum's birth. I can't judge how "Auntie" Alice felt—whether she carried with her any sense of guilt or not—but I feel sure that Mum, because of the way she was treated by the family, felt shame throughout her life. She was the scapegoat. Regardless of that, she seemed to have a need to connect with her sisters and returned as often as she could to the place of her childhood.

Sometimes during the long summer days, Mum would get Roy and me ready, and we would set out to walk from Mow Cop to

Mossley, through Dales Green, up to the top of the ridge of hills that separated Strafford from Cheshire (called Corderwell), and along the steep, hilly slopes of Congleton Edge. Here the track was stony and narrow, and care had to be taken not to slip over the edge of the rocks and down the steep slopes covered with heather and bilberry bushes. It was quite dangerous, but we were used to playing on and climbing up steep sided rocks and were as sure-footed as a pair of mountain goats.

Mum sometimes had a plan in mind when we reached these grassy slopes. She would produce a couple of bags, and we would carefully scramble down from the path to pick the black, juicy bilberries. It was a slow, laborious job; the berries were so small it took ages to fill even a corner of the bag, but we persevered, in spite of pestering flies, until Mum declared that there was enough to make a bilberry pie when we got home. The job was slow, but the rewards were wonderful. Bilberry pie was, and still is, my favourite. Mum's pastry was brown and crispy on the top of the delicious berries and covered in thick, sweet custard. Reminding myself of such delights would double my efforts and stop me shovelling the odd handful into my mouth whilst still on the slopes. We would arrive at one of the aunties' houses after our trek tired and sweaty, but we'd soon revive after a drink and a biscuit.

Some memories are specific to each of the aunt's homes. The garden was always the attraction at Auntie Jessie's, but the time would come when we were called inside: "Hands washed! Make sure shoes are clean! Sit down!"

I remember a large AGA range in the kitchen, and slab tiles, but in the hallway leading to the immaculate living room, the walls were panelled in dark brown oak. A grandfather clock sent its loud ticking into the dark shadows at the corners of the hall, and the door was (in my mind) hidden in the panels. I was terrified of being trapped in there, because I couldn't find the door handle in the dark. If we were invited to tea, the china would be brought out and set carefully on the table. There would be sandwiches and tea and usually a cake of some sort. A large teapot brought in from the kitchen would be used to pour the tea into the delicate china cups. It always tasted fine, but I hated such occasions, because I was painfully shy.

One day I disgraced myself by swallowing a gulp of tea too quickly and choking. I ended up with tea pouring down my nose, all over the front of my top and, horror of horrors, a few spots splashed onto the tablecloth. My mother was embarrassed, Auntie Jessie was open-mouthed with shocked disapproval, and I wanted the floor to open and swallow me. Having no children of her own, Jessie was unused to such displays of "bad manners."

Visits to the other aunts were a little less stressful for me, and each had their attractions that provided me with escape strategies. Auntie Sarah's garden was not as exciting as Auntie Jessie's, but nevertheless that's where I liked to go! It was a long, narrow garden at the back of the house, with a lawn surrounded by flowerbeds. The fence had a gate in it, and I loved to lift the latch and disappear into the back half of the garden, which was semi-wild and full of London Pride: red, white, and bluebells. Auntie Sarah didn't mind me picking a few of these to take home.

One sunny day, I made my way out to the garden, where there was a fold up deck chair covered in a bright, stripy material sitting on the lawn. I decided to sit there for a while before disappearing into the "wilderness." The deck chair was adjustable and could be notched up into a sitting position or laid back to recline on. While sitting on it, I reached my hand back along the frame to find how to adjust the position, and suddenly the whole thing collapsed, trapping my hand in the frame as it concertinaed together. My fingers were really squashed and poured with blood, and my loud screams fetched everybody running out of the house to see what disaster had befallen me.

Auntie Fanny's house had a long, sloping lawn at the back, but it wasn't her garden that fascinated me—it was her front room and its contents. I don't think this room was generally used at all, and it was filled with staid pieces of heavy furniture, highly polished and standing at attention around a large, expensive rug. At one end of the room was a china cabinet, filled to brimming with beautiful pieces of porcelain, fluted cups and saucers, highly decorated dishes and plates, teapots, and crystal jugs and vases. It wasn't the contents of the cabinet that intrigued me but rather what sat on top of it! Here, a huge glass dome covered the kneeling figure of a little boy who was gazing into a lily-filled pond that also contained a beautiful white swan with half-outstretched wings. It was an impressive display that filled me with awe, and I'd sit for a long time gazing into the depths of the dome to see what I could spot among the fronds and ferns around the pond.

These homes and their contents were a million miles away from my stone cottage and the well-worn pegged rugs and second-hand pieces of furniture, but I was always delighted to return to it. It was my home.

I wonder where "home" was for my mother. Was it in Mossley, with her sisters, where her birthplace was? Or was it at Mow Cop with her in-laws? She was looked down on by her own family, but things weren't any better in Mow Cop. There she was considered "posh" and a foreigner of sorts. Yet again she was on the outside, even with some of the Ecclestone family.

Even as a child, I could recognise my mum's reticence within the family. There were sometimes comments or muttered asides directed at her, but she never rose to them because she hated confrontation. She did have one champion, however: my Uncle Sam, who was married to Auntie Ruth. I believe he loved my mum, and he would always support and defend her against the others.

Uncle Sam and Auntie Ruth had three boys: John (about my age), Michael, and the baby, Allan. I loved to visit their house. These visits were as far removed from the Mossley visits as chalk from cheese. Auntie Ruth was a great cook, and I was always invited to stay for a meal if I was playing with the boys. My best mate amongst the boys was Michael. I was a tomboy as I grew up, and Mike and I would wander for miles together. He was a great naturalist and knew birds and wildlife and nature with a broad knowledge beyond his years.

We climbed trees, fished in the streams and canals, hunted for (but never destroyed or raided) birds' nests with their eggs. We discovered where the owls roosted and then dissected the pellets to see the tiny bones inside the bundles of fur. We took a small bucket down to the pond in the Sludge and caught crested newts, which we took home to put in my mum's rain butt. When they were discovered, she made us catch them and take them in a bucket full of water back to the pond. We whittled sticks and played fencing down in the Big Wood, and I can clearly remember the day he said, "No, I can't play fencing with you anymore, 'cos you're a girl and I might hurt you."

We played with the rabbits in the hutch at the back of Michael's house, and I marvelled at the softness of their fur. I remember enjoying a wonderful stew at Auntie Ruth's one day when I was invited to stay. "What is this, Auntie Ruth?" I asked as I spooned the delicious gravy into my mouth.

"Oh, it's one of the rabbits," she said. "We decided to make one of them into lobby." Down went the spoon at the side of my dish, and even when she laughed and said she was joking, my appetite had completely gone.

On the odd occasion I would stay overnight, and the evening always ended as we crowded together on the settee, and Uncle Sam told stories and sang songs in his wonderful deep baritone voice. A prayer would finish our day and send us off to bed utterly content.

A couple of the families lived too far away for me to just drop in. Uncle Lloyd had married Doris, and they lived on the top of the hill in Mow Cop. They had two delightful little girls, Ann and Joan, and I loved to play with them when a family visit was made. Uncle Jim and Auntie Daisy had a farm in Goldenhill, and I remember going round the shippens and seeing the cows in their stalls and having loads of fields and meadows to play in with cousins Brian and Barbara.

I enjoyed spending time with my cousin Dorothy, who lived across the fields from us. She was older than me and introduced me to stubs of lipstick and face powder that she had finished with, and I discovered a new game of making myself up when I got back home and was tucked away in some quiet corner.

We didn't socialize with Auntie Nellie and Uncle Sid very much, although they lived so close. Uncle Sid was lovely but very quiet, and he didn't say much. Auntie Nellie talked all the time—and grumbled a lot. I remember staying overnight with Dorothy on one occasion and having a nosebleed during the night. Auntie Nellie was really cross and was still grumbling the next day. I scuttled back across the fields as soon as I was dressed to the safety of my place. Knowing how cross she could get, I don't know how I had the temerity one day to pinch some crocuses from under one of the trees in her garden—but pinch them I did. When my mum found out, she made me take them back and confess to Nellie what I had done.

Uncle Winston and Auntie Miriam lived a little way from the village, down at the Bank, and had two children, Colin and Maureen. Maureen was disabled and not very verbal. Auntie Miriam idolized her and attended to her every need. Their home was often used for get-togethers, and Miriam was a great cook and enjoyed putting on a spread for the whole family. After a meal, the men played darts in the kitchen, the women gossiped, and we children played out until dusk fell and we were called inside. The evenings were spent in talking, singing, telling family stories and anecdotes, and reciting. If Uncle Jim was there, he would recite long poems, which were hugely entertaining—many of which he had written himself. He was an inveterate comedian and performer and was in his element in a group of people. He liked to label himself as the "black sheep" of the family, probably because he liked the odd drink, and chapel was a strong advocate for being teetotal. But in truth, he had a heart of gold. Strangely enough, although my mum preferred to take a back seat, she too was a wonderful reciter of poetry, and would do so if encouraged to take her turn at entertaining us.

"Who shall it be? Who shall it be? I looked at John, John looked at me," told the story of two parents having to choose which child they were going to give away, to give a better chance of survival because they were so poor. A sad story, which might have struck a chord with those gathered who knew all too well what poverty meant. I think a slice of bilberry pie was welcome after that to raise our spirits!

A visit to Grandma's was like none other! I don't know how old she actually was at the time I'm remembering, but to me, she was always OLD. She could ever be seen dressed in a long, floor length black skirt covered in a pinny, with a matching black top, hair pulled away from her face and tucked into a bun, and specs on her nose. She was quite large and moved slowly and deliberately, slippers dragging across the floor. A black curtain separated the shop from the small living room, and if the shop bell tinkled to herald the arrival of a customer, she sometimes shouted, "Who is it? What do you want?" If the customer didn't warrant her attention, she would shout, "I'm busy. Cart off across to Hall's shop where you went last week!" Nobody was exempt from the sharp, cutting edge of her tongue.

The shop contained a mixture of all sorts of things, from potatoes and bundles of sticks to paraffin, bread, cough mixture, biscuits, sticking plaster, crisps, and sweets. The narrow, curtain-covered doorway opened onto a very small living area with a table, a couple of chairs, Grandma's rocking chair, a sideboard, and a cupboard in the wall. A tiny buffet where I used to sit was perched close to the grate, where a fire always roared up the chimney. Another doorway led to a kitchen with a sink and then to yet another back kitchen, where a dolly tub, mangle, and slopstone were housed. The back door opened onto a small yard where the toilet crouched in a dark, brick shelter.

At some point she took in lodgers. One was called Hobson, and the other was Mr. Rowbotham. Hobson died, and she actually married the other, Sam Rowbotham. They must have been very thick skinned, because she verbally abused them all the time, calling them all sorts of names and accusing them of being lazy and good for nothing! I should think they must have been in a desperate need of lodgings or they would never have stayed.

If I was not well enough to go to school, I was sometimes left at Grandma's for the day. She had a homemade remedy that seemed to deal with all ailments, from sore throats to stomach aches. She called it brimstone and treacle. I had heard of brimstone in chapel services, in relation to a dreadful place called hell—and one small teaspoon of this thick, black potion could evoke the flames and stench of hell like nothing else. Amazingly, my illnesses never seemed to last more than a day, and the next morning would find me more than ready to tackle the steep School Bank on the way to school.

Two things I did enjoy when visiting were her lobby stew and her chips. The lobby was delicious, and the chips fat and succulent. A few chips and a spoonful of peas, together with a slice of bread and butter, were always well received. But her scones! She might have been a dab hand at making lobby, but her baking left much to be desired. She kept them in a large tin box in the kitchen, and I remember lifting the lid one day to discover a couple of leftover scones that sported a light green mould!

She gave me one of her scones as a snack one day as I sat on the buffet waiting for the day to pass. "Here," she said. "Get that down ya." I took a mouthful and moved it round in my mouth, wondering how I was going to swallow it without heaving. I waited until she disappeared into the kitchen, and I quickly stuck the whole thing up my knicker leg. She came back, and I pretended to be gathering up the last crumbs on my plate while the heat from the fire melted the butter and warmed up the scone in my knickers.

At last, she went out to the kitchen again, and I shouted, "I'm just going outside for a bit, Grandma," and carefully disappeared through the curtain and out of the shop, leaving a Hansel and Gretel trail of crumbs. I hid behind the cobbler's shop across the way while I scooped the mass of crumbs out of my underwear into the grass, and then, after a bit, made my way back, scuffing the tell-tale crumbs out of sight with my sandals.

If Granny was in a good mood, I'd ask if I could play in the shop. If she agreed, I'd close the curtain behind me and pretend I was the shopkeeper. If anyone came in, I'd stand back until they'd been served and then continue to play—moving a few tins on the shelves, pretending to weigh out the potatoes on the scales, tidying the counter and window display, and so on. My interest in the shop was twofold. Not only did I enjoy playing there, but I was interested in the contents of the large jars on the counters and the boxes in the window. They were full of sweets! After rationing, there was no need for the quarter-pound rationing coupons, and sweets were available in all the shops in the village.

Very occasionally, Grandma would hand me a couple of sweets—but one day, while alone in the shop, I eyed the large jars with the screw top lids and imagined chewing the caramels or the lemon sherbets they contained. I wondered how tight the lids were fastened and whether I'd be able to undo them if I stood on tiptoe. I decided to have a go, just to see, and was surprised to find they turned quite easily. In fact, the lid came off the jar with comparative ease … and the caramels were right there. I could actually reach them if I pushed my hand inside. Before I knew it, I had secreted four caramels into my pocket, and the lids were back on the jars. They were the Dainty Dinah caramels I've mentioned before, with red and shiny gold wrappers, each one a succulent mouthful. It was at that point I made my escape. "I'm going home now, Gran!" I called through to the living room. "I'll see you tomorrow." I wouldn't have skipped home with such glee if I'd realised that my shrewd granny had been watching my carryings on through the curtain! There would be a reckoning!

Unaware of the Damocles Sword hanging over my head, I sat in the sun at the side of my house and took out two of my sweets, unwrapping the first one carefully and then popping it into my mouth. I sucked slowly, enjoying the sweetness that oozed onto my tongue before I started to chew it, and the flavour filled my senses.

Before I could tackle the second one, Roy appeared around the corner of the house.

"Do you want a sweet?" I asked. "Grandma gave me two while I was visiting."

I felt a strange satisfaction that Roy, though completely unaware, was joining me in my treachery.

The booty had been completely demolished, and the sun-filled afternoon had passed pleasantly. Then my mother returned, having called at Grandma's on the way home. It was the first thing she greeted me with.

"Have you been pinching sweets out of your grandma's shop?" she asked in a shocked voice.

The game was up. My crime had been discovered. Mum didn't shout and rail at me. She didn't smack me. She just said one single sentence that made me quake in my boots and send me scurrying for shelter: "Just wait until your dad comes home!"

I watched for his return, and eventually the front gate swung open and I saw him making his way up the path and in through the front door. A little time passed before Mum opened the door and shouted my name.

"Jean, come in right now!"

I slowly made my way in, feeling like a condemned man on his way to the gallows. Dad was sitting at the table, waiting for his tea, cutlery laid out, while Mum was getting things ready to serve in the kitchen. Dad just looked at me and said, "Sit down." I sat on the settee behind him, and Mum brought in his tea and put it in front of him on the table. I heard every clink of the cutlery on the plate, every mouthful as Dad worked his way through the main course of the meal. Then the cutlery was placed on the plate, and Mum took it away. In came the pudding and *click* went the spoon around the dish. Mouthful by mouthful. Out went the pudding dish and in came the cup of tea—black, two sugars—and the teaspoon stirred the tea slowly round to dissolve the sugar. *Slurp, slurp.* Dad drank his tea and clinked the cup back on the saucer. Silence. He then slowly turned and looked at me.

"I hear you've been taking sweets out of Grandma's shop. Is that true, Jean?"

"Yes," came a whisper from somewhere inside me.

A pause. Then, "Well, don't ever do it again."

That was it. Nothing else was said. But I cannot express the shame I felt. Just the quiet, sad look on his face told me of the disappointment he felt. I'd let my superhero down, and that knowledge was more effective in dealing with my misdemeanour than any beating or scolding could ever be.

It was the last time I played in Grandma's shop—but, unfortunately, it wasn't the last time I needed to be chastised for my naughtiness.

CHAPTER FOUR

A Bit of This, and a Bit of That!

I lived down the Hollow until I was about five or six, when we moved up into the village itself to 116 the Flat. Some of my memories have become intertwined over the years, and it's hard to separate certain happenings and lock them into a specific location. Other things are crystal clear. Being down the Hollow added an extra half mile or so to our school journey, but it meant we were much closer to our favourite place to play: the Sludge.

It was a glorious place of adventure for us children, but adults viewed it with some misgiving, as a place fraught with danger—as indeed it was! Tucked away amongst the grassy slopes and wooded areas were at least two mineshafts, disused coal mines long abandoned. These were covered by pieces of wood, rotted in parts, which certainly wouldn't have supported even the weight of a small child. We were shown these mines and warned about them, and, with the inbred knowledge that we had as country children, we obeyed to the letter. We knew the lay of the land. We knew our way around the twists and turns of the different tracks. We knew where to go and what to do to keep ourselves safe, even from a very young age.

Shrubs and bushes and brambles were hidden between the undulating grassy slopes, the brambles yielding a bountiful harvest of luscious blackberries in the summer that filled many a pie in our mum's kitchen. The main track led to a rickety old bridge across a stream, which fed into the canal at Scholar Green, while to the left there was a wood of larch, silver birch, oak, and elder, wonderfully carpeted with drift after drift of glorious bluebells during late April and May. The sight and the scent can still fill my senses.

This is where Mike and I came to fish and catch the sticklebacks to take home in a jar. This is where we caught the newts and dissected the owl pellets. This is where Uncle Jack, Auntie Lizzie, Esther, and our family came on one of our Sunday evening jaunts and somehow disturbed a wasps' nest along the canal bank. They made a "bee" line for Uncle Jack, stinging him in various places. The sight of him swinging his shirt around his head as he ran across the fields at full pelt while the angry wasps formed a swirling funnel and gave chase is indelibly printed on my mind.

We sometimes (but not on that occasion) called at Esther's house on the way home from such excursions. Their house seemed exceedingly old and was largely black and white timbered. It had small paned windows and deep windowsills, because the walls were really thick. Inside, the walls were covered in white distemper, and cold tiles covered the floors. There was the familiar range and wooden cloth-covered table with a few chairs dotted around. A door led from one side of the room into another room, which had a bitumen-covered floor, whitewashed walls, and was a favourite play area for us girls. This room always amazed me because it was completely empty, but it was a marvellous place where our imaginations could run wild. The garden was also wonderful, full to bursting with scented poly-antha flowers, potatoes, peas, and beans. We could hide between the rows of peas, which grew to a height of five to six feet, and rifle as many pods as we wanted, undetected, until summoned from the doorway: "Come on, it's time for home."

We would return via the roadway, avoiding the hazards of the Sludge, past the farm with its milk churns waiting for the following morning's collections, until we arrived back home.

Apart from family members and Esther's family, I don't remember visiting anybody else's home, but I clearly remember certain people visiting us! There was Mr. Barton with his large case, bulging with haberdashery. He would flick open the catches and fling back the lid, and various articles would fall out onto the table. There were vests, liberty bodices, pants, socks, pinafores, and more, all crammed into the case. He was quite large and very jolly, always smartly dressed in dark trousers and tweed jackets, a cap covering his hair, and spec-tacles balancing on his nose.

I watched, fascinated, as he meticulously lifted out piece after piece of clothing to show my mother, waiting for any flicker of interest to be shown. Mum would sometimes buy a pair of socks or new pants for one of us—or even a pretty wrap-over pinafore for herself—before Mr. Barton carefully folded each article and piled it back into his case. It was only then that the constant stream of sales patter would cease and he would fish into his pocket and pull out a paper bag, from which he handed Roy and me a few chocolate drops. He would then haul his case off the table and stumble out of the door. Mission accomplished—over and out!

He was the only salesperson I remember coming to the house, except for Alf, who parked his ice cream van at the corner of the house, on the Hollow, to tempt us with his delicious golden Cornish ice cream.

"Oh please, Mum, please, Mum," we would plead as Mum looked for any spare coins in her purse. If our pleading—and Mum's search—were successful, we would dash out to hand over the coins and watch as Alf scooped the ice cream out of the container and piled it high onto the cornets, our mouths watering in anticipation. We would then go our separate ways to wallow in enjoyment as we licked the mound of ice cream round and round to make sure no dribbles were lost down the sides of the cone. My favourite bit was the very last tip of the cornet, soaked in melted ice cream, before lips were licked and every vestige was removed from fingers. There was nothing to compare with the golden delights of Alf's little yellow ice cream van.

Roy hated the next visitor who came to the house! Mr. Hanley, short and wiry, was an organ teacher who came to give Roy lessons on Dad's organ. For a good half hour before he arrived, Roy would moan and groan and shout and cry: "I don't *want* to play the organ. I *hate* playing the organ. I *won't* play the organ"—until a knock on the door would bring an uneasy calm, and Mr. Hanley would be smilingly invited in by Mum to begin his unenviable and unappreciated task.

I would stand on the other side of the table from the organ, while Roy sat on the tall, thin-legged piano chair. I would carefully study Mr. Hanley's face as he watched Roy's fingers on the organ keys and examine the large wart that straddled the bridge of his nose. I fancied he looked something like one of the gnomes out of the Enid Blyton storybooks. My reverie would come to a discordant end as Roy hammered out several strangled chords, accompanied by a look of pain from Mr. Hanley. Roy would only have been about nine or ten at this point, and his legs would hardly have reached the pedals that blew wind into the pipes of the organ. I don't think he had an idea what all the stops were for, which altered the tone and the volume of the instrument. I recall that one of the tunes he tried to play was called "Home Sweet Home," and eventually, to maintain the equilibrium of our own home sweet home—and the sanity of Mr. Hanley—the lessons came to a swift end.

Another man, Leone, sometimes called to sit and chat for a while. He would always sit on a chair by the open door, bent over his walking stick, white hair and long white beard covering his hands that held the stick. He wore big boots and a khaki-coloured long overcoat, and he was a familiar figure up and down the Hollow. He looked as ancient as the hills to me, and if I had been asked, I would probably have guessed he was at least one hundred years old. Mum always enjoyed his visits, and she told us he was extremely intelligent and widely read. He was a neighbour of Auntie Lizzie's, and she helped him with his everyday needs.

Mum helped the old man, Mr. Mitchell, who lived next door to us. She would take meals round to him and help him with washing and other household chores. He was a small, bespectacled man with a moustache, and a spotted kerchief round his neck. He could sometimes be seen sitting outside on a chair in the sunshine, smoking his pipe. I had no idea that Mr. Mitchell was in difficulty of any kind, until something happened that left me extremely puzzled and my mum in floods of tears.

I was sitting in a sawn-off tree trunk that gave me a wonderful viewing point right across the fields and the Sludge, and it enabled me to see into the three back yards and gardens at the start of the track across the fields to the farm. I was probably practicing my "peewit" calls that sounded, to my ears, exactly like the birds as they flew across the treetops, when I spotted something going on over the hedge. A couple of strangers came up the other side of Mr. Mitchell's house, went in through his door, and started to remove pieces of furniture, which they hauled down the path into a waiting truck. This went on for quite some time, until all the furniture had been removed. Then, to my astonishment, they led Mr. Mitchell out of the house and banged the door shut. He was crying and wailing as he shouted to my mother: "Dunna let 'em tak' me, Missus, please dunna let 'em tak' me."

My mother watched, helpless, over the hedge, before she disappeared crying into the house.

My mother never explained, and I never understood until many years later. In Britain, there used to be workhouses where those unable to support themselves were given accommodation and, in the earlier years, employment. They were cruel places, where men and women were separated, and children were taken away from their parents. People there were given the most basic of rations. At the time of this incident, most of the workhouses had either been abolished or reassigned as hospitals for the elderly. There was one such building quite near to us on Turnhurst Road, Chell, which eventually became Westcliffe Hospital. I would pass it every day on the bus ride to Brownhills High School from Mow Cop, when I'd passed my 11+. I should imagine that this was where poor old Mr. Mitchell was taken when he had no family to support him. For quite some time, the empty house seemed to exude sadness, which crept through the dividing wall and affected the whole of our family.

But little by little, normality returned, and routine took over. Mum kept the house ticking over—cooking and baking, cleaning and mending, washing and ironing, and making sure that we children and Dad had everything we needed. Dad continued to oversee his work at the Iron and Steel factory, ensuring the constant flow of raw materials to the munition factory at Radway Greed. And Roy and I made our daily pilgrimage to Woodcocks' Well School, up the Hollow and down the Hollow, up and down, with our strong little legs making light work of all the steep hills.

We never dawdled on the way to school in case we were late, but at home time, after coming down the School Bank and into the village, I sometimes took my time to investigate the hedge banks on the last stretch home. Several of my school friends lived in the houses at the top of the Hollow: Irene and Nancy and her little brother, Raymond. Being several years younger than us, Raymond wasn't allowed to join in any of our games, which probably annoyed him at times. So, he got his own back by teasing us. One day while I was meandering down the last stretch of my homeward journey, I spotted Ray tucked behind the wall that bordered the field. He was creeping along in the grass, out of sight, then jumping up and waving his arms and shouting names before bobbing down again and appearing further along the wall. I watched carefully, noting where he was likely to appear again. I sprinted along the wall, and as he bobbed his head back up, I shot a smart left hook, smack into his eye. Shocked, he came out from behind the wall and made his way home to explain to his mum who he'd been fighting with, and what mischief he'd been up to that resulted in a black eye. I don't remember him doing it again!

It was on the journey to school that I sometimes collected "treasure" to show the teacher: a wonderful blackbird's speckled blue egg that had dropped out of a nest, a few primroses, or an interesting stone out of the tiny stream of water running down the gutters on either side of the road. They would be placed on display on the teacher's desk or the nature table. It was while daydreaming my way home one day that I thought of a *real* treasure that I could take to show everybody, and I picked up the pace and ran the rest of the way to share my brilliant idea with my mum.

Because I was born in 1937, which was the year of the coronation of George VI and Queen Elizabeth, I had received a blue tin money box with a silver crown coin inside. The box was square with a slit in the top and a little lock on the front, so the special coin could be locked away and kept safe. As I had started school at four-and-a-half, I was in a class of children who were older than me, and I was the only one to possess such a wonderful money box. My mother said I could take it to school, but I was to bring it back the same day. I could hardly contain my excitement as I made my way to school the following morning, the box tucked securely under my arm. I presented it proudly to the teacher, who put it on her desk for safekeeping, and there it stayed for all to see throughout the day.

At home time, I collected it and started to make my way home. About halfway down the Hollow, I met up with Ernest, who lived at the farm across the fields, and he asked me what I was carrying. I proudly showed him and told him how special it was, because it had been sent to me from the Queen, who lived in the palace in London. He gazed at it for some time and then said, "Well, that's nothing. Look what I've got in my pocket." He pulled out two knuckle bones. Knuckle bones were from the butcher's shop—short, flat bones about eight inches long, which were scrubbed and cleaned before use. They were then rattled and clicked between the fingers of one hand to produce a sort of musical sound.

"Go on then," I said. "Play them." And he did. I was mesmerised by the smart way he handled those bones and at the wonderful sound that he produced. "Wow! Can I have a go?" I asked, and he placed them between my fingers and showed me how to hold them. I couldn't make them work or produce any sound at all, but he reassured me that it needed practice, and that in time I'd be brilliant. I was more than ready to do a straight swap, and I handed over the coronation money box in exchange for the magical knuckle bones.

Mum was waiting to greet me at the gate, and as she watched me travel the last few yards, a quizzical look came over her face.

"Where's the money box?" she asked.

"Oh, I swapped it with Ernest for a pair of knuckle bones. Look—" I got no further.

"*Well*," she said, "you just go right on across those fields and *swap them right back*!" I don't know if Mum ever realised that she was responsible there and then for scuppering my chances of ever becoming a famous solo knuckle bone player!

The only time we didn't make the daily trek up the Hollow to school was when the roads were impassable with heavy snowfalls or if we were ill. I'm sure we had all the normal childhood illnesses, but there were three I remember well, for different reasons. It was either before I started school or in my first year that I had the measles. In those pre-NHS days, parents had to use their own initiative and depend upon friends and neighbours for advice, together with the odd bottle of medicine or packet of pills, if they could afford to visit or call the doctor.

I remember feeling sick and being unwell and tossing and turning through the night, but then my dad had a cunning plan! They knew that strong light had to be avoided or measles could damage the eyesight. So, he rigged up a tent over the settee. We had acquired a second-hand settee and armchair, and a large sheet was somehow strung over the settee, rather like—to my mind—a Bedouin tent. My pillow, bed covers and blankets were brought downstairs and stuffed into it, making a delightful hidden cave, dark and cosy. When I was recovering, I imagined all sorts of scenarios taking place under that sheet. Aladdin's magic carpet couldn't have carried me to more exciting places than I visited whilst there.

Mum tried hard to keep me entertained as I improved. The best idea she had was to provide me with a cardboard box, some bits of old material, and a couple of clothes pegs. That motley collection became a bed, replete with bed covers, and a beautiful doll whose face had been drawn on the top of one of the pegs and who was dressed in clothes that I cobbled together from the scraps of cloth. I was disappointed when I was declared fit enough to go back to my normal bedtime routines and was sad to see the Bedouin tent demolished and the settee returned to its normal function.

The next two illnesses I recall were when we had moved from the Hollow up into the village. Roy got yellow jaundice first, and then I too became ill with it. I remember the weirdness of looking at Roy when he was yellow: yellow skin and eyes and, when Mum lifted up his pyjama shirt, a completely yellow chest and tummy. A dreadful nausea accompanied the yellowing of the skin, and we were not allowed to eat any fat of any kind.

An illness that was dreaded among the village families was scarlet fever. The doctor had to be notified about this disease, because it necessitated being sent away to an isolation hospital for several weeks. The nearest one to us was Bucknall. The name might as well have been in a foreign climate—we had never heard of it, and it was as good as across the other side of the world to us. Scarlet fever started with an intensely sore, white-spotted throat that lasted for some time before the skin started to peel off. Mum was as scared of this illness as we were, and she never reported it to anybody when Roy and I caught it, either school or doctor. But I can clearly see her in my mind's eye, peeling strips of skin off our hands and feet, backs and tummies. We were never sent away, and thankfully we both lived to fight another day!

Our make-believe games, and the scenarios we imagined, all paled into insignificance when Grandma introduced something into the village that nobody had believed possible: television! It was only introduced into the UK in 1936, one year before I was born, and Grandma bought a nine-inch TV in about 1944 or 1945, while the production of television was still in its infancy. She became famous overnight in Mount Pleasant. Everyone was desperate to pay her a visit. Old friends made a reappearance, and new ones lingered by the shop counter, hoping for an invitation beyond the curtain to see the wondrous sight.

It was tiny. A little box with a black and white screen. When it was working, only a few programmes were available: *Annette Mills and Muffin the Mule*, a lady sitting at the piano and singing to a large puppet on the lid of the piano, whose strings were clearly visible (along with the occasional hand of the puppeteer); *Mr. Pastry*, a slapstick comedian rather like Charlie Chaplin, who stumbled into stepladders, and fell over chairs, and was soaked with buckets of water that were thrown over him. But most of all, the screen showed the still picture of a little girl in a dunce's pointed cap, who held a baton which she pointed at a blackboard. The caption read, in large letters, "Normal service will be resumed as soon as possible." Another breakdown!

Regardless of that, the villagers loved it and squeezed into the tiny living room. The fire would be roaring up the chimney, and people would stand shoulder to shoulder, squashed together so that not another square inch was available, and not another body could have wriggled its way into the sweating crowd of folks, all craning their necks at the tiny screen. I'd sometimes wander up to the village to watch this phenomenon, and I would be squeezed in right by the fire, on the buffet in the corner. My legs would be covered in red circles where the fire had burned them.

We would stay as long as we wanted. Dad could have that extra cuppa with Gran before bedtime, after everyone else had trickled out. Time didn't matter. We would eventually say goodnight and make our way out through the shop, the bell tingling as we banged the door shut. Darkness surrounded us as we made our way to the top of the Hollow—no stars, no lights, only the impenetrable thick cover of blackness filling every space. We'd stand for a moment before we plunged into the downward slope of the journey home. I'd reach my hand out and slip it into my dad's strong hand, and he held me tight as we strode home together. Utter safety! Utter trust! The darkness held no fear, because I knew that whatever happened, Dad would protect me and keep me safe 'til we got home.

How marvellous is that relationship between a father and his child! It was a wonderful pattern to me throughout the coming years and laid the foundations for yet another vital relationship. I was eighteen when I heard the invitation from John's Gospel to follow Jesus, the Good Shepherd, who promised to lead his sheep to the safety of the sheepfold and protect them from all harm. All they had to do was hear the call and follow him—and I did just that. Metaphorically speaking, I reached up my hand and slipped it into the hand of my Heavenly Father. Utter safety! Utter trust! Journeys down the

Hollow are long past; times spent with my dad are now just precious memories. But my journey with my Heavenly Father continues, and I'm still exploring the hedge banks as we travel along, looking for the treasure in hidden places, and still curious as to what may lie around the next bend.

"One more step along the world I go
One more step along the world I go
From the old things to the new
Keep me travelling along with you.

Round the corners of the world I turn
More and more about the world I learn
All the new things that I see
You'll be looking along with me.

As I travel through the bad and good,
Keep me travelling the way I should
When I see no way to go,
You'll be telling me the way I know.

Give me courage when the world is rough
Keep me loving though the world is tough
Leap and sing in all I do
Keep me travelling along with you."

– Sydney Carter

CHAPTER FIVE

A Change of Location
(116, The Flat)

I t seems strange that despite the fact that the house in the Hollow had been such a secure haven for me, I have no recollection of packing up and moving out. I would have been around six, and the only thing I can assume is that we children spent the day elsewhere, either at a friend's or relative's house. Similarly, I don't remember moving *into* 116, the Flat, although I do remember something on the very first day of being there.

The previous owner and occupant was the elderly mother of Uncle George from Mossley. Because she wasn't able to look after herself anymore, Uncle George was taking her somewhere to be cared for. We weren't aware of any of the sale's arrangements or talks that had gone on previously—the only thing I did know was that it had cost £300, which seemed a colossal sum of money to me.

What does stick in my mind are all the things that had been cleared out of the house and left on the lawn outside the back door: items of crockery, pots and pans, jugs and basins, cut glass salt pots, and several cruets. They were left so that we could take anything we wanted before the rest was taken away and disposed of. To my surprise, there was no sink or inside tap in the kitchen, just an outside tap to collect water from. If we wanted to boil a kettle, we had to go outside the back door to fill it and take it inside to boil on the fire. Because of the inconvenience of this arrangement, an inside tap and stone sink were soon installed in the kitchen.

Downstairs there was a living room, entered by a front door, which had a coal fire in a small range, complete with hobs, oven, and mantlepiece. The large table, organ, settee, armchair, and wooden chairs had all been transferred from our other house, so it immediately felt like home. In between the living room and kitchen was a pantry and stillage on the left, and stairs leading to the two bedrooms on the right. The kitchen was much larger than our previous one, with a covered boiler built into one of the corners for Mum to do her washing in. Underneath the boiler was a recess where a fire could be lit to heat the water—a very small metal door had to be swung open in order to shovel in the coal, and, as with the range, the ashes had to be shovelled out after use.

Upstairs there were just two bedrooms, but there was a change in the sleeping arrangements. Roy had the small back bedroom to himself, while I had a single bed in the same room as Mum and Dad. Furniture was very sparse in the bedrooms. Roy just had a single bed, while there were two beds—a single and a double—and a large set of drawers with a swing back mirror on top in the other bedroom.

A chamber pot was installed underneath each bed because, once again, the toilet—a two-seater this time— was in the back yard. A large garden comprising quite a lot of land surrounded three sides of the house. There was a wooden shed outside the back door, and a tumbledown, roofless stone structure covered in yellow stonecrop, which formed part of the boundary of the back garden.

To me, the most exciting part was a magnificent hawthorn tree soaring into the sky, which would soon become a wonderful replacement for my secret den under the table—with a much improved view point.

Our new location was just a few yards from Grandma's shop and was far more central. Coming out of the front door, down the yard and steps, and through the little wrought iron gate, we could turn right and walk along a raised path, incongruously called the Flat, which led past Triner's farm and up School Bank to Woodcocks' Well School and St. Luke's Church.

If we turned left at Triner's farm, we could go down a little road, named the Intic, that brought us to Hall's shop and Mount Pleasant Chapel. Left here would lead us back along the main—and only— street of the village to Grandma's shop. Opposite was Whitehurt's (Spudder's) shop, and climbing back up to the Flat would bring us home. There were four shops along the main street: Grandma's, Farmer's Newsagents and Sweet Shop, another little one further along (I've forgotten the name), ending at Hall's on the corner. Two pubs—The Crown and The Millstone—lay at either end of the village, which to me were places of ill repute that I viewed with a sense of horror. At one side of The Millstone was a factory that made velvet and was called the Fustian.

Our house was only a few hundred yards from the factory and pub at that end of the village and was the first one along the Flat. When we moved in, the garden was largely neglected, but after a while, Dad (although no Alan Titchmarch) had knocked it into shape. The triangular end plot was usually planted with potatoes, while the front garden had both vegetables and flowers. If you came into the garden by the front gate and steps, there was a small lawn to the left, surrounded by narrow beds of perennials, while peas and beans filled the right side. A hedge divided the front garden from the lawned area at the side of the house, and Mum grew love-in-a-mist and marigolds along the hedge.

I mustn't forget the thin strips of garden that edged the path leading to the steps from the front door. They contained Dad's prize collection of carnations. Beautiful flowers in various colours— yellow with a thin red stripe, pink, red, white, and lemon. Lovely to look at and wonderful to smell as we returned home and lifted the latch on the gate after a busy day at school.

The shed, where we kept the coal, provided the boundary for the back garden, where more vegetables were planted. A rain butt sat by the back door, which had contained—if only for a few short hours—the unfortunate crested newts. Mum washed our hair in the rainwater because she said it made it shine, but I didn't like how the surface was always covered by dead flies and bits of debris that had been blown into it and which had to be scooped off before use.

Dad used to encourage Roy to help him in the garden. They collected tall, straight sticks to support the peas and beans, and they would stick them into the ground when the plants were just a few inches high. As they grew, they had to be fastened to the sticks by string so they wouldn't flop over in the wind. The ground had to be dug and the soil turned over with the spade before the seed potatoes were put in. I loved seeing the flowers on the potato plants—tiny white stars with a yellow centre—but it was when the flowers died that we knew the potatoes were ready for harvesting. Oh, the joy of standing and watching Dad as he dug deep with the wooden shafted garden fork and drew out a mix of soil, plant, roots, and handfuls of delicious new potatoes. We would scramble to pick them out of the soil, rubbing the dirt and skin with our fingers to reveal the white flesh underneath. We would take our haul into Mum in the kitchen, knowing that in an hour or so we would be enjoying a veritable feast of new potatoes smothered in golden butter. Food fit for a king!

Not all of Roy's gardening memories were so pleasant, though. One day during the school holidays, Dad had left instructions for Roy to start forking the soil over in the vegetable patch ready for planting. He'd done a few rows when there was a terrible yowling. Mum and I raced to find out what had happened and discovered, to our horror, that Roy had driven the garden fork into his foot, one of the prongs going right through his shoe and into the flesh between Roy's big toe and the next one. There was instant washing and cleaning and some sort of bandage applied, but I don't think the thought of a tetanus injection was even considered. In fact, I don't know if they were even available at that time.

If you had the opportunity to climb high in the sky in an air balloon over Mow Cop and the surrounding area, you would look down on the end tip of the Pennine Mountain Range. It makes its way down the central spine of Britain, ending in small, rocky outcrops. Mow Cop, nearby Congleton Edge and the Cloud (which just measures in at one thousand feet), lie to the west of the southernmost tip of this range, but there is still a lot of evidence of rocky slopes and outcrops in these local areas. Such evidence could be found right outside our back door! The whole area was called "The Rocks" and was an immediate replacement for my erstwhile favourite play area, the Sludge.

The stony path leading up to the Rocks followed the rough stone wall at the end of our property and led up to the level grassy area at the top via some flat blocks of sloping rock that had been eroded by the passage of many feet. As we became familiar with this place, we rarely chose to use these steps but scrambled our way up the rock face, negotiating the footholds and searching for the niches where we could cling on— sometimes by the tips of our fingers. We found comfortable perches in little basins of rock, where surfaces came together and formed tiny catchment pools of rainwater. If some of the rock faces were too sheer, with no promise of hand or footholds, we would work our way along cracks, lodging our toes in the spaces and using the flat of our hands to steady us. There was always such a sense of achievement when we scrambled onto the grass at the top and rolled over on our backs to catch our breath. Peering over the edge and looking down, we could see where we would have landed if one of the holds had not been successfully negotiated: piles of large rocks and slopes of scree that had fallen in wind or rain lay menacingly at the bottom of the climb.

The danger of disused mine shafts had been replaced with the hazards of rock climbing. No wonder Mum often forbade us to go! No wonder, on the occasions when she did allow us, we left home with dire warnings ringing in our ears! No wonder we sometimes didn't tell her so that she wouldn't worry about our safety!

There were two similar rock faces—the one behind our house, and the other further up, near to The Millstone pub, which was very sheer, very high, and very dangerous. I watched boys climb this, including Roy, and I determined to master it. I watched where they found the holds and how they managed the sheer flat surfaces by changing direction—going sideways rather than climbing straight up—and my resolve was strengthened.

I tried several times, climbing up a bit before jumping down when I got stuck, and hadn't gone too high. I could never resist a dare! I'd jump across the widest streams, climb the most difficult trees, scale the sheerest rock face, and this one wasn't going to be any different. The first time I did it, I was with either Roy or some friends. One stood at the bottom, shouting instructions: "Look to the right, there's a little ledge. Get hold of it. Then slide your left foot across and feel for a little crevice." Another one of them lay flat on their tummy at the top, shouting encouragement: "Come on! You're halfway up … you've only got a third left to go … you're nearly there!"

There's always that point of terror when you get halfway and there's no turning back, and you have to teach the butterflies in your stomach to fly in formation. But climb it I did, and many times again after that first trek up, never being able to resist the challenge.

Lots of adventures and escapades took place on those rocks: mountaineering between rock faces in our wellington boots after a heavy snowfall, with an old broom handle as a trekking pole; playing in the rock pools found in flat surfaces, where the rock had been eroded away; just laying, daydreaming on the springy green grass that covered large areas.

But there were occasions when the whole village community carefully scaled the sloping steps to gather on the grassy area on the rocks behind our house. One such occasion was Bonfire Night, when wood and crates, tree branches and rubbish of all kinds were hauled up there in preparation, days before the fifth of November. A soaring bonfire was built—by both boys and dads—and crowned with a stuffed Guy Fawkes, resplendent in somebody's old trousers and jacket, and bound together with string. Flashlights and lanterns bobbed their way up the steps to the waiting gathering, before somebody's dad lit the kindling, and the paraffin-drenched wood shot sheets of flame and smoke high into the sky. Fireworks were lit, and we watched rockets scream upwards, while dads lit bangers in a clearing, away from the flames. Laughter and screams, and potatoes thrown into the flames. These were to be rescued several hours later and eaten, blackened, without any butter or salt, but thoroughly enjoyed because of the excitement and occasion of it all.

A huge bonfire was also lit on a spare piece of ground at the top of the Hollow to celebrate victory in Europe (VE Day). The whole village turned out, fireworks were lit, and the village street was alive with crowds of people going in and out of the pubs to celebrate the end of a dreadful time of war and deprivation. I only know of two people who didn't join in with these celebrations: my grandma, who sat alone and grieved for Raymond, who would never be returning to enjoy the victory, and me, who was only allowed to join the crowds for a short while before being taken home to bed. Mum thought there would be a lot of drunken brawling, and I would be better off at home. I remember forlornly gazing out of the bedroom window and watching fireworks zoom into the night sky before putting on my pyjamas and climbing into bed.

On other national days of celebration, fires were sometimes lit on high geographical points, and burning beacons could be seen from Land's End to John O' Groats.

But my secret place, my place of solitude, was found right back home in my garden, high up in the branches of the hawthorn tree. I loved my brother and the company of my friends, but it was hidden amidst the lipped twigs and branches that I was free to explore the "labyrinthine tunnels of my mind"[1] and lose myself in flights of fancy. When we first moved in, the tree was virtually impossible for me

---

1   *The Hound of Heaven*, by Francis Thompson

to climb, because the trunk was too tall and had no obvious hand-holds. Roy made it possible by hammering a sturdy chisel halfway up, which enabled me to swing my leg up and pull myself into my leafy hideaway.

The first thing I discovered was what a marvellous tree house it made; right at the top of the trunk was the entrance and living area, while further up in the branches were two bedrooms, one to the left and the other to the right, following the direction of the branches. I often took a book up there, secreted in one of my pockets, and I'd sit and read to my heart's delight. At other times, I'd climb right into the crow's nest in the topmost branches and "sail" along the main street of the village. I could spot people going in and out of shops, children playing hopscotch and skipping rope on the road (stopping if a car came by), boys on their bikes, mums hauling heavy bags home—and I could clearly see anyone coming up my front path.

I used to sit up there and watch for my dad to come home from work. The P.M.T. bus would stop at the top of the Hollow, and if it was the right time of day, my dad would get off. I'd watch how he walked up the slope to the gate, how he climbed the steps to the front path. Was his head down? Did he look tired? Was he walking slowly? By noting these things, I could determine if he was feeling ill or not. He suffered with dreadful headaches and severe stomach pain, and for years I was riddled with worry about the state of his health. I would watch him refuse food and sit doubled up in pain with his head in his hands, while Mum would fetch the tablets for his head, and the Aludrox bottle of medicine for his stomach. After years of suffering, he underwent major stomach surgery, and half of his badly ulcerated stomach was removed. After a long recuperation and convalescence in Grange-over-Sands, we were all relieved, and greatly delighted, to see a much healthier Dad.

It was a couple of years after moving to the Flat that I started to be plagued by the annual recurrence of hay fever and asthma. It started after a sunny afternoon of playing "roly-poly" down one of the slopes in one of the fields. The grass was high and bursting with pollen, and afterwards I sneezed my way home, eyes streaming and nose running. The asthma followed and was most acute at night. I gasped my way through the long hours, propped up by several pillows, with my mum by the side of the bed, encouraging me to "just fight for the next breath, come on, it's nearly over." All through the years and into later life, I dreaded the acute asthma attacks that blighted the months of May and June.

After his illness, Dad returned to work at Shelton Steelworks, and Mum continued to work for a nearby family at their farm down The Bank. During the school holidays, Roy and I were left with a few chores to do, and then we were free to do whatever we wanted … within reason! Mum would leave us with many instructions as to what we could have for lunch and what we were and were not allowed to do.

One particular day, she gave me an errand to run. At lunchtime, I was to go to the Co-op and ask Mary there for the six custard tarts she was saving for us. The morning dragged, and I watched the fingers of the clock go round. Time seemed to stand still. I couldn't wait for twelve o'clock to arrive, and I scampered off across the street to the Co-op a few minutes early. Mary had put the custards aside for me to collect, and I retraced my steps slowly, careful to carry the paper bag with its precious contents as level as I possibly could, so as not to crumble the tarts inside. As instructed, I put them inside the pantry on the cold stillage to keep them fresh.

Mum had said I could have one after my lunch, so I gobbled up my sandwich and took one of the tarts outside and sat with my back to the wall in the sunshine. I was going to enjoy every delicious morsel. First the frill of pastry round the edge, nibble by nibble, crumb by crumb. Then the slow excavation of the glorious golden custard, my tongue relishing every last drop from the pastry shell. Last of all, the pastry itself was carefully demolished, and I gathered the odd crumbs from the foil dish.

I was content for a little while, but then a picture seemed to fill my mind: the plate of custards in the pantry. There were five left on the plate. I counted off in my head: one for Dad, one for Mum, one for Roy—that left two spare ones. I went into the pantry to check I'd got it right. One, two, three, four, five. Yes, if everybody had one, it left two over! They didn't belong to anybody—I'd have another! It was just as delicious as the first. I licked my fingers clean and then started to play one of my games.

Strangely enough, after a while the vision of the remaining spare custard began to torment me. If that wasn't intended for anyone, it wouldn't be missed.

It wasn't long before only three custards remained on the plate. Later in the afternoon, another one disappeared, because I reasoned that Roy didn't really deserve one; he could sometimes be a bit mean. Two remained: one for Dad, one for Mum.

As the afternoon wore to a close, a realisation came to my mind. My mum was so kind. She could never sit down to eat her meal and enjoy a custard tart if I hadn't got one. And would Dad sit there and eat one if he was the one left eating by himself? I couldn't imagine it.

After they had all gone, I felt a bit sick—and a bit scared. How was I going to get out of this one? It took me a while to devise a plan. This is how the plan unfolded:

Mum arrived home.

"Did you collect the custard tarts from the Co-op?"

"No, Mary hadn't saved any!"

Off went Mum to the Co-op.

On her return: "She says you picked them up at 12:00 p.m."

"No. She hadn't saved any."

"Right, come with me."

I was taken across to the Co-op, where I stood, shamefaced, before an angry Mary, before being taken back home by a furious Mum: "Just you wait till your dad comes home."

Mum and Dad each had their distinctive roles in the family. Mum was the caregiver, seeing to our needs—cooking, baking, cleaning, washing, and ironing—while Dad was the main breadwinner, who spent a great deal of his time at work. However, looking back, I realised that together they taught us the essential principles of life. Dad established standards and beliefs, making church and Sunday school an integral part of our weekly routine. But it was Mum who taught us to pray and have the faith to believe that if we took our needs, however small, to God, they would be met. Together they gave us the building blocks to establish our lives on a living faith.

Likewise, they dealt with authority and discipline. Mum would guide and encourage, but it was Dad who meted out punishment in a unique way. Neither of them believed in corporal punishment (unless pushed to the limits!), but Mum would sometimes resort to a rant and shout if she was angry. Dad, however, only needed to turn and *look* at us for us to know that we had reached the limits. I should imagine that the custard tart incident warranted a very hard look indeed! One thing I do know—the custard tarts brought an end to my petty pilfering, and I remember exactly the moment the line was drawn.

It was a Harvest Festival at the chapel, and Dad was taking me to the morning service. We sat on the very front row, as I liked to do, so I could see everything clearly. The display was set before us in a riot of colour, and the distinctive smell of Harvest Day filled the church: a mixture of ripe fruit and golden corn that carried with it the memory of hay fields and loaded carts and glorious hot summer days. Just before the services started, Dad leaned over to me and, in a whisper, said, "You won't touch anything, will you, Jean?" I'm sure he was warning me not to set the piles of apples tumbling down the aisles, or the tins of fruit from toppling over, but in my mind, he thought I was going to steal something and sneak it into my pockets. I was horrified! It was like a stone had dropped into my stomach. My dad thought I was a thief! That was the moment that a firm resolve took hold of me: I would never ever give him any cause in the future to doubt my integrity. I never stole again.

I suppose it was fitting that the chapel was the place where this epiphany took place, as it was one of three platforms on which my religious knowledge was founded: home, school, and church.

Harvest Festival was the only occasion when the chapel was decorated or embellished in any way. The Sunday school was quite ordinary: bare, wooden floorboards, pews, and a small, raised platform with a table and organ on it. Inside the chapel, however, it was beautifully painted and decorated. Pews were highly polished and covered with patterned, red baize runners. Carpeted aisles led to a raised pulpit, which was within a railed communion space, and coloured light from one or two stained glass windows was reflected back from the two large, highly polished brass vases standing on either side of the pulpit area. There was also an upstairs gallery with an organ and choir stalls, from where we could lean and gaze down on the tops of heads below and count how many people were in the congregation. The numbers were limited on a weekly basis, but anniversaries and choir festivals and performances of *The Messiah* brought forth huge crowds that had to squeeze into every available space.

I had one or two ways to entertain myself if I was bored during long sermons. I would take my handkerchief out of my pocket and make different shapes by folding it in different ways. The other thing I liked to do was to pick the fluff off the red baize seat runners. During a very long, boring sermon, I could amass quite a large ball, which I then had to hide in my pocket to dispose of after service.

There was the weekly Sunday school routine of hymns and Bible stories, culminating in the annual prize-giving of books for good attendance. But there were other highlights of church life dotted through the year.

I always had a new dress for the Sunday School Anniversary, which was made by Auntie Ruth. A stage was erected in front of the pulpit, and we children would parade in at the start of the service, resplendent in best bib and tucker. Uncle George was the conductor, and he had to climb onto one of the pew seats in the middle of the church, from where he stood and waited until he had everybody's attention before he started to wave his baton about. I often sang a solo, and Roy and I joined together to sing duets. I don't know about Roy, but I hated singing these solos and duets and was nearly sick with nerves beforehand. Auntie Ruth and my dad had no such fears, and their voices rang out from the choir across the congregation and were admired by one and all.

A week before the annual anniversaries, we had "walking round" Sunday, when choristers and children, plus my dad and Uncle George, walked from Mount Pleasant village up to the top of Mow Cop, stopping at intervals to sing to anybody who cared to listen. Dad would pull his tuning fork out of his pocket so we could pitch the tune in the right key before we sang. But the best bit was when we arrived at the square Wesleyan chapel at the end of our musical tour, and we would be regaled with drinks of milk and the most delicious sugar buns before starting our descent into the village on the way back home.

Uncle George's day job was at Cowlishaw Walker and Co., an engineering company, and Dad's was directing trains at Shelton, but their common passion was music—Dad with his choirs, his organ, and his singing, while Uncle George was a wonderful pianist. He also composed music and lyrics for many of our Church Anniversaries. It was wonderful to be with them, Uncle George on the piano and Dad standing by his side, singing the hymns from Moody and Sankey: "Out of the Ivory Palaces," "Jerusalem," "All in the April Evening," and many others. Sometimes a friend, Bob, joined them, and he brought his violin. I remember watching Bob play, his eyes closed, completely lost, while wonderful music poured from the strings of the violin as he lovingly drew the bow over them. It was during one of these glorious times that I heard Massenet's "Theme from Thomas Tallis" for the first time, and I've loved it ever since.

In my memory, those times always took place in the front room at Auntie Dorrie and Uncle George's. They always seemed to be hot summer afternoons, windows open, curtains moving in the breeze, and the scent of flowers from the garden floating in to join with the chords and cadences of the music. How privileged we were to have so much musical talent in our midst.

Our anniversary services with the choir, the music, and the visiting speakers drew people from surrounding villages. But for me there were other delights apart from sugar buns, music, and the annual new dress connected to such occasions. On those special Sundays, we always had a marvellous spread at tea time: ham or tongue sandwiches, salad, Mum's baking—which always included little pastry tarts filled with her wonderful lemon curd—and tinned fruit with Carnation milk poured onto it. The only downside was that we always had to entertain the visiting speaker, and we had to wait until he'd been served before we could have our turn. I would wait nervously with my eye on the plate of ham, or the homemade cake and tarts, and I'd watch the fruit served out, hoping he wasn't too hungry and that there would be some left when it came to my turn.

But these were highlights of the year, and village life generally was made up of the mundane and the ordinary: school every weekday, home routines, friends and family, daily chores, and the ever-rotating peaks and troughs of rural living.

Over the years, I have sometimes listened as people have shared unhappy recollections from their sad childhoods; looking back, I marvel at my own "golden years," which formed such a wonderfully solid base and foundation for all that the future held. I also think that if I had known what the future held—and that when I started school at four-and-a-half I'd be going for the next fifty years—I wouldn't have been so eager to skip merrily up the School Bank to enter the portals of education housed at Woodcocks' Well.

CHAPTER SIX

School Part One:
The Beginning of a Fifty-Year "Stint"

It's hard to imagine myself at the tender age of four-and-a-half making my way up that very steep School Bank on the way to Woodcocks' school. I know how I felt inside, but it's difficult to get a picture in my mind, as I don't know what I looked like as a little girl. Roy has drawn a thumbnail sketch, which gives me a vague idea:

"Red, curly hair and sturdy."

"Fat?" I ask.

"No, *sturdy*," he insists. "Not thin, but not fat. Just *sturdy*."

So now I have a clearer picture. This little red-haired girl, with a few curls poking out of her bonnet, gas mask slung over one shoulder, her hand in Mum's, makes her way on her sturdy little legs up the hill to start a lifetime of school. Although I was excited and full of anticipation for all that lay ahead, I do remember holding quite tightly to my mum's hand, because it was a bit overwhelming to think that in a very little while I was going to be left on my own in a place I didn't know, with people who were strangers.

The school lies halfway up the hill that goes from Mount Pleasant village to the castle at the top of Mow Cop, and it faces St. Luke's Church. On coming to the top of School Bank, a sloping incline leads up to the head teacher's house and gardens before dropping down again as it comes to the school entrance. It was up this slope we walked, through the gate of the head's garden, and right into his house. I don't remember any conversations, but it was from here that Mr. Lowry, the head, relieved Mum of her charge and escorted me into the reception class to be introduced to my teacher, Mrs. Hampson. Six-and-a-half years of school stretched before me in this stone-walled building—vitally important years of learning and growing, developing and planning. A rich seam of my life that had to be dug and excavated but that would reveal priceless treasures for later life.

Have you ever sat in front of a globe and spun it round and round on its axis? Rivers and streams, countries and continents, seas and oceans fly round unseen, flashing by in a blur until you put your finger out to bring it to an instant halt. Then every detail is clear, and a particular place stands out: names, hills, highs, lows ... all are high-lighted. All is known.

So those years flew by, with multitudes of facts, masses of learning, loads of experiences, all making up my education. The foundation, the backdrop of my life. But then there are times when the world seems to have stood still, and I remember words and feelings and places and people in minute detail. It's these happenings and events that stand out as I look back over those years, and it's these occasions that I'll try to bring to life for you.

I think that because I could already read when I went to school, I found some things a bit boring. There were lessons that were dedicated to learning and writing letters. Large cards containing a picture with a letter underneath had to be carefully copied: "A for apple," "B for ball," "C for cat," etc. One day, tired of such repetition, I lined up by the teacher's desk to ask her a question.

"Please could I just draw the pictures and colour them in, and leave the letters?"

She answered, to my shock and horror, by smacking me across the face!

"Just go sit down and get on with what you're supposed to do."

I went back to my desk with cheeks burning, not only from the smack but also from embarrassment at being so humiliated in front of the class.

Most of the time, I just got on with my work, discovering that there was a particular treat for those who finished their work early. At the side of the classroom sat a marvellous rocking horse, which must have stood three feet tall, beautifully painted, with a mane and tail of hair. Anyone who had done their work well and finished early could be given the chance to have a ride on the marvellous creature. It was such a joy to be lifted up onto his back, feel the reins in your hands, and lean forward to stroke his mane before taking off at a steady canter, and then a full gallop to who knows where. It was quite a surprise to hear the teacher's voice break into the adventure with a reminder that "time is up" and it was time to come back to earth!

Reception class was not an adventure for everybody, and it certainly wasn't for my friend Esther, who started at the same time as me and was a few months older. Her mother had to bring her right into the classroom every morning because she was so upset. She clung onto her mum's coat, screaming and crying. The teacher would get hold of her and unlatch her from her mum before sitting her down into her desk, all the while encouraging Esther's mum to leave because, "Es would be fine in a minute!"

But she wasn't!

She continued to scream until the teacher sent her out into the cloakroom, making sure the outside door was firmly shut. One day, tired of the screaming outside the classroom door, she sent me out to quieten her.

"Jean, go and make Es be quiet—or there'll be trouble."

I made my way to the cloakroom where Esther was huddled on the bench under the coats hanging on the pegs. I put my arm round her shoulders and hugged her, while telling her to, "Shh, shh now. It won't be long before your mum comes back to fetch you."

She continued to cry.

"Hush," I said. "We can play together at playtime. It's nearly playtime now."

The sobs continued. Then, in desperation—

"If you stop crying, I'll give you a banana when we go home."

I had never seen a banana—never even smelled a banana—but to me, it was one of those exotic fruits that people talked about in storybooks. An object to be greatly desired. Sure enough, the promise—though impossible to be fulfilled—had the desired effect. The crying stopped, Esther wiped away her tears, and the day continued without any calamity falling on us!

The infant department consisted of two classes: Reception, where my story began, and Class 1 next door. These two classes were in their own building, set apart from the juniors. The teacher in the next class must have taken a shine to me because there would sometimes be a knock on the dividing door, and Miss Bailey would poke her head through.

"Could I borrow her for a bit?" she would ask my teacher. If all my work was done, there would be a nod of agreement, and Miss Bailey would take me through to her class. If she was telling a story, she would sit me on her knee while she read to the class. At other times, she would hold me in her arms while she listened to tables being chanted, or spellings being practised. An unusual thing to do—and one that made me feel a bit conspicuous—but one that sticks in my mind nevertheless.

Two daily routines became a familiar part of our school life: morning playtime and its bottles of milk, and midday, when lunch was served. Every morning round about ten o'clock, the school caretakers would haul in a large crate full of bottles of milk. In the reception class, there was an open fire with a protective iron guard around it (sometimes little knickers could be seen on this after an unfortunate accident), and the crate would be placed in front of this. The bottles were small—one third of a pint—with a cardboard disc set into the neck of the bottle with a hole in the centre where a straw could be inserted. In Class 1, there was a large, black pot-bellied stove, with a large, black pipe reaching from the stove into the ceiling—also surrounded with a protective guard—and their crate would be placed in front of this. I never liked milk time, because instead of being cold and fresh, the milk, because of its proximity to the fire or stove, was always slightly tepid, and it made me feel a bit sick. Nevertheless, all excuses aside, the bottles had to be completely emptied before they were accepted back in the crates.

Dinners were cooked on the premises, and the kitchen adjoined the infants' block. Just before twelve, work was put inside the desks, and a monitor would go round each class and cover the desks with little oil cloths that smelt of wet paint and varnish. The dinner ladies would then bring large trays in and place them on the teacher's desk and nearby surfaces: potatoes, vegetables, and sometimes a delicious meat pie, together with jugs of gravy. Pudding followed, with spoonfuls of thick custard, spotted dick, fruit, sponge, or jam tarts. Wholesome and filling and appreciated by sturdy little people like me. The downside of the dinners being served in the classroom was that right through the rest of the day—even at story time at the end of the afternoon, while we were imagining exploring Sherwood Forest with Robin Hood and his merry men or wandering through the Big Wood with Winnie the Pooh and Tigger—instead of breathing in the sweet forest scents, our nostrils were still detecting a faint smell of cabbage or meat pie.

In Class 1, a large weather chart hung on the wall by the door. The squares were filled with pictures drawn by the children to depict the day's weather. But there was a mystery surrounding the weather chart that I couldn't seem to solve. Every morning, someone was sent outside to find out which direction the wind was blowing. One particular boy—we nicknamed him Sparrow Legs, for obvious reasons—was often chosen to go outside for this task. He would go out and come back in and say, very confidently, "Northwest," "Southeast," "West," "South," etc. and I would gaze at him in awe, and wonder how on earth he knew. One awful day, Miss Bailey turned to me:

"Jean, go and see which direction the wind is blowing."

My knees were knocking and my palms began to sweat as I made my way through the cloakroom and out of the door to the small yard outside. I looked up into the sky for a clue but could see nothing. Then I remembered something Sparrow Legs had said when I asked him how he did it. Like he did, I licked my fingers and held them up in the air to see if I could detect the movement of air. Nothing. I repeated the process several times with no success before, in desperation, making my way back into class and reporting, as confidently as I possibly could, "The wind is blowing from the Northwest."

"Good," said Miss Bailey as she marked it down on the chart. "Well done, Jean."

It was only sometime later, when I spotted the weather cock on the top of the junior building, that the mystery was finally resolved.

Other mysteries were encountered in Miss Bailey's class, one of them being knitting. One afternoon in the week was dedicated to craft, when the boys would do some sort of handicraft, and the girls would be taught knitting and embroidery. Small squares of Aida cloth would be used for embroidery, and we would take our needle and thread and weave the silk in and out of the holes in the cloth. Items such as bookmarks and little mats would be carefully stitched, and the completed items would be taken home at the end of term and proudly presented to our parents.

Sewing was fine, but when it came to knitting, I was completely flummoxed. The needles seemed to have a life of their own, and when it came to introducing the wool, I was lost. I listened to the teacher's instructions: "Needle into the stitch, wool around, needle back, stitch off—and start again!" I found myself winding the wool round and round in desperation, and when it came to taking the stitch off, the whole thing untangled, and I'd be left with two needles and a heap of wool on my desk. I never managed to resolve the knitting problems while I was in the infants' block, but later, in the junior classes, light dawned and the penny dropped. Eureka!

Something else puzzled me in Class 1. Because we were a church school, affiliated to St. Luke's Church of England across the road, certain things were an integral part of our religious education syllabus. We had to learn, off by heart, the Lord's Prayer, the Ten Commandments, and the Apostles' Creed and catechism. Several afternoons ended with the whole class reciting one or other of these before we said prayers at the end of the day. Now that's not what puzzled me. It was what Miss Bailey did while this was going on that intrigued me.

A mirror was placed on the windowsill between the desks and one of the wall cupboards, and the teacher would comb her hair and put on her makeup, then stand with her back to the radiator and pull little bits of fluff and cotton off her green corduroy skirt and let them fall, one by one, on the floor where she stood. When our chanting came to an end, she would choose someone to go and fetch the dustpan and brush and brush all these bits up and put them in the wastepaper basket. Why would she do that? I asked myself many times. Why didn't she just stand by the side of the wastepaper basket and drop the bits straight in? Perhaps it was good training for us not to be so heavenly minded that we were no earthly use, and that when our minds came down from the higher planes, a menial task or two would be good for us! Who knows?

I happily stayed in these two infant classes until the age of seven, by which time I was quite proficient in the three Rs and more than ready to scale the greater heights that the junior school presented.

I should imagine I felt very grown up as the term began for me to go up into the juniors. There was one entrance to the whole of the school, but that day I would turn right instead of left and go down the steps into the big girls' door that led to the junior classes.

There were four classes altogether, and although there were separate entrances for boys and girls, and separate cloakrooms and washrooms, the classes were mixed— although sometimes boys and girls would be separated for certain lessons.

Older girls would continue with needlework and craft, while the boys did gardening in the allotment (or Mr. Lowry's own garden). On certain days, a bus would draw up in front of the school, and a class of boys would be taken to the Congleton schools for metal or woodwork while the girls went to be taught cooking. The same bus journey would be undertaken to take us to the open-air swimming baths in Congleton, which were freezing cold. We would be sent to get ready in the changing rooms before trooping out, blue with cold and covered in goosebumps, to sit along one edge of the baths until the teacher shouted for us to jump in one at a time. If anyone was too timid, there would be a not-so-encouraging hand on the back to catapult us off the edge and send us sprawling, frog-like, into the icy depths. I *never* learned to swim!

I have much fonder memories of my junior years back in Woodcocks' Well: history lessons, with all the time charts round the classroom; geography, with the colourful atlases showing brightly coloured maps of unknown countries and continents; maths, with mental arithmetic and the challenge of finishing first with an unspoilt total; reading endless books from the library; and spelling quizzes.

Books and stories were always my first love. I remember unforgettable story times with Mr. Lowry when he came to read to us at the end of the afternoon. I watched him come into the classroom, a man of ample proportions, clutching a small book of Rudyard Kipling's *Just So Stories* under his arm. Grey suit, a pocket watch in one waistcoat pocket, and an Albert chain stretched tautly from one button across his corpulence to a button on the other side of his waistcoat. I breathed a sign of anticipation as he perched himself precariously atop the tall teacher's chair, one foot on the spindles, the other bracing himself, toe reaching the floor. He opened the book and began. My mouth dropped open in surprise. I heard the story of Rikki Tikki Tavi as never before—and never since! A stream of words shot out of his mouth as though fired by a machine gun. The room was filled with a cloud of warring vowels and consonants that ricocheted from the walls of the classroom before sliding down and hitting the floor in submission. I didn't understand anything of the story except for the animal sounds he made as he described the *tck tck tck* of the mongoose and the sibilant hiss of the two cobras, Nag and Nagaina. At the end of the afternoon, we said prayers before stacking the chairs on our desks, children from the front row wiping their damp faces as we trooped out to breathe in lungs of fresh air and make our way, shell-shocked, down the hill toward home.

At hometime, a couple of the teachers would leave through the main entrance and make their way past the railings on the incline to Mr. Lowry's house. When they reached the top of the School Bank, they'd turn left and follow a narrow track along the top of the Rocks to go to Dales Green, where they caught a bus to take them home. Unbeknownst to them as they were hurrying across the rocky path, much skulduggery was often taking place behind the rocky mounds and grassy slopes—a veritable war of the counties! The boys from the Board School in Staffordshire and the boys from Woodcocks' in Cheshire would often meet to do battle on those high grassy slopes of the Rocks. When a cry went up—"Watch out: teachers!"—they would take cover behind the nearest rock or dive into a tall patch of grass to hide till the danger had passed. Then out they would come—Woodcocks' boys with their backs to their home county, and Board School boys with their backs to theirs, and they'd start to hurl stones at each other.

All this was unknown to me, but Roy tells me that the stones were chunks of rock, not small pebbles. "Oh, they never did real damage," Roy recalls. "Just a few stitches here and there!"

I don't know how long this enmity between the two schools had gone on, or even what caused it in the first place, but it was a very real vendetta—one that lasted as long as I was in the primary school.

Sometimes during school assembly, which always took place at the start of each day, Mr. Lowry would ask certain boys to remain behind afterwards. We would gaze pityingly at them as we filed out, knowing what fate awaited them. If he'd heard about them fighting, there would be no mercy. It wouldn't just be one hand but two that received the heavy *thwack, thwack* of Mr. Lowry's cane, meting out (in his eyes) the just punishment. According to Roy, Mr. Lowry's cane was painful, but apparently not as deadly as that given by the deputy head, Mrs. Dale. That was apparently to be avoided at all costs. I never heard of any girls receiving such punishment, but it was quite a normal sight to see some boy or other hugging a bright red puffy hand under his armpit to try and ease the pain.

It was in those junior years that we girls became aware of the boys. This was the time when, instead of playing all together in a group, special friendships began to grow, and one or two girls would become best friends, while certain boys would begin to stand out from the crowd. Esther and Dorothy were my best girl friends, and we played together both at school in the playtimes and when we got home, after tea. As for boyfriends, Jimmy and Johnny alternated throughout the time I was in the junior classes, fickle affections often determined by a square of chocolate or a kali dip handed over at playtime.

I remember singing lessons. While the teacher was concentrating on the piano keys, and we were carolling the story of "Sally Malone selling her wares in Dublin's fair city," billet doux on scraps of paper would be passed from desk to desk. *"Meet me behind the cobbler's shop after Dick Barton"* (a radio programme). Such assignations would be innocent affairs: an arm around the shoulders for a hug and a stolen kiss or two before we joined the rest of the village crowd in their boisterous outdoor games.

Yes, great fun was had both in the village and in school. But there was one occasion during the year when I hated the sound of the school bell ringing to hail the start of a new school day, and I would drag my feet up the School Bank and wish myself a million miles away. The misery would have begun a day or two before, when we were issued with small, pink forms that had to be taken home and signed by our parents.

"Mum," I would plead, "please don't fill it in! Don't give your permission! My teeth are fine."

It was the dreaded annual visit of the school dentist. A couple of days after the distribution and return of the forms, a mobile van would arrive and park in front of the school entrance. Children were called in class by class for inspection first, after which parents were notified of any filling or extractions that were needed. Then began the BIG WAIT, till it was my class' turn. Because I hated the dentist so much, they were days of unmitigated dread. By the time my name was called, my insides were jelly, and my whole body seemed to tremble. The inside of the van seemed full of instruments of torture surrounding the large black chair. No Mastermind chair could hold as much dread and fear as did that dentist's chair in my child's mind.

Then the little mirror was held inside my wide-open mouth, and the needle hovered in mid-air before sinking into my gums—not once, but two or even three times. A little wait before the main tools of torture started to crunch and grind the offending tooth that needed extracting out of my numbed gum.

"Spit in here," the dentist said, pushing a spittoon to the front of one arm of the chair.

I spat into a pool of blood and broken bits of tooth that filled the vile container. I then made my way back to class, a piece of wadding packed into the gaping hole in my gum, to sit in my desk and carry on with my work. Experiences like that were probably the reason that visits to the dentist have always been a torment to me throughout my life.

Other health visitors who came to the school were the doctor, who came perhaps once a year, and the "Nit Nurse," who came two or three times annually. But these didn't fill me with dread like the dentist did. The health visitor who came to inspect us for head lice was particularly nice. She would come into each class and find a convenient chair to sit on before calling us one by one to come and kneel in front of her while she gently parted our hair, lifting curls and holding up plaits, and looked for any evidence of the head lice. If she looked at the teacher and nodded during an examination, the child would be given a letter to take home so that their mother could deal with the problem.

Although it was a common problem in those days, I never seemed to catch nits from anyone in class—until one memorable day. I know the specific date because it was my seventh birthday: September 23, 1944. And it was my mum who discovered the unwelcome visitors. She was combing my hair and putting in the ribbon that I wore when she suddenly stopped.

"Just stand still a minute," she said as she began to inspect my hair lock by lock. I held my breath as she searched carefully front to back, and back to front. "There!" she exclaimed. "It's a nit."

I was horrified, and so was she. And so began a routine that was repeated several times each day over the next few days: a saucer of vinegar, a nit comb, and Derbac soap to wash my hair before going to bed. After two or three days, my scalp was red raw, my hair was radiantly clean and shiny, and the nits had disappeared— thankfully never to return!

Fortunately, such traumas were short lived and soon forgotten. There were so many things to look forward to: a new storybook to curl up with, a special outing with a friend, gaining top marks in a test, high days and holidays. Although I loved school, it was always wonderful to have a day's holiday for one reason or other. One such occasion was on Ascension Day. Being affiliated to the church, it was reckoned to be a special day for our school. We would go to school as usual in the morning, but soon after going into the classroom, we were summoned into the hall, where a visitor awaited us. I guess he must have been from the school board, or the church PCC, and he came to ask us questions about the Bible and check whether we knew the Ten Commandments and the Apostles' Creed etc. Afterwards, we all lined up and trooped over to the church for a short service, after which we were allowed to go home for the rest of the day. We grabbed our coats from the cloakroom and ran home in great excitement at the prospect of having an extra day's holiday.

Toward the end of my time in junior school, I was responsible for giving the whole school half a day's holiday, which I'm sure made me a very popular girl for at least a day. But let me explain. Most children spent the whole of their primary years at Woodcocks', starting at five, and leaving when they were fourteen. In 1948, the leaving age was extended to fifteen. Roy was in that particular year group, so he left, like all the children in his year, when he was fifteen. He went as an apprentice to Richard's Tiles in Tunstall and began to learn the skill of carpentry. He later became an experienced carpenter and gifted wood turner, as well as following in his grandad's footsteps to become a wonderful preacher.

But at the age of ten, children were given the opportunity to take the 11+ examination, which, if successful, would open the door into high school education. The exam was in four stages: maths and mental arithmetic, then written English, followed by general knowledge and, lastly, an oral examination. I was entered for the maths and had to go into enemy territory to take it at the Board School. After a few weeks, I heard that I'd passed it and was asked to go to a Kidsgrove Secondary School to take the written English. On passing that one, I was sent back to the Board School to take the general knowledge portion and, being successful, was notified that the next round was the oral. I was surprised to learn that instead of me going to another school, two inspectors would come to Woodcocks' to interview me. The head decided to give the whole school a holiday, I suppose in order to guarantee a quiet atmosphere in which the exam could take place.

I remember it vividly. They were really nice inspectors who, although I was extremely nervous, tried to put me at my ease. They asked various questions before giving me a laminated picture of the inside of a country cottage, with range and mantelpiece, a rocking chair, table, etc. and an old lady—looking rather like my grandma—preparing vegetables in the sink. Well-polished brass jugs and candlesticks adorned the mantel and windowsills, and the two men asked me questions about the scene. One question was, "How do you know this is a well-kept cottage?" Another asked about what time of year I thought it was—the garden could be seen through the half open door. I found no difficulty in answering until, out of the blue, one of them asked, "What does *cacophony* mean?" I couldn't answer and was convinced that the failure to do so meant that I'd failed the whole thing. Imagine my delight several weeks later when a brown envelope dropped through my letterbox to say that I'd passed the 11+ and was offered a place at Brownhills High School for girls. I was the only pupil who passed that year from my school and was delighted at the thought of stepping out into the realm of a big new world outside the confines of the village.

Looking back, I am so grateful to have been part of such a wonderful school community as that found in Woodcocks'. It, like the village, was like an extended family, teaching, guiding, and caring for all its members. Five generations of my family have spent time within its confines, learning not only rules and regulations, facts and figures, but also the basic principles of life—concepts that make the world go round and make us better people to travel in it.

CHAPTER SEVEN

Village Characters and Capers

After hearing news of my 11+ success, there were several months before I left Woodcocks' and started my life in pastures new. Things were about to change for me, but the village and its characters remained steadfastly the same. A trusty rock in my about-to-change world.

Part of that stability came from well-established institutions that had been there for many decades, like the church along the street and the school up the hill—or from families whose ancestors had lived there for generations, and from trades and traditions that had been forged through many years. There were the farmers who still depended on tried and trusted ways to till and plough and produce their crops and look after their animals. There were the cobblers—we had two in the village—who sat by their hot open stoves to mould and shape the tips to go on the clogs before hammering them on with little tacks. I liked going into the wooden shack of Mr. Howell, the cobbler at the far end of the village, to watch him at work.

It was a tiny workplace and hot because of the stove, and it was full to overflowing with tools and leather and pairs of shoes and clogs waiting to be repaired. Every surface was covered, every available space and shelf occupied. Mr. Howell was a man of very few words—partly because he wasn't used to very much company through his working day, and partly because his mouth was often full of little nails or tacks that he hammered into the shoes and clogs. I'd watch as he carved and shaped the leather soles until they were a perfect fit, letting all the shavings fall onto his knee before joining the mounds on the floor by his feet. The tools, some of which hung on hooks on the wall, were deadly sharp, while others—like pincers and hammers—lay on the bench, ready for action when required. He wore a strong leather apron with a large pocket around his waist, which protected him from accidental slips of the knives and cutting tools. When he'd had enough of my scrutiny, he would grunt through his tacks and indicate that it was time for me to be on my way.

There were the publicans, who never seemed to emerge out of their taverns into the light of the day until the arrival of the dray carts with their load of wooden barrels, which they would roll around the buildings and drop into the cellars, before disappearing out of sight again.

Then there were the shopkeepers with their familiar faces, who dispensed sweets out of jars, vegetables out of bins and baskets, and who weighed sugar and flour to be put into bags, and wrapped loaves of bread into pieces of tissue paper, before taking the money and handing back the change.

All the small shops in the village were more or less the same, but the Co-op was different. For a start, it was much larger and central to the village. A large stone step graced the entrance, which led into a spacious and impressive interior. The first thing to capture the shopper's attention was the large bacon slicer that was housed behind a glass screen to avoid accidents with curious fingers that might have been poked over the counter. A wooden handle turned the circular cutting machine, and the hunk of bacon was pushed as closely as possible to the machine. "Thick or thin?" the assistants would inquire, before turning the handle and expertly catching the bacon slices as they fell onto the outstretched piece of greaseproof paper, before handing them over the counter.

All sorts of groceries filled the shelves around the shop—some hiding behind glass doors, others filling large barrels in front of the counter and covered by heavy wooden lids. Most things were loose and had to be weighed and bagged in the shop, which made shopping quite a lengthy process. Bread and cakes (and custard tarts) were kept behind a glass-fronted counter, away from the inquisitive fingers of hungry children.

After purchasing all that was needed, the prices were added up and the bill given to the customer, who then handed over the money to the assistant. Then a very strange and fascinating thing took place: she placed the money in a metal box-like container that was suspended on a wire quite high up over the counter. She would pull another wire, and the box would zing along to a cashier, who was in a tiny, enclosed space where all the money was kept. The currency in those days was pounds, shillings, and pence—extra tables for us to learn and recite at school. Twelve pence equalled one shilling, twenty shillings equalled one pound, and so on. Because shopping took so long in the Co-op, there would be large queues, especially on Saturday mornings, after most people had received their week's wages the day before.

Apart from the grocery shops, there were also two butchers: one right by the Co-op, and the other at the top of South Street, where we were usually told to go. I loved watching the butcher hacking away at the joints of beef to produce mounds of stewing beef, or slicing chops from legs of pork or lamb, or, best of all, holding up strings of sausages before curling them onto the scales and cutting off the required number to wrap in paper and mark the price on one corner. My ambition, while I watched him, was to be either a teacher (my first love), or a butcher when I grew up. The first one won out in the long run when my fascination with handling raw meat became a distant and distasteful memory.

Just around the corner from the butcher's, down South Street, lived my best friend, Dottie. She and I, together with Esther, spent most of our spare time together corking on a cotton reel, fashioning outfits for dolls, making secret societies, and devising codes and different ways of communicating with each other. One summer we taught ourselves sign language and delighted in passing private messages to each other—much to the annoyance of anyone who might have joined the gang for a day or two. To my surprise, Esther and Dottie didn't enjoy climbing rocks or scaling trees, or jumping from the roof of our garden shed, or off some high bank across wide streams, so I had to rely on Mike or a gang of boys to join me in those activities.

Evenings brought a whole lot more outdoor games, a favourite being "Dickie show your light." A gang of us would split into two groups, each group having a torch. Then we would go in different directions around the village, in and out of people's yards and gardens, up and down the different streets, behind buildings and sheds. Every now and then, one of the groups would stop and point the beam of the flashlight up into the sky, and the other had to run toward it to find out where they were hiding. Of course, by the time they'd got to the point where they thought they'd seen the light, the first group had disappeared again. But suddenly the mad activities would come to an abrupt end as a loud voice would be clearly heard through the darkness: "Dick Barton! Dick Barton's started!"

Dick Barton, Special Agent, was an extremely popular programme on the wireless. It started at 6:45 p.m. and lasted for just fifteen minutes. At 6:45 p.m., the village would miraculously clear, and every child would dash home to hear the antics of crimefighter Dick and his sidekicks, Snowy and Scott. Just after seven o'clock, the village would be overrun once more, as those who were old enough were allowed to stay out "just for another half hour," while the less fortunate had to begin their bedtime routines.

Because none of the families possessed a TV, the wireless was not only a vital means of communication, but it also provided a great deal of entertainment. There were lots of comedy programmes, like Tommy Handley in the famous *ITMA*, Elsie and Doris Walkers— alias "Gert and Daisy"—and *Take It From Here,* while the well-known singers were the Forces' sweetheart Vera Lynn, Yorkshire born Gracie Fields, and George Fornby with his ukulele. We listened to them all, amazed at the fact that we could sit around the strange looking little box and hear voices and conversations from some-where else in Britain, perhaps hundreds of miles away. Dad would hush us into silence when the news came on, and we listened to the news readers with their posh voices, informing the listening public about the most recent happenings or announcements. We weren't allowed to twiddle the knobs at the front of the wireless, or else the channel would be lost in an ear-splitting stream of hisses and crack-les, and Dad would be furious. It would take him ages to re-tune the channel, and we would be threatened with early bed if we touched them again. We children also liked to listen to stories and plays, and *Children's Hour* at teatime, but one of my favourite memories was listening to the honeyed tones of Bing Crosby singing, "I'm dreaming of a white Christmas …"

But we weren't content to sit for long listening to the wireless during the day. Outside activities were far more exciting! Hopscotch on the road, whip and top, jumping "doubles" with a skipping rope, or finding new ways of catching, throwing, and bouncing a ball. Because we walked—or ran—everywhere, and because we were so active, I don't remember any children who were obese, or even tubby (perhaps sturdy, but never fat!).

Roy had his own set of friends. I particularly remember Norman from across the village, whose mother used to grow rhubarb in her front garden. On occasions, my mum would send me to buy "six penn'orth of rhubarb" from Norman's mum, and I'd come back from the errand with a bundle of rhubarb wrapped in newspaper under my arm, ready to pop into one of Mum's wonderful pies. It was only in later years that I heard tell of some antics Roy and his friends got up to in their absences: swimming in the canal; diving off canal bridges; walking along the frozen surface of the canal (known as "the cut"), cigars or cigarettes in their mouths. Mum and Dad would have been horrified, just as they would have been if they'd ever discovered he'd had the cane at school. Family discipline and school authority being held in such high regard, it would probably have warranted more punishment when he got home. "You must have done something to deserve it," my dad would have said!

Roy and his gang might have taken part in many dangerous escapades that could have ended badly for them, but there was never any malice or ill will toward others in any of their antics—unlike one shocking incident I remember with dreadful clarity.

It happened at the same time that I tasted my very first custard cream biscuits. We were going away on one of our short stay holidays to Bulwell, to visit Auntie Alice and Uncle Ted. Bags were packed, arrangements were made for Mary next door to feed the cat, and off we set. While we were waiting to catch the bus on the first leg of our journey, Mum popped into Gran's shop, leaving us at the bus stop. She came back, the bus arrived, and we climbed aboard feeling very excited. The holiday had begun! Roy and I, followed by Mum, went to sit on the back seat, and Mum produced a paper bag out of her holdall. Custard cream biscuits! We had never seen them before, and when Mum gave us two each, we slowly nibbled around the top biscuit before taking tiny bites at the custard-covered layer. What luxury to start our trip!

We spent the next week at Auntie Alice's before making the return journey and arriving home in the early evening. We collected the key from next door, where Mary told us that the cat, Ginger, had not had his food for the last two days and hadn't been seen in the house or round the garden. Knowing the independent nature of cats, Mum wasn't too bothered at first. But when a week had passed and he'd still not appeared, or even been seen, we were all really worried and started a search of the village. I don't know who discovered him, and I don't know who came to bring us the news, but eventually the horrid truth filtered down to us children.

It seems that some of the village boys had caught him, taken him into the air raid shelter, strung him up, and thrown stones at him until he was dead. They'd actually stoned him! We couldn't believe it! The whole village was appalled at such cruelty and made their feelings very clear to the culprits when they finally confessed to their coldblooded killing. We were naturally heartbroken, not just because he'd died, but even more so because of the *way* he'd died. I remember the conversations in Grandma's shop and along the street as people showed their disgust and disbelief at such carryings on. People were used to death, but not to cruelty.

As I think back on the different people in the village, names flash into my mind: Tilly, next door to Grandma; Gussie, Nora, Alicia, Arthur, Vera, Billy, Jo. I remember the sort of people who made up the community of Mount Pleasant Village: good, honest, caring folk. And, for the most part, law abiding. But not exclusively so! There was Joey, the local "jail bird," who had apparently served time in prison for some unknown offence. Mums would warn their children not to venture down The Sludge alone if they'd seen him go down The Hollow. I would view him with a curiosity and a real fear as he disappeared behind the door of The Crown, certain that anybody who'd been to prison *and* went into a pub must be beyond redemption.

On my errands to and from the Co-op, I would often gaze at the windows of the last house I would pass before I arrived at the shop. The curtains never stirred, the door never opened, the occupants were never seen. People said a recluse lived there. I had no idea what a recluse was and wondered what "it" might look like. Was it big or small? Was it even human? I was riddled with curiosity—until one amazing day, all was revealed. The front door opened slightly, and a *very* old gentleman made a half appearance. The instantly noticeable thing about this "recluse" was his shock of snowy white hair and a long white beard. He was spotted several times before he made a full appearance, opening the door and standing in full view, leaning on his door post as he gazed at the village. I saw him several times and realised that he wasn't scary at all. In fact, he looked very shy, and his blue eyes twinkled as he smiled at people passing by. My mum explained to me what a recluse was and said he was known to be a very nice, but retiring, gentleman called Mr. Boote, and I had no reason to be scared when I saw him.

So when he smiled and beckoned me over one day, I went close to the door to see what he wanted. He was holding a well-worn little book of Robbie Burns' poetry in his hand, which he offered to me. Apart from "My love is like a red, red rose," I couldn't understand any of the other poems, but I spent a long time pouring over them, probably while perched in the leafy realms of my Hawthorn Tree. Over the next few months—and with my mum's permission—I ventured into his front room, where he showed me a huge collection of books, stored higgledy piggledy in every possible nook and cranny of the room. After that summer, I didn't have as much cause to go to and fro along the main street. I changed schools, and when I arrived home, I had too much homework to do, so my sightings of and encounters with this well-read, well-educated gentleman came to an end.

There were also two very old ladies who sparked my interest. One lived on the other side of Granny's shop, sporting the typical long black clothes and specs and walking stick. She was hardly ever seen, and rumour had it among the children that she was a witch who spent her time sitting at a sewing machine, pedalling away with just one leg because the other one was crippled. Stories abounded, and our imaginations ran wild. Some of the boys sometimes threw stones at her windows, and she would fling open the door and hobble out, waving her walking stick and shouting curses at the culprits.

A similar looking lady, in the usual long black garb and a bonnet on her head and cape around her shoulders, would sometimes be seen slowly wandering up School Bank, with her shopping bag clutched in one hand and walking stick in the other. I sometimes offered to carry her bag and would walk her back to her cottage across the fields of Rock Side, halfway up the hill. She'd reward me with a six pence for my trouble.

Just as the people in the village were amazed by Grandma's TV, they were also delighted and incredulous when the Parish Room at the top of the intic started to show films—black and white Charlie Chaplin movies. It seemed as though every youngster in the village and surrounding area, together with a good sprinkling of curious adults, would begin to congregate at least half an hour before the show was due to start. They would queue down the intic and all along the Flat, with their entrance money clutched in sticky little palms, and watch for the doors of the Parish Room to swing open. Then there was a rush, and a push, and a grabbing of seats. We would watch the man with his film camera perched on his tripod as he attached the spools of film, and a hush would descend as the lights were switched off and the film began to roll. The rotating spool could clearly be heard, clicking and whirring while the film was shown, only ceasing when the man stopped to change the reels. They were black and white silent films with captions at the bottom of the screen, but we were thrilled, and would still be chatting about the antics of Charlie as we arrived home to have a bite of supper before diving into bed to dream of a peculiar little man with a bowler hat, walking stick, and black handlebar moustache.

Although people from the village wouldn't be so eager to attend services at the chapel as they were to go to the weekly film shows, I reckon they all knew about and were proud of the connection of Mow Cop with the birth of Primitive Methodism. Methodism actually started with Hugh Bourne, who was a member of the Wesleyan Society. He was converted at the age of twenty-seven, in 1799, but because he became such an exuberant and zealous preacher, he was frowned upon by the Wesleyans. He moved from Bemersley to take over a chapel in Harriseahead and conducted powerful revival services, where many were converted, one of whom was William Clowes, who would eventually join forces with Bourne. Together, they began to conduct open air services, which attracted many followers and could be heard all over Mow Cop. These open-air rallies became the catalyst for the famous camp meetings, the first of which was held on Mow Cop in 1807 and attracted over four thousand people. It was out of these open-air camp meetings that Primitive Methodism was born and, as a consequence, Hugh Bourne was expelled from the Wesleyan Society.

Although they had lost some of their popularity by the time I was a child, I remember camp meetings taking place every Easter time, and huge crowds still attended. There are still two chapels on Mow Cop: one Wesleyan, called the Square Chapel because of the shape of its building, and the other a Primitive Methodist. My parents used to attend the open-air meetings on the slopes of the castle, walk home for tea, and then return to church for the evening service. It was in this chapel that my brother became a Christian when he was twenty-four and very soon decided to give up his job as a carpenter to go to Kenley Bible College, before devoting his life to the ministry.

Camp meetings still take place on the castle slopes but are a pale shadow of those conducted by Clowes and Bourne, having lost much of their religious power and fervour over the years. All has changed, and we live in a post-modern society, where there are no absolutes. People have stepped out of traditions and beliefs that have been held in high regard for many generations. Some consider it progress, while others yearn for the old moral codes and the tried and tested ways of living.

Similarly, at the end of that summer of 1948, all was about to change for me; I was about to step out of rural primary school into the lofty realms of high school education. Out of the safe confines of village life into a big new world. Out of a small circle of trusted friendships and into unfamiliar relationships. I was about to leave behind all that was familiar and step into the unknown—and I was going to make this journey completely on my own. It was like sitting at the top of one of those long slides in the children's playground: perched high, precarious expanse of slide in front, people pushing impatiently from behind.

"Go on, then," someone cries. "You can't turn back now. You've got to let go!"

And so I did. I took a deep breath, let go, and plunged forward into the unknown world of high school.

CHAPTER EIGHT

School Part Two:
High School Years (1949 –1956)

The new autumn term at the high school started in September, but the excitement began several weeks earlier. It was when we received a letter telling of the uniform regulations and requirements that the whole thing became real to me. We were given directions to a shop in Trubshawe Cross, just below the high school, where all the necessary items of clothing were stocked.

Mum and I travelled to Tunstall by bus and then had to walk the rest of the way to Trubshawe, passing en route a very grand, red brick building, with a notice board by the entrance gates stating, "Brownhills High School for Girls." I gazed in awe at a very large building surrounded by tennis courts and grassy playing fields, a couple of extra side buildings, and a tarmac-covered car park. This

was where I would be coming in a couple of weeks' time—alone—
and I wouldn't be passing the gates. I would be going right through
them to enter an unknown world. I shivered in anticipation.

We found the shop not very much further down the road. It was
small and poky, filled with packed shelves, towers of boxes, and
samples of uniforms displayed on coat hangers. The lady must have
kitted out thousands of apprehensive new pupils and went confidently through the list we had, producing each item from box, shelf,
or cupboard, and placing them on the glass counter. It seemed she
knew the size required just by a glance and, sure enough, when I
tried them on, they all fitted perfectly.

The list was comprehensive, including underwear (substantial
brown knickers), socks, and a tie. The winter uniform was a brown
skirt (knee length, no shorter), cream long sleeved blouse, and
a brown and cream silk tie. A brown cardigan was recommended,
and a blazer with a school crest on the pocket was optional. In the
summer, the skirt could be replaced by a brown and cream checked
cotton dress with a small white collar. The item that struck me as
peculiar was the brown pork-pie hat with a brown and cream band
around the brim. Apparently, it had to be worn "at *all* times" as part
of the outdoor uniform, and anyone seen on the street or in the town
without it after leaving the school building would be severely repri-
manded. We grew to hate them, and as soon as we deemed it safe,
they would be stuffed in bags or satchels, out of sight.

The complete uniform was really expensive, and I sensed, rather
than heard, my mother's gasp of surprise. But she paid the bill with
her usual smile, as though she did this sort of thing every day of the
week. She never mentioned anything to me, but it probably took a
few extra shifts of overtime at the Steel Works, or a day or two of
additional cleaning at the farm to fund the expense.

Over the coming weeks, name tabs had to be laboriously stitched into each item, but eventually all was finished, and I was ready to launch into my big adventure. On that auspicious day, the first thing to cause both excitement and apprehension was the bus journey from Mow Cop to Tunstall. It was only a five-mile journey, but I couldn't imagine travelling to school every day on a bus instead of climbing the School Bank on my sturdy legs. Apart from that, I think it was the first time I had ever travelled on a bus by myself in the whole of my life.

I waited at the bus stop at the top of The Hollow, nervously clutching my satchel—Mum waving from the gate of #116—until the bus lumbered along the main street and stopped for me to get on. I climbed aboard and showed the conductor my bus pass before sitting down near to the front. My new school life had begun.

The journey took about half an hour, the bus meandering through Dales Green and Harriseahead, Newchapel and Pittshill, past the old workhouse buildings, before dropping down the hill toward Tunstall. The journey came to an end in the town square, where everybody got off the bus. I spotted several girls in B.H.S. uniform, so I fell in step behind them and found myself going down the road that Mum and I had taken when visiting the uniform shop. By the time we arrived at the school gates, there were many groups of girls, all in the same brown uniform, all heading in the same direction: *through* the gates and across the yard to a semi-covered entrance.

The building was designed as a large quadrangle, which surrounded an open space containing a few shrubs. Classrooms and cloakrooms lay along the corridors on each side of the quad, while a large hall ran along the middle of the enclosed area, joining the two long corridors in the middle. While the older pupils went into their classrooms, all the new children—probably one hundred in total—were shepherded into the hall.

I gazed at the large expanse of oak-block floor, the rolls of honour displayed on the top wall, the grand piano on the raised platform at the far end, and the rows of chairs down each side, and marvelled at the size and grandeur of it all. As we stood in the middle of the hall, clutching satchels and pump bags and wondering what was going to happen next, the door near to the platform swung open, and in swept an imposing looking figure. Sensible brogues, modest attire, short, cropped hair, spectacles on nose, and a large black cape that swung and swirled as she walked up the steps of the raised platform to take her elevated place behind the dais—Dr. Bright, the highly respected, greatly feared principal of B.H. School for Girls. We listened, awestruck, as she welcomed us into her school, laid down a few rules, told us of the high standard of behaviour expected from us and emphasised how privileged we were to have been chosen to attend such a prestigious high school—the "cream of the Potteries!"

After delivering her monologue and disappearing through the swing doors, three members of staff appeared and selected the children who were going to be in their classes. I was called into the group headed up by Miss Greaves, a slim, bespectacled lady whose plaited hair was coiled into two discs that sat on her ears like ear muffs. I later discovered that this softly-spoken teacher ruled with a rod of iron, suffered no nonsense, demanded very high standards, but was extremely fair and very understanding.

Miss Greaves led her class (1G) out of the hall through the same door that Dr. Bright had disappeared through. We stepped out onto what I was to discover was "holy ground!" A large area of floor was covered by a mosaic of black and white tiles, which separated the hall from Dr. Bright's office and the office of the school secretary. We were told that the only time we stepped onto those tiles was when we were going to the hall or either of the offices—and we were *never* allowed to cross them from one corridor to the next without a very good reason!

We were taken into our classroom, the very first one past the secretary's office, and seated alphabetically around the room in the large wooden desks, with their lift-up lids and inset pot inkwells. The rest of the day passed in a whirlwind of exercise books, pens and pencils, textbooks, and other supplies being distributed. Of being led into cloakrooms and given a peg where we could hang pump bags and satchels. Of dinner times, when we sat self-consciously on tables of eight in a large dining room. And of playtimes, when we stood on the edge of crowds of older children and wondered if we would ever get used to such an enormous school and so many children.

At least that's how I felt. I had come from a small rural school with a total of around fifty pupils, and here I was in a crowd of hundreds. From a place of total familiarity to somewhere completely alien, where I didn't know one other person. My home was in a small village on the slopes of Mow Cop, and the majority of these girls were from the local towns. I felt as though I was re-enacting the tale of the country mouse visiting his sophisticated friend, the town mouse, and I felt completely out of my depth. Would I ever feel comfortable in this place? Would I ever find my way around? Would I ever find a friend?

At home time, I walked back to the town square to catch my bus home, bought an ice lolly to console myself, and anticipated going back to my comfortable and familiar surroundings, while wondering—with trepidation—what the next day would hold. If I could have gazed into the future, I would have realised that the years spent in Brownhills would give me wonderful friendships that would last a lifetime, and furnish me with experiences and learning that would give me the keys to a wonderfully satisfying career.

I think the main contributor to building strong, lasting friendships was the fact that from Second Year onwards, we stayed together in the same forms, or classes, right through the school. In different years we might study different subjects and attend different classes, but we always started the day together for registration and school assembly.

Assembly was rather a grand affair. All the classes would line in, one at a time— we First Years right at the front—and the teachers would sit on the chairs at the end of the rows of children, watching closely for any unacceptable behaviour. Each of the members of staff wore their robes and silk-lined hoods, showing which university they had attended. Either Mrs. Fleetwood or Mrs. Doorbar would be playing the piano as we lined in, and when all had gathered, there would be a pause before Dr. Bright made her entrance. Hymns, prayers, and readings would be followed by notices before we all trooped out again to our separate classes, when lessons would begin.

Unbeknownst to us at the time, First Year was a time of sifting and sorting, when we were constantly tested and appraised before the end of term exams. After the year's coursework and exam results were finished, we were split into three streams: the top stream took Latin, the second German, and the third Domestic Science, while all streams took French. I ended up in the Latin stream, where I stayed for the rest of my school career until I went into the Lower and then Upper Sixth.

Because the classes were re-sorted in Second Year, our alphabetical position around the class changed, and I found myself sitting second from the front, in front of a girl called Gwen, who became my best friend all the way through school and into later life. She later told me that she spent a lot of her time gazing at my thick red plaits (my baby curls had gone by then) and nearly cried when I had them cut off, replaced by a mass of curls as a result of a perm during one weekend.

Contrary to my fears, I soon knew lots of the girls, and a loose gang of half a dozen or so met up with each other during playtimes and dinner times: Sheila and Steph (two girls from Biddulph); Margaret, Monica, Gwen, and myself, together with a sweet girl from nearby Longport, named Dorothy. During the first couple of years, Dorothy and I visited each other's homes on occasions, and I discovered that her background was quite similar to mine: chapel go-ers who sang in the choir and held familiar beliefs and traditions. She had a lovely older sister named Florence who, many years later, became Dorothy's carer when she developed M.S.

But my constant friend and companion was Gwen, and I had many sleepovers in her home, where I got to know her mum and dad very well. Her mum had dreadful asthma attacks and was often gasping for her breath. Because she was so ill, Gwen had to do many of the chores, not only when she arrived home, but before she left for school, when she tried to leave everything in place for her mum during the day. Although it seemed hard at the time, it developed her into the character she is today and made her an extremely caring person.

But back in First and Second Years, we were still settling into these friendships and relationships, as well as learning subjects we had never considered before, like foreign languages. I didn't mind French, with all its verbs and vocabulary that had to be committed to memory, but Latin was never easy for me. The first year was reasonable. I still remember a little poem Miss Mitchell taught us, written in Latin, which made us laugh when it was read out loud: "Caesar adsum jam forte, Brutus et arat, Caesar sic in omnibus, Brutus sic in at!" That was probably the highlight of my prowess in Latin, but I had to continue studying it until O Levels, when it was the only exam I failed! I was probably a constant source of frustration to Miss Mitchell. I remember the exasperation in her voice one day as she returned my Latin homework: "Jean Ecclestone, if you were a nurse and were as careless with your drugs as you are with my Latin verbs, you'd kill everybody off!" I think she took it as a personal affront that I never managed to conjugate her verbs correctly.

Nevertheless, I excelled in First Year, attaining 100 per cent throughout the year in Maths, and was awarded a form prize. Oh, how proud my mum was to come into the "hallowed halls" of B.H.S. on Prize Giving Evening and see her little girl climb the steps and walk across the platform to receive a prize from Dr. Bright in all her formal robes.

It was only during First Year that we took needlework under the tuition of Miss Bennison. We had to walk halfway to Tunstall in a long crocodile to have our lesson in an old building, which also housed the cookery classes. The first thing we had to make was a cookery apron from a pattern that we had to cut out of a newspaper. My newspaper was in two pieces that I had to pin together, but when I came to cut out the material, I cut along the row of pins and ended up with the apron material in two pieces. When I took the separate pieces to show the teacher, she took it, scowled, then threw it at me, telling me how stupid I was. I sat for the next few lessons with the bits in front of me, having no idea how to rectify my mistake. Even to this day, I have little confidence in my sewing ability.

But it was probably in Second Year, when needlework gave way to cookery, that the walk up to the building gave Gwen and me a brilliant idea. We were both fans of Wimbledon tennis championships, and particularly of Ken Rosewall, the Australian champion. After lunch one day, we formed the crocodile procession with the other girls, but when we arrived at the doors of the old building, we held back until everybody had gone in. Then, instead of joining the class, we continued to walk on up to Tunstall, where we caught a bus to my house and watched Ken Rosewall playing tennis all through the afternoon. I don't remember any explanations we gave to my family when they came home to find us there, nor do I remember being found out in our misdemeanour by anyone from school. Our naughtiness went undetected, and we had a wonderful afternoon.

I don't think I enjoyed playing tennis as much as watching it. When we started to play tennis in Second Year, we trooped onto the courts under the tutelage of Miss Mellor and Miss Smith, swinging our racquets confidently, with high aspirations of future achievements. Our dreams were instantly dispelled with the first flail of the racquet as the ball bounced straight past us, and we were left rooted to the court. I don't think my racquet had any contact with a tennis ball, apart from the first stroke when I started what was supposed to be a rally. In spite of the teachers showing us the technique little by little, and trying to teach us the strokes, I never really succeeded, because I had an insurmountable problem!

The problem started when I went home from school and announced that we were starting tennis lessons, and I needed a racquet. Mum didn't say much, but a look of concern came over her face. She never told me at the time, but it turns out that she had to sell her new pressure cooker in order to have the money for a racquet. The following weekend, we made our way to the sports shop in Tunstall to look at the different styles of racquet. We had no idea what we needed to look for, and the shopkeeper offered no advice, so we came out of the shop with a very substantial looking racquet, plus a press to keep the strings at the correct tension. I took my racquet very proudly into school for the next games lesson and walked onto the court, ready to soar to new heights with my expensive equipment at the ready. But I hadn't taken one important factor into account: it was unbelievably heavy! When I held it in my hand and stretched out my arm, my arm dropped helplessly toward the ground. I tried to hit a coming ball, but it was like holding a sledgehammer. I watched other girls flicking and twirling their racquets about with the greatest of ease, and when I asked if I could hold one, it seemed as light as a feather in comparison to my monster. I quickly lost interest in my dreams of not just watching Wimbledon but actually playing there, and never really got past that first round.

I had more success with hockey than tennis and became the goalkeeper for the school team at one point. I probably felt a bit safer in the nets, because I'd been given a black eye while playing on the wings one game by an overly enthusiastic opponent who was swinging her hockey stick like a golf club!

One girl in our group achieved great heights in other sporting events. Monica excelled in track and field, especially javelin, and she gained many accolades for her success locally and even in national events. We were very proud of her and her achievements and cheered loudly when she received any school awards.

We might not have been great athletes (apart from Monica), but we all adored Miss Smith. We jostled to be in her group when the class was split for games and listened to her every command with puppy-dog devotion. I imagine she was my first schoolgirl crush, which lasted for a season before dying a quick death when we became more interested in boys.

Monica was the first one of our gang who started to show interest in boys. She initially had a crush on a young man named Joey, who drove a truck near to where she lived, but when that obsession faded, she began to talk about a boy named Tony, from one of the nearby boys' high schools. This was no passing fancy, because she ended up marrying him and was enormously proud when he became a scientist and was awarded a doctorate. She managed to combine her love of sport and her love for Tony by becoming the wife of Dr. Hartland as well as being on the board of directors for Stoke Football Club.

B.H.S. expected its pupils to do well in the outside world. They provided the sort of education to equip us to be "high flyers," and they did their best to guide us in our career choices. Teaching was the profession most of us were encouraged to pursue, while such practical occupations as nursing were actively discouraged. Nevertheless, many girls ignored the advice given and followed their own choices. Some became nurses, tax officers, secretaries, and office workers. One brave soul even left in Fourth Year to get married and start a family, much to everybody's shocked surprise.

I would imagine that most people looking at us now—elderly and (mostly!) respectable—would be shocked to know what naughty girls we could sometimes be. From my own experience—I soared in First Year and dive-bombed in Third—my report book paints a graphic picture of my academic demise.

I don't know exactly how it happened, but 3L became a disreputable class. We baited the less assertive teachers, played pranks on new members of staff, were inattentive, noisy, and, I should think on some occasions, rude. And our work suffered for it. Of course, not all the staff were intimidated by us. Some bastions of authority and order were able to suppress our exuberance and quell us into submission.

Looking back, I have to admit some shame but also confess to the fact that that riotous time was great fun. Biology, for instance, when we split into groups to dissect rats, inspect slides under microscopes, study flora and fauna in detail, and also manage to do all sorts of things that weren't work related, under cover of equipment set out on the benches. History, with a timid young teacher who actually left the classroom in tears one day when we hid a plastic pile of dog poo by her desk! We were sorry afterwards, and a couple of girls went to her to apologise, but I'm afraid the damage was done, and her confidence at least temporarily shattered.

When that memorable year came to a close, we were given one of the stricter teachers to be form mistress for Fourth Year, and our wings were very definitely clipped as we began to return to working hard, behaving sensibly, and picking up our work grades. We slowly began to get back on target so that we could achieve the grades we required to follow our preferred careers.

Sometimes, however, the wrong behaviour was not found in pupils but in members of staff, like when the French teacher took a dislike to Monica and constantly goaded her during class: "Monica P. Recite the poem to the class that you had to learn for homework!"

Monica would stand up and begin, "La cigale et la fourmi …" A long pause before she tried again. "La cigale et la fourmi … err …"

The teacher would approach Monica's desk and stand over her while she stopped and started before finally giving up and sitting down. But Monica refused to be squashed, and many times retaliated—much to the aggravation of Miss M.

There was also the Maths teacher (our Fourth-Year form teacher), who was greatly irritated by Gwen. She would only have to see her walking down the corridor, or entering the classroom, or getting a book out of her desk, before she would pounce and accuse her of some misdemeanour or other.

But such incidents were soon forgotten over an outdoor playtime on the field, or an indoor dinner time, when we would be allowed to go into the hall and dance to LPs put on the turntable: Elvis Presley and Chuck Berry, Bill Haley and the Comets, and the melodic tones of Pat Boone. It was here I learned to jive and rock and roll, as well as waltz and foxtrot, skills I perfected to a degree in later years when attending Teacher Training College.

It was between Third and Fourth Year that my family moved house again, to Mosslands, Biddulph Road, Mossley. Mum had come back to her roots. Dad continued to work at Shelton Iron and Steel, taking the bus there and back each day. We never had a family car. Mum took a job as a machinist in one of the mills in Congleton, while Roy continued his apprenticeship at Richard Tiles. My school route changed—still catching the bus, but now going from Mossley to Biddulph to Tunstall. Sheila and Steph travelled on the same bus from Biddulph, so we were able to travel together.

I thought it was a wonderful house move. It had three bedrooms and, for the first time ever, a bathroom and inside flush toilet! The bath was an old iron one on four legs, which was quite rusty when we moved in. Dad solved the problem by painting it with ordinary gloss paint, which peeled off when the bath was full of hot water and stippled our bottoms, much to everybody's annoyance.

Instead of attending Mouth Pleasant Sunday school and church, we now went to Biddulph Road Methodist, at the bottom of the hill where we lived. This was where Mum and Dad had first met in the days of their courtship.

It was just opposite to the chapel that I caught the first of the buses on my new and extended school journey. I didn't mind the extra time travelling, because it sometimes gave me a chance to finish off homework or do a bit of extra swotting if it was exam time.

Mum and Dad always worked hard but never had extra money to spare for anything but the necessities. Just as we never had the convenience of a family car, we never went away on family holidays either. A day out to Bellevue Zoo in Manchester would be a delightful highlight, but apart from staying at Auntie Alice's, we never visited a B&B or hotel at the seaside. So when Gwen invited me to go on holiday with her family in the summer after Fifth Year, I was thrilled.

They went every year to a B&B in Llandudno, Wales, which was owned by Mrs. Williams. I would stay overnight at Gwen's house in readiness for the journey the following day, when we would travel by train from Stoke Station to Llandudno Junction. The journey itself was exciting because I didn't often go anywhere by train. An early morning start added to the excitement, and Gwen and I jigged about on the platform, waiting for the train. I think Gwen's mum had packed us a sandwich to eat en route, but I couldn't wait to catch my first glimpse of the sea. I spent most of the time gazing out of the window, watching the world chug by, and the great plume of steam that swirled past from the engine at the front of the train. I remember turning a bend on the track and seeing the shimmer of the ocean lying in a thin line beneath the horizon, and marvelling at the wonder of it all. I was going to be so near to it over the coming week that I was going to be able to dip my toes in it, to paddle along the edge where the ocean met the sand, to gather shells that Gwen said were hidden in the rock pools, and even to brave the waves in the new swimming costume I'd got tucked in my suitcase.

We took a taxi from the junction and walked the last little way down the avenue to be greeted by a smiling Mrs. Williams, who knew the family from the previous years. We trundled our cases and bags up the stairs, and Gwen and I were delighted to go right up to the third floor to a small dormer room under the eaves. There we could hear the harsh call of the seagulls who winged their way across the rooftops in search of abandoned scraps of food they could plunder.

We quickly changed our clothes and made a hasty exit to walk along the promenade and down the steps onto the beach, determined not to waste a moment of our holiday.

It was a joyous week spent exploring the beach and gathering shells and walking or riding up the steep hillside of the Great Orme to feel the strong wind in our ears and the green springy turf under our feet. Investigating the delights along the pier, such as shops selling kites and balloons, souvenirs and candy floss. Discovering an orchestra at the end of the long pier, where we fell under the spell of a piccolo player in the wind section whom we named Piccolo Pete, returning several times to be mesmerised by his charms. On one of the evenings, Gwen's mum and dad took us to a concert in the pavilion, where we laughed and cheered at each performance before wandering back to the boarding house, clutching steaming bags full of fish and chips.

It was while we were enjoying such a holiday that Gwen and I received a telegram informing us of our GCSE results. We were pleased to have passed six each, which secured us both a place in the Sixth Form to continue our studies. It seemed no time at all before we were back home and at the end of the school holidays, when a new term beckoned.

Another holiday springs to mind, which doesn't conjure up completely happy memories: The French exchange, which took place in Fifth Year. Those still taking French were invited to take part in a holiday when we opened our home up to a French student for three weeks before travelling back to France with them to stay with their families. The area we would be visiting was Cosne Sur Loire, a little village in the beautiful Loire Valley.

I was paired up with a girl called Martine, who lived with her parents and younger brother, Paul, over the draper's shop in their three-storey house. It was a beautiful village that virtually sat on the banks of the Loire. Cobbled streets, tall, antiquated buildings with shuttered windows and heavy doors with impressive looking door knockers.

The family were delightful and went out of their way to make my stay happy—but Martine was very different. She had already spent three weeks with my family in England, so she'd had her holiday and wasn't at all interested in making my visit enjoyable. She would abandon me and go off to join her friends when we were out; she would play tricks and try to make me look silly; she would spin complicated stories and tell lies to her parents while we sat round the table for the evening meal. She was a nightmare! The thing that saved the whole holiday and turned it into a great experience was that the family took us on a trip to visit many of the chateaux in the Loire Valley, ending up in the South of France, and visiting Nice and Cannes and Monte Carlo. Martine was not a pleasant companion, and her friend behaved in exactly the same way with my friend, Monica, also along on the exchange trip. But her family, and the wonderful trip around the South of France, rescued the experience from being an utter disaster.

Apart from all the wonderful things I saw, it also achieved other goals in my life. First of all, it greatly increased my world horizons! Who would have thought that I would cross the Channel, explore a foreign country, and speak—however haltingly—a foreign language. Another perhaps timelier achievement was that it greatly improved my conversational French, boosting my success in the GCSE exam to a commendable credit!

And so we sailed through the external exams and into the Lower Sixth. Some friends left—Dorothy went to begin her secretarial training, while others left to pursue nursing careers etc.—but those wanting to be teachers, or go even further in their education, stayed on to continue their studies.

Here in the upper echelons, the atmosphere was much more relaxed—apart from the fact that, once again, and much to Gwen's dismay, we were under the keen eye of Miss Ball. It was at this point that we chose the subjects we wanted to do for A Levels. Unfortunately, it wasn't always possible to be accepted into one's first choice because of the limitation of numbers, and I found I was unable to do Religious Education. I had to be content with carrying on in Biology to A Level standard (much to my horror!), along with my chosen subjects of English, OL Geography, and the General Knowledge paper. Unbeknownst to me at the time, it would take all my powers of concentration to achieve the required grades in these subjects, due to a major distraction that was waiting for me in the Upper Sixth.

But here in the Lower Sixth, there was plenty to keep us busy and occupied. There were extramural activities introduced to our timetables, such as visiting meetings at other high schools (both boys and girls), when quite a lot of socialization took place. Monica enjoyed these afternoons because she often had the opportunity to meet up with Tony. On other occasions, some of us were invited to sell tickets for concerts at the Victoria Hall, which gave us a wonderful chance to hear many marvellous choirs and musical performances: male voice choirs, the Vienna Boys choir, and the classical works of many famous composers such as Mozart, Chopin, and many others.

Back in class, I was enjoying my English lessons, reading Thomas Hardy, Matthew Arnold, Chaucer, and Shakespeare. We had studied one of Shakespeare's plays in each grade, but in the Lower and Upper Sixth, we went into greater detail and tackled the wonderful tragedies of *King Lear*, *Othello*, and *Macbeth*. English was the subject I would continue to explore in college—a natural progression, I suppose, in a lifetime of developing a love for reading.

Another privilege was attendance at the Sixth Form Society, where speakers were invited to stretch the boundaries of our minds and make long speeches about a variety of topics. Each time, a girl was chosen to give a vote of thanks to the visitor at the end of the session. The Geography Mistress was always present to see that this was done properly.

This honour fell to me one memorable day. I happened to be sitting by Monica, who was fidgeting about and making it quite hard to concentrate on what the gentleman was saying. I began to get more and more nervous as his speech drew to a close, and I frantically tried to remember what I was going to say. He finished speaking, and Miss Metcalf stood up to introduce me. My mind went blank as I rose from my chair. I could see Monica hunched up in her chair, shaking with laughter, while my knees shook with fear. I took a deep breath and began, as an expectant hush fell around the room:

"Mr. ----, on behalf of the Sixth Form Society ..." My mind froze. I began again: "Mr. ----, on behalf of the Sixth Form Society, I would ..."

The words disappeared out of my mind. I kept sitting down and then standing to try again until I just gave up and stood in mute horror, gazing at the poor embarrassed speaker and the mortified Miss Metcalfe. There was silence, apart from the suppressed choking sounds coming from the creased-up form of Monica next to me. Miss Metcalfe hurriedly apologised for my performance and thanked him profusely for his wonderfully interesting talk. I filed out with the others, trying to avoid her furious gaze as she watched me leave.

I tried to avoid her for several days, but eventually my misdeed caught up with me. She caught me going down one of the corridors.

"Miss Ecclestone, whatever happened to you the other day? What an extraordinary performance! I hope you don't disgrace yourself like that again!"

She did choose me again at a later date to give the vote of thanks, and I managed to give an acceptable performance, having made sure I wasn't sitting next to Monica!

It was at the beginning of Upper Sixth that my concentration was taxed to its limits, and it happened during the course of an ordinary weekend. I'd invited Margaret over so that we could go to a dance at the Congleton Town Hall in Congleton one Saturday night. But when we arrived, we discovered, to our dismay, that it had been cancelled. We had a quick wander through the town before deciding to go back home. It was as we were nearing the bus stop that we saw there was a dance taking place in the nearby Drill Hall, a meeting place for the guides and scouts. All ideas of returning home were abandoned as we joined the crowd of dancers in the hall.

We danced together for a while before two young men made their way over to us and asked if we would care to dance. I found myself partnered with a pleasant looking fellow called John. I remember two things very clearly, the first being the fact that I noticed he was wearing black patented dancing shoes.

Oh no, I thought. *What a sissy!*

The second thing was that he was repeatedly tripping over my feet. When he said, "I know all the fancy steps to this dance," I retorted with, "Well, shall we try and sort out the basics first?"

After such a miserable introduction, I was surprised that he continued to partner me through the evening, and then asked if he could walk me home. Margaret caught her bus in Congleton, so we meandered up the hill from Congleton, chatting as we went, until we arrived at my front gate. After a short while, he asked for a date the next night, to visit the cinema. When I said I wasn't sure if I was free, he said he was going back to his Air Force base after that, so I rapidly changed my tune and agreed to meet him in front of the Town Hall.

When the next night arrived, I stood in front of the Town Hall, gazing at everybody passing by, because I wasn't sure I could remember what he looked like. He rolled up, thankfully minus the black patent shoes, in a lovely cream cable-knit sweater, and yes, I did recognise him! He told me later that that first walk to my house, and then back home, was complete agony, as his feet were crippled in those dancing shoes. I couldn't resist a smile!

We continued to meet on occasional weekends, and I discovered he lived in Congleton, and his father was one of the local chemists. John was away quite a lot, because he was an aircraft apprentice at the RAF base at Aylesbury, but he came home as often as possible, and we continued our relationship.

But there was still work to be done back in school, as we were preparing for our A Levels. I suppose our relationship couldn't have started at a more inconvenient time for me and my studies. I spent a lot of time daydreaming and doodling names on the back of exercise books but fortunately still managed to attain the grades I needed in order to go on to teacher training college.

I applied to three colleges and was called for an interview at my first choice: Nottinghamshire County Training College—Eaton Hall—in Retford. The day eventually arrived when I had to travel to Retford, a long circuitous journey on four buses, which took me from Biddulph to Stoke to Derby and Nottingham and then on to Retford. Christopher Columbus couldn't have felt more apprehensive when in 1492 he "sailed the deep sea blue." I felt like I was crossing the globe and arrived at the college totally exhausted. Two or three more candidates were already there, and we were given a meal before being told to wait outside an oak-panelled door until our names were called.

When it was my turn, I was ushered into an impressive looking office, and in front of an imposing looking principal, who reminded me of Dr. Bright back at school. She greeted me and shook my hand, pointing to one of the chairs in front of her desk. There was another chair nearby, on which lay a huge tabby cat, resplendent on a plump cushion. It was later rumoured that if anyone dared to try and sit on the cat's chair and remove her from her cushion, it meant an instant fail and immediate curtailment of the interview. Fortunately, that didn't happen, and the interview was brought to a satisfactory conclusion, which I eventually discovered had gained me a place in Miss Warren's college "for refined young ladies."

The year 1956 brought my school career at B.H.S. to an end. The last day was filled with a flurry of goodbyes; of filling autograph books with everyone's address, and promising faithfully to write and keep in touch; of hugs and tears; of a hitherto unknown familiarity with members of staff; of clearing desks and exchanging gifts; of stuffing as much as possible into bags and satchels (including our pork pie hats); of waving our last goodbyes, and disappearing through the gates to make our ways home.

I see clearly now that the girl who came out of those gates on that day was very different from the red-haired little girl with pigtails who had walked through them six years previously. I had made wonderful friendships that have lasted more than sixty years; I had achieved the necessary qualifications to enable me to follow my chosen career; I had broadened my horizons in many ways; and I had met the man I was going to marry. I had grown my wings, and I was ready to fly!

CHAPTER NINE

College Days
(1956–1958)

Just as a breeze snatches the seeds from a dandelion head and scatters them far and wide, so the end of that last term dispersed our gang of six to various universities and training colleges the length and breadth of the country. Margaret had chosen Eaton Hall in Retford along with me, and it was great to know there would be one familiar face amongst the strangers.

A friend of the family offered to take me on my first journey to college, so cases and bags were piled into his car, I waved my goodbyes to Mosslands, and we set off. I was leaving home for the first time, and it was a completely unique experience. I wouldn't be coming home every night, hopping off the school bus, and hauling my satchel full of books over my shoulder in order to do my homework and return to school the next day. I was going to a completely new setting, living with people I didn't know, and wouldn't be seeing my family for several weeks. I swallowed hard and concentrated on the journey through Leek and Ashbourne, Marlock, Worksop, and eventually onto the smaller country roads that led to the college in Retford.

It was as I remembered from my previous visit: a large, red brick, spacious hall, set in its own grounds, far away from town or city and, I thought as the car pulled up in front of the main entrance, in the middle of nowhere. The village of Retford was a little distance away—probably a twenty-minute walk—and the Hall itself was set in the middle of fields, with the River Idle running nearby. A bus stopped outside the college gates, which would take you into Retford in one direction, or Gamston and Markham Moor in the other. Even the names of nearby towns sounded strange and foreign to my ear. Cars were arriving from all directions, packed full of people, cases, bags, and belongings of all sorts.

My friend helped me unload my things from his old car, and we made our way through the doors, where he then left me, surrounded by my cases and bags, in the entrance hall. I was on my own, but not for long, before a friendly looking older student made her way to me and asked my name. She looked down her list before helping me gather all my things together, telling me cheerfully to follow her. She led me to a small room down one of the corridors on the ground floor and told me to just wait there for a while, and somebody would come and give me a hand.

The "somebody" was a lovely girl called Ann who, it turned out, was my college "mum." The college had a wonderful system whereby a second-year student would be given the responsibility of looking after a new first year, introducing her to college ways and gradually easing her into the system over the first weeks. Ann was friendly and comfortable to be with. She took me around the building, told me where everything was, and gave me directions to the refectory, where we would eat our evening meal at the end of that first day and where I would have to make my way the next morning for breakfast.

Back in my room, after Ann had dropped me off, I left my things as they were and went to see if I could find Margaret. When she arrived, it turned out that she too had a room on the first floor, not too far away from mine, so we were highly delighted. Ann was a great help in those initial weeks, but it's amazing how quickly the new becomes familiar, and in no time at all, Margaret and I felt like old hands at it all. When timetables had been distributed, students had found their place in their subject groups, classrooms had been located, and we'd actually started our studies, we settled comfortably into college life.

My room was small, containing bed, desk and chair, built-in wardrobe, and a wash basin and mirror in the corner. Several communal shower units and toilet blocks were spaced out on two floors. There was nothing fancy, but I found the bed quite comfortable and the room itself conveniently placed for access to various parts of the building. The shower was a novel experience for me, but I soon realised it was far superior to my paint-shedding bathtub back home! There were also a couple of kitchens on both floors where we were able to boil kettles and make drinks, as well as do a little bit of basic cooking on a small stove. In the weeks that followed, most evenings would find groups of us in the tiny kitchens making our favourite evening snack of beans on toast. The toast was either well and truly brown or, if it had been rescued too soon, a pale imitation of toast as it should be—but we loved it. I can't imagine we were really hungry, because college food was cooked in the kitchens on the premises and was delicious: homemade soups and stews, pies and meat dishes, as well as plenty of stewed or fresh fruit, custards, and rice puddings. I think it was the newly formed friendship groups getting together and enjoying the novelty of cooking for ourselves and eating together that drew us around the little stove.

My friendship group was quickly formed in the very first weeks and consisted this time of a gang of five, plus some extras who came and went at various times. There was myself and Margaret, Joan, Barbara, and Margaret B (whom we called Bunny), who formed a tight knit group. Then there was Pam, Joyce, Sally, and Jackie who joined us on occasions. We were all studying different main subjects but came together for other general lessons, as well as meals and social activities. I was doing English as my main, and Margaret Maths, while the others were split between Biology, Sport, and History. Although some of us studied the same mains together, it was our evening get-togethers that brought us close together.

After our evening meal, we would eventually end up in our individual rooms to do any homework we had been given. After showers, we would change into our nighties and dressing gowns, having decided earlier whose room we were congregating in that night. Over mugs of tea or cocoa, we would discover something of each other's backgrounds, or we'd share stories that had everyone rolling around with laughter. Occasionally there would be a knock on the door to tell us to be quiet, or at ten o'clock, when the member of staff who was on lock-up duty would parade down the corridors, switching off lights, checking windows and doors, and declaring it was time for "lights out!" We would always retreat to our rooms at this point, wishing the staff member a courteous, "Goodnight!"—but sometimes, after checking the coast was clear, we would reassemble, making sure to keep the sound level down.

We were like birds let out of our cages, tasting the exhilaration of real freedom. We felt so grownup, able to make up our own minds and our own choices. There was no school uniform that took away our individuality and made us all look the same. Instead, we gloried in the fashions of the day and proudly strutted our stuff down the catwalks of the corridors. There were the full mid-calf skirts and shirt, waister dresses, pencil skirts and long-sleeved blouses—often with Peter Pan collars—flat ballerina shoes, and ankle socks. More often than not, the girls chose short hair styles, but fringes were not popular, and long hair and ponytails were the exception rather than the rule. I think the grand dames on the college staff tried to reel us back a little with their edict over the sports kit. When being measured up for our games equipment, the length of the skirt was determined as we knelt on the floor, and the mistress measured where the skirt fell: exactly on the knee, and not a centimetre shorter!

I occasionally went home for a weekend break, but more often wrote letters to Mum and Dad to tell them how things were going, and in return they passed on news of my family. Almost at the same time that I had started college, Roy had been conscripted into the army. He had been allowed to complete his apprenticeship before being called up, but at the age of twenty-two, he joined the Cheshire Regiment. After a while, he was drafted to Berlin where, on occasion, he was put on sentry patrol to guard the war criminal Rudolf Hess in one of the main German prisons.

Meanwhile, John had completed his apprenticeship as an aircraft engineer at Aylesbury and gained a commendation for outstanding work and progress. Over the course of a weekend, I returned home and travelled down to the Air Force training base with his parents to witness the passing out parade and the award of his commendation. Afterwards, much to our mutual delight, he was posted to nearby Waddington, so he was able to make frequent weekend visits to Retford.

I think I was the only one at that time with a regular boyfriend, and the girls were very interested in the relationship and keen to know how we spent our weekends when he travelled up from Waddington. He would meet me at the college gates after travelling by train, and we would wander down the road to the nearby village, more often than not ending up at a favourite haunt of John's—a cafe run by a jovial Italian woman named Belinda. Over the course of the two years, Belinda became very fond of the familiar young man who visited her establishment, and she made him mouth-watering meals, his favourite being a mushroom omelette and chips, with the omelette literally bursting with fat, juicy mushrooms. When I went with him, it took me ages to finish the huge meal, and I would plead with John to take his time and eat slowly so I could keep up.

We ate, walked, and talked our way through the weekends, and I was always sad to see him off at the railway station. I would quickly become re-immersed in the weekday routine back at college, though, and the homework and private study that needed to be done after each lecture, as well as all the social gatherings with the girls.

My main lessons for English were taught by Miss Clarkson, a very refined, well-spoken lady who could be very cryptic and sarcastic. She was the one who made me realise that I spoke with an accent that was quite distinctive. There were only about a dozen students in our lectures, so everybody had plenty of opportunities to contribute to discussions. After one such time, she asked me where I came from.

"Congleton," I replied.

She raised her eyebrows and repeated, "*Congleton,*" with heavy emphasis. "Where did you do your home study?" she asked.

I had visited a local residential school over the holidays, so I replied, "Buglawton Residential School for Boys."

"Oh," she trilled, "*Bug*lawton. *Bug*lawton, was it?"

I remained silent for the rest of the discussion. Later, as she was distributing parts for Bernard Shaw's play, *Joan of Arc,* she turned to me and said, "Miss Ecclestone, you can take the part of the soldier."

I did, with the realisation that, in Miss Clarkson's eyes, my northern accent was not quite acceptable.

Nevertheless, she was an extremely good lecturer who knew her subject through and through. And apart from her ability to reduce her students to pulp at times, she also managed to bring out the best in us academically.

There were one or two subsidiary topics that all the students took, such as Sport, Religious Education, Environmentals, and Music, but the other major one was Education, which included Health and Child Psychology. This, of course, was vitally important to us as we began to prepare ourselves to teach children ranging in age from five to eleven and twelve to sixteen years. We needed to know and understand the way that children developed mentally, physically, and socially before we could begin to teach them successfully.

Running parallel to all the teaching and theory behind the social and emotional development of children, we young ladies were experiencing our own social development. We were dipping our toes into hitherto unknown waters and enjoying the experience. Apart from the friendship groups and social activities within the college, there were also the extramural activities outside, visits to local places of interest, jaunts to nearby towns, visits from the Physical Education students from nearby Loughborough Sports College, college dances, and more. John came to the dances when he could, but I don't think he really enjoyed them, because they were often rather formal. I think he much preferred wandering around the locality and visiting Belinda's. But some jaunts we girls made were extremely exciting. I remember two or three of us going to nearby Doncaster, to a Lonnie

Donnegan concert. We hitched lifts there and back, waving lorries down from the side of the road. I never shared that experience in my letters back home!

John and I wrote to each other several times a week, and the girls soon recognised his letters on the letter board. "Another one from John," they would call as I came out of the refectory after breakfast. They were easily spotted because he drew "Chads"—a little cartoon character—on the top corner of the envelope and coloured them in with brightly coloured inks.

Because of his frequent visits, he too became quite a familiar figure whom the girls came to recognise—as did certain members of the staff. I was called into the principal's office one day and given the third degree by Miss Warren:

"Is it your young man I have seen loitering around the college ground?" she asked.

I presumed it must have been John, so I nodded.

"Are your parents aware of this young man and his visits?" she continued.

"Oh yes," I affirmed, "they are. They are very fond of him."

"Mmmmm," she concluded. "Well, make sure that he doesn't interfere with your work." And with that veiled warning in my ears, I was duly dismissed.

I think the staff kept a close look out for the presence of strangers in the grounds because the college was quite close to Rampton Psychiatric Hospital, and occasionally there were reports on the local radio that one or other resident had escaped. On such occasions, the staff were very on edge, and lock up times at night were attended to very thoroughly. Windows and doors were double checked, and the member of staff on duty would parade nervously up and down the corridors until satisfied beyond a doubt that everyone would sleep safely and uninterrupted throughout the night.

It would have been during the second year there that I tested the security of the college—and found it wanting! By this time, my room was on the second floor, together with all my friends, but I still knew girls whose rooms were on the first floor. This information came in very useful on one particular occasion. I had been out with John, and for one reason or another, we arrived back at college after lock-up. Fortunately, John's "loitering" habits had given him a good knowledge of the lay of the land, so we crept around the residential block, keeping well into the shadows, until we came to the side of the building where I knew one of my acquaintances had her room. It was then essential that I counted along the windows of the down-stairs rooms to make sure I came to the right one. I tapped lightly, my heart in my throat, then tapped again a little louder. It seemed ages before the curtain was drawn aside and a familiar face peered out. I breathed a sigh of relief as she opened the window and, with John's help from behind, I heaved myself over the windowsill before disap-pearing into the room and waving him a hasty goodbye.

During that first year we learned a lot, not only about ourselves, but also about what would be expected from us as we launched into our teaching careers. We didn't just learn about the theory of education but were guided and instructed in how to put it into prac-tice. There were essays to write, texts to be scrutinised, the works of famous educationalists to be discussed and debated, time to be spent in the library, lectures to be listened to, exams to be revised for and undertaken, and school practices to be experienced.

School practices—when we actually put our learning into action and met real pupils for the first time—were the most important times in our college education. But at the end of the first year, during the summer holidays, something of great importance happened in my personal life.

I was at home for several weeks, and John, still at Waddington, learning about the new Vulcan Bomber Aircraft, would come home to Congleton for his weekend breaks. Before one weekend, as a P.S. in his letter, he said, "Oh—when I see you on Friday, remind me to ask you something."

He arrived home on Friday, and we decided to go to Trentham Hall the next night, where a dance was taking place. In my excitement at our plans, I forgot about the P.S., and it was only when he rolled up in his dad's car on Saturday that I remembered. He just brushed away my question and said, "Oh, it'll wait," as we made our way to the lovely Trentham Hall, which was situated in beautiful grounds.

The dances were wonderful occasions, led by well-known orchestras, and we danced along to the tunes of popular singers such as Dean Martin, Paul Anka, Duane Eddy, and Rosemary Clooney. Every now and then while enjoying a cold drink and getting our breath back, I remembered that he'd got a question of some kind to ask me. But each time he just said casually, "Oh, later." So I forgot about it, and we continued to jig our way through the evening. About half an hour before "The Last Waltz," he said, "Let's go outside for a breather."

It was a lovely night, bright stars pricking through the darkness, showing outlines of fir trees. We stood in the shadows enjoying the crisp, fresh air.

"Oh, by the way," I said. "What *was* the question you wanted to ask me?"

His response completely stunned me, just four words that took my breath away.

"Will you marry me?"

I stood in silence for a little while before I gasped, "Oh, I don't know, you'll have to ask my dad."

My lukewarm response was due to the complete unexpectedness of the question and not due to the lack of desire! So consequently, after a conversation with my dad, our plans were formed.

It was during the same holiday that we made an excursion to nearby Rudyard Lake, a local beauty spot. As we walked by the side of the water underneath the trees, he slipped an engagement ring on my finger.

The whole of that summer break was extraordinary, a crossroads where decisions were made and the direction of our lives determined in the space of a heartbeat, by a single choice. After John returned to base, and before my holiday finished, I was listening to music on the radio and jiving in my room with my doorknob as a dance partner. Mum and Dad were away, and Roy was in bed. When the programme finished, it was followed immediately by a service broadcast from a Manchester church, led by a minister called Nelson Parr. He was reading from John Chapter 10: "I am the Good Shepherd. The sheep hear my voice and follow me."

Childhood memories stirred, stories from Sunday School telling of that good shepherd leaving the flock to search for the one that had wandered away. I remembered times when I had felt the safety of walking down the Hollow, my hand in the hand of my dad, and a longing took hold of me to put my hand in the hand of that Good Shepherd and entrust my life to him. That night, I heard his voice calling me, and I decided to follow him. I became a Christian not just by name, but by experience.

John was curious when I shared with him, and over the course of one weekend, we went to listen to two deaconesses who were preaching in the Primitive Methodist Church in Mow Cop. At the end of the service, they gave an invitation for anyone who wanted to "come and see" what it meant to be a Christian to talk to them afterwards. John accepted their invitation, and he too made the momentous decision to follow Christ that night. After some life-changing choices had been made, we settled down to make other plans regarding our future.

We decided that I would start my teaching career when I finished college the following year, while John would continue in the RAF and sign up for twelve more years. Both families were pleased with the developments, and the future looked rosy, but there was still work to be done before our plans could be realised. And for me, that meant finals to be passed, and a major school practice to be success-fully undertaken.

After the allocation of schools, the forerunner to our school prac-tice was the initial visit. After a good breakfast, the bus picked us up, our bags containing all that we would need for the rest of the day. We set off to schools that were regularly chosen to play host to the college students, located in towns whose names would become very familiar to us: Markham Moor, Worksop, Mansfield, Ollerton. The bus travelled along country roads and up and down town streets, dropping off groups of two or three students at the gates of the different schools. We who were left watched them go through the gates and across the schoolyard, before disappearing through the main entrance, knowing it would soon be our turn to discover what lay before us over the next month. I was in one of the last groups to arrive at my destination, which was a primary school in Ollerton called Whinney Lane. Only two students, including myself, were left there. Upon arrival, we were taken to the headmistress, who took us into the staff room to be introduced to the rest of the teachers and to find out whose classroom we would be in.

I had a really nice teacher, who greeted her class when they came in and said that I was going to help teach them over the next four weeks. There were a lot of curious stares and a few comments to friends behind cupped hands, but they seemed a nice enough class. They were warned to be on their best behaviour. During the course of the day, I became familiar with the basic layout of the school but spent most of the time sitting and listening to the class teacher and noting the behaviour of the children. There were obviously one or two I would have to watch—boys, of course—who appeared to do the minimum amount of work with the minimum amount of effort but a lot of fuss.

The day seemed long, and although I had done very little other than observe, I felt exhausted and climbed thankfully onto the bus when it returned to pick us up. The reports from the students varied widely; some had been to wonderful schools, while others had landed in staff rooms of unfriendly staff or found themselves with the daunting prospect of boisterous or unruly classes over the next weeks. I felt lucky that Whinney Lane didn't seem to be as bad as that.

Back at college, the next few weeks were full of lectures from the Education lecturers, giving help on specific topics relevant to our needs: lesson plans and notes, and preparation of materials and visual aids that we thought we should need. When the day came to begin the practice, we set off once more. This time our bags were bulging with all the aids and materials, notes and plans that were going to be so important to us when, for the first time, we would stand in front of the class, responsible for being in charge of twenty-five to thirty-five children who relied on us to have all the answers. As hoped on the visit, my class were a pleasant and orderly bunch—with the odd mischievous exceptions—and I got on well with them. The nerve-wracking times came when a college lecturer arrived, always unannounced and unexpected, to observe and comment on our teaching, lesson preparation, and the way we handled the discipline of the children. Later, back at the college, we would have an audience with the staff member to be encouraged or redirected, according to how the lesson had gone.

Isn't it amazing how time varies its pace? At times it can crawl along in heavy, hobnailed boots, as though ploughing its way through thick swampland, while at others it picks up pace and gallops along, light feet hardly seeming to touch the floor. That school practice was not unpleasant, but it was very long, very arduous, very tiring, and it seemed to last forever. The end report, however, was good, and I was pleased that I had done a satisfactory job.

It turned out it had actually been more than satisfactory, however, because I was called into the principal's office a couple of weeks later. Once there, Miss Warren told me that it seemed I had a way of dealing with pupils who were underachieving and asked if I would consider studying for an extra year to gain qualification to teach such children. I thanked her but said I was engaged and had plans to marry soon after leaving college. During the course of my teaching career, her assessment was proven to be correct, and I often ended up with the poorer students who needed that extra help and encouragement. I always enjoyed it and was delighted when they began to thrive.

With a successful school practice tucked safely under my belt, I now turned my attention to which section of my main subject I should tackle for my thesis. After much thought, I decided to do poetry. Looking at some of my favourite poets, I narrowed it down to poets of the early twentieth century. I loved Dylan Thomas and W.B. Yeats, and in that era were the war poets, who had always fasci-nated me, like Wilfred Own and Edward Thomas. Having come to a decision, I booked a slot with Miss Clarkson and set out an outline of my plan with her. She listened to my ideas and said, "What will your title be?"

"Poets of the Early Twentieth Century," I replied.

"Hmm," she deliberated. "Don't you think 'Early Twentieth Century Poetry' sounds so much better? It's a matter of *style*, you see."

That re-phrasing has resonated in my memory and mind over the decades, and I sometimes, even now, find myself turning or adjusting a phrase in my mind and thinking, "Sounds better now—it's a matter of style!"

And so began my journey into the war poets.

Wilfred Owen's "Arms and the Boy":

> "Let the boy try along this bayonet black
> How cold steel is, and keen with hunger of blood."

Or Rupert Brookes' "The Dead," *1914:*

> "These hearts were woven of human joys and cares
> Washed marvellously with sorrow, swift to mirth...
> Felt the quick stir of wonder; sat alone
> Touched flowers and furs and cheeks.
> All this is ended."

As I browsed upon these poems, so full of beauty yet so interlaced with anguish at the waste of young life, I thought of Uncle Raymond, who lost his life along with so many other young eighteen- and nineteen-year-olds. Their swift, untimely end came not by blade or bayonet but with bullet, but the end was the same: wasted life.

I didn't linger there long. I hurried to lighten my spirit in the stanzas of Dylan Thomas' "Under Milk Wood," and his saucy characterizations, or—best of all—in the wonderful stanzas of W.B. Yeats' "Cloths of Heaven":

> "Had I the heavens' embroidered cloths
> Enwrought with gold and silver light
> The blue, and the dim, and the dark cloths
> Of night and the light and the half light
> I would spread the cloths under your feet
> But I, being poor, have only my dreams
> I have spread my dreams under your feet
> Tread softly, because you tread on my dreams."

Wonderful poetry that even decades later stays in my mind and stirs my imagination! But back then, with a deadline to meet and much work to accomplish, I didn't spend too long musing over the beauty of the poetry. It was a case of many long hours spent in the library and over my desk, burning the midnight oil. The disheartening experiences were to slave away at some section or other, only to have Miss Clarkson spatter the pages with question marks or red lines from her biro, with comments like, "Would you like to think about how you could rephrase this section?"

Nevertheless, it was eventually completed and accepted into the hallowed realms of Miss Clarkson's study to be appraised—and hopefully not assassinated!

Not all the work was completed, however, because final exams loomed. Students became tired and short tempered as they spent time revising and researching, getting nervous as the exam dates drew near. The "gang of five" still met for bean suppers in the kitchen, but we all had different exam timetables and needed to revise at different times. Bunny was the one who spent hours and hours, evening after evening, in the Biology Lab, and we teased her that she was going for gold!

At last all was complete. Thesis and work finished, exams done, books returned to the library. The die had been cast. We had done the best we could, and we would either be found wanting, or we would have achieved our goal. All we had to do now was wait for the results, which would arrive through the post after we had left college and returned home.

Before that happened, though, there were end of term festivities: jaunts into now familiar towns, afternoon wanderings down nearby lanes and fields, late night feasts and noisy shenanigans, and lots of talking, laughter, and stories from the past two years. But, at last, our rooms were cleaned for the final time, and bags and cases were packed. There were lots of hugs and some tears as we said our good-byes and made our way to the nearby station, or to waiting cars and taxis. We were homeward bound!

Arriving home was a strange mix of joy as we re-entered the familiar family routines, and loss as we looked back and viewed that which seemed so recent and present, but was gone forever. College and friends, studies and lectures, had been the reality of our lives for two years but were now reduced to memories. The first couple of weeks passed slowly, but then the anxiety of waiting for the post to bring results set in. Just like eight years earlier, I waited for a brown envelope to settle on the mat, and I looked out daily for the post-man's visit—until the day it finally arrived.

I took it upstairs to my bedroom and shut the door, ripping open the envelope and quickly scanning down the list of names. It was in alphabetical order of course: A, B, C, D, E ... and hallelujah, there it was! Jean Ecclestone, in the list of successful students who had gained a fully qualified teacher's certificate.

I breathed a huge sigh of relief and began to go down the lists in a more leisurely fashion to check that all my friends had also passed. All were there—with one horrible exception. Bunny! I retraced the list of names several times with no joy. Bunny, the one who had spent hours and hours doing extra work in the lab, was the only one who had not passed. I was flabbergasted. I wonder now if she had received a warning to step up her work and that was the real reason for the extra lab work. Whatever it was, it was all to no avail, and the gang was gutted for her. The die had indeed been cast. For us, it meant standing on the launchpad of a brand-new career. For Bunny, it meant retracing her steps and, en route, picking up her broken dreams to try and reshape her future.

As the poet Matthew Arnold said, "Wandering between two worlds—one dead, the other powerless to be born."

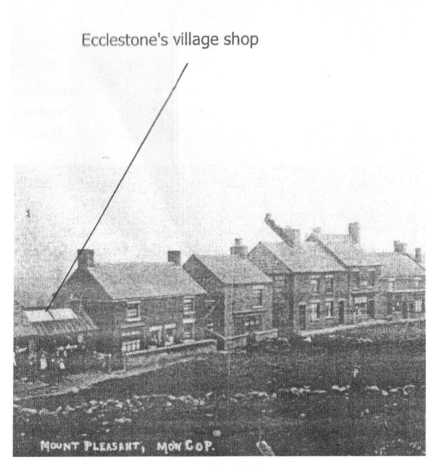

Ecclestone's village shop

MOUNT PLEASANT, MOW COP.

My grandma's shop

Grandma Ecclestone and one of her children
(possibly my dad, as he was the firstborn)

Grandad Ecclestone

Mow Cop Castle

Playing an organ like my dad's

JEAN MCLELLAN

An old fire range

Our family of four, taken on my ninth birthday

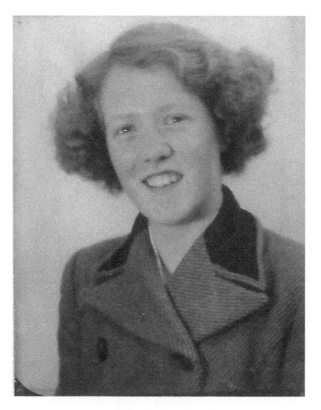

Me at age ten

Dad and I, taken when I was around fourteen

French exchange holiday in Nice

Holiday with Gwen and her family in Llandudno, Wales

The high school "Gang of Six" (I'm second from the right in the back row)

John and I while courting

Our wedding day, 1960

The happy couple

In full regalia!

College friends (I'm third from the left)

Our bungalow in Cyprus

Roy and Eileen's wedding

Our little family at Biddulph Road
(L-R: a little friend and Cathy in the back; Sally, myself,
and Lesley in the middle; David in the front)

A snack stop on holiday (L-R: Cathy, Lesley, Sally, David, me)

A holiday photo from Kinlochleven, Scotland

Family beach fun at Woolacombe sands

Camping in Glencoe, Scotland

John and I at a favourite haunt in Bakewell

First adventure on John's motorbike

Family photo in 2009
(Back Row, L-R: Ben, Emma, Erin, Laura, Jen, Sophie, Megan, Joshua, Kyle
Second Row, L-R: Daniel, Lesley, David W, Michael,
Richard, David M, Tina
Third Row, L-R: Cathy, myself, Sally
Front Row, L-R: Ayana, Moses, Alicia
Dogs, L-R: Bracken, Mac, Rosie)

Visiting 116 the Flat in 2021

Standing at the "big girls' door" at Woodcocks' Well School in 2021

Visiting Woodcocks' Well School in 2021

CHAPTER TEN

Back to Square One

Like Mow Cop, Mossley sat on the boundary line between Staffordshire and Cheshire, so when I started to apply for my first teaching post, I had to decide which county I wanted to work in. I had heard that Cheshire was considered to be less favourable to work for than Staffordshire, so it was to Staffordshire that I decided to apply. I received a speedy reply from the Education Offices and was called for an interview in Staffordshire. Imagine my surprise when I discovered that the interviewer was Miss Bowie, who had been the German teacher at Brownhills High School for Girls!

Although I had never studied German, she recognised me as soon as I arrived and greeted me warmly. There was nothing official or intimidating in the interview at all, and she studied the list of vacancies in front of her before coming to a rapid decision: "How would you feel about a lovely little country school affiliated to the local Church of England church?" she asked. The wheel had come full circle! It sounded wonderful! Before I had the chance to say anything, she added, "And it's only about three miles from where you live!"

Well, there was nothing more to say, except to thank her for her time and accept the offered position, thinking it would be like returning to Woodcocks' all over again. The vacancy was for a reception teacher in Biddulph North Primary School, a small stone building that sat adjacent to the church and its surrounding church yard. The church was squat, slightly raised on an incline above the school, stone-built with its square Norman tower housing the church bells. Because of its slight elevation, it seemed to be guarding the school and its pupils, as apparently it had done in the previous century. It was reported that Cromwell's men had fired their cannons from the ridge of Congleton Edge during the Civil War and badly damaged the church, smashing the stained-glass windows. Apparently, the vicar at the time collected as many fragments as possible and preserved them. They were later fitted into the east window of the church and can still be seen today.

Although sixteen years had lapsed, I didn't feel I had travelled far! My first primary school had been on the slopes of Mow Cop, steeped in the history of Primitive Methodism and its battle against the established church, and here I was in my first teaching appointment, housed in buildings that had been under attack from Cromwell and his infamous roundheads as they took up arms against the Crown and its establishment.

The thought of ancient history was still in my mind as I was taken to see my classroom on my first day. A partition separated it from the class next door, and an old upright piano sat in the corner. What astonished me was a basket at the side of the teacher's desk filled with old slates, chalks, and cloths. Were these children still using chalk and slates to write with? It turned out that I needn't have feared: pencil and paper were generally used, and the slates only occasionally made an appearance during afternoon crafts.

The head, Mr. Whitehurst, and his staff of three, Arthur, Audrey, and Ken, were very welcoming, and after a quick look around the four classrooms and the general layout of the school, I was handed a cup of tea along with my timetable.

Although I had been trained to teach seven to eleven year olds, I was thrown in the deep end with a reception class! That first morning for me was also the first morning for twenty-four brand new, very scared, very tearful little five-year-olds. Some of them weren't just crying—they were screaming and hanging onto their mums as if their lives depended on them. I couldn't believe it. It was a nightmare! The head and secretary came in to give a hand, shooing away the mums and assuring them that all would be well, while retrieving the scared infants and shepherding them into the classroom.

That first day passed in a haze of cries and tears, sadness and sodden handkerchiefs, and the next few days began in a similar way. But slowly and surely, the whirlwind abated, and by the time ten days had passed, the majority of the children had settled. Just the odd one or two, like a little girl named Yvonne, still needed constant reassurance, and even my presence with her during the play times. But at last she too was happy to wave her mum goodbye at the gate and make her way into the classroom. I loved teaching reception, but even twenty years later, I still found that until the new children had settled down, I myself wasn't happy.

One of the first questions I was asked was if I could play the piano. "Only a bit," I admitted.

Apparently that "bit" was a bit more than anybody else. Just before going to college, I took some lessons with my friend Steph's mum, who was a piano teacher. But I hadn't progressed much further than the basics. I liked to play a little on Dad's organ, which had travelled with us through the years from house to house, and I could knock out one or two hymns from his Moody and Sankey hymnal. But organ and piano are very different to play and require a different touch on the keys. Regardless, I was asked to play for some of the assemblies, but when Mr. Whitehurst realised that my repertoire consisted only of, "O God, Our Help in Ages Past" and "The King of Love My Shepherd Is," he asked less frequently.

Because there were only three classrooms in the building, there was quite a lot of doubling up, with many rooms having a dual purpose. Ken's room was also the staff room where we had coffee or tea at playtimes. Audrey's was used as a dining room, and her children had to pack their morning's work away at 11:50, in readiness for the dinner ladies to carry in the large containers of food to be served at lunchtime. My room doubled as an assembly hall, where we started the day listening to a member of staff bringing a "thought for the day" and a prayer, and perhaps a lilting melody from the old piano! Arthur's class was housed in a mobile out on the schoolyard, where he reigned as king of his own little castle, undisturbed by anyone passing through and surrounded by half-finished craft projects that, to the uninitiated, seemed like chaos. The head shared his small space with a part-time secretary named Joan, who arrived after lunch to help with accounts and various tasks.

Before lunch saw the arrival of two dinner ladies from nearby Woodhouse Lane, Mrs. B. and Mrs. T. They were quite well-to-do, motherly souls, who did the job of watching the children at playtime because they loved them and not because they needed the money.

They were wonderful characters who knew all the parents and the families going back over many years, and I found their snippets of information and advice extremely useful at times.

At playtimes, staff took turns on a duty rota while the children played on the schoolyard, with the reception class at the back of the building, and older ones at the front. But in the summer, they enjoyed playing on the large field at the back of the school, behind Arthur's mobile and the toilet block.

Just like Woodcocks', it was like belonging to a large family. There was a wonderful atmosphere throughout the whole school, and the children were happy to be in such comfortable and relaxed sur- roundings. There was an ethos of caring and encouragement that brought out the best in the children, and they did well with their studies as a result.

In my reception class, much of the practical equipment was quite old fashioned (although not quite as bad as the slates and chalk). The previous reception teacher had made collections of buttons, beads, bobbins, and counters to use for counting in Maths, and I unearthed a huge collection of old pictures and charts that looked as though Noah had used them in the ark. The reading books were from the *Janet and John* and *Dick and Dora* schemes, with several homemade packs of flashcards to help with word recognition, plus individual sound cards for phonics. It was all quite out of date. Nevertheless, that was the equipment I had, and I had to make the best of it.

After settling down, the children seemed to do well, mastering the first steps of the three Rs, and enjoying work in general. Most afternoons were craft and activity based, when they were allowed free choice to develop their independence and social awareness. For me—and for the children, I think—the best part of the afternoon was story time. I would sit on a small child's chair as they gathered round me on the floor, sitting with knees crossed, a rapt expression on their faces as they lost themselves in another world. I found it was almost a magical experience, when at times it seemed I was communicating with their innermost being. I remember being fascinated with the psychology of language and the way information was communicated. The way thought was converted into language, and then changed back again into thought and imagination. I loved the feeling that I had a captive audience who were completely lost in the moment, eyes reflecting what was going on in their imagination. It's a thrill I never grew tired of during all my years of teaching, and even now, when I speak to adult gatherings, I can still recapture the feeling.

That first year was the best possible launchpad I could have had into my teaching career. The children enjoyed it and did well with their first steps into numeracy and literacy, and I learned so much. I marvelled at the way they latched on to new concepts, especially the skill of reading, and I loved it when I could see the light dawning as they moved from repetition to understanding. I was as thrilled as they were when they began to read with fluency, and I would watch them, delighted, as comprehension brought a half smile to their faces.

Over the years, I taught different ages for short periods of time but have always maintained that the bulk of the hard work happens in reception, as children make a start on the ladder of the three Rs.

It was in that first year that I too learned concepts and philosophies that would continue for a lifetime: the art of listening empathetically, the way to inspire and provoke curiosity, the way to communicate and hold attention, and, above everything else, how to encourage and build confidence. I believe that any child, regardless of ability, can be helped to make progress if we can find even one small attribute to encourage and praise.

By May of that first year, I began to be confident of my ability to teach and be responsible for a class of twenty-five reception children. But alas, pride comes before a fall, and I was about to take a tumble.

On the first bank holiday weekend in May, the school had a tradition of holding a fête, which was open to the public. If the weather was fine, it was held out on the field, where games were set up and stalls selling bric-a-brac, cakes, and refreshments were inside the school. The previous reception teacher had established the tradition of teaching her class to dance around the maypole, and apparently it had become the highlight of the afternoon. The photographer from the *Biddulph Chronicle* always made an appearance, and photographs filled the centre pages the following week. Imagine my dismay to be handed the dubious honour of training up my children to be the central players in this tradition, of which I was totally ignorant.

Once the maypole had been erected in the grounds of the neighbouring vicarage, we set to work. A portable wind-up gramophone was carried out onto the lawn, and we began by listening to the music. No ribbons were on the pole at this point. Boys and girls were paired up, and I encouraged them to skip around the pole, some going around in a clockwise fashion, while others criss-crossed around the other way. We repeated this performance over the course of many P.E. lessons until some semblance of order appeared and the children were familiar with the music, the skipping, and the direction they had to follow. But one fateful day we trooped out to find that dozens of multi-coloured ribbons had been attached to the top of the pole, hanging down to reach the ground.

We formed the circles, and I apprehensively handed out ribbons to the pairs of children. I instructed them to weave in and out of each other the way we had practised, keeping a firm hold of the ribbons, which had to go up and over, up and over, all the way around until they had been interlaced in a beautiful pattern down the length of the maypole, at which point the dance would be ended, and the spectacle complete. As the weeks progressed, the children danced, trying valiantly to keep in time to the music while at the same time learning how to weave the ribbons without knocking each other over, and avoiding me, who was usually running around the outer circle, whistle in my mouth to call a halt if things got out of hand.

Despite all our hours of rehearsal, I was still not sure that we had the central attraction of the maypole dancing under control when the day of the fête finally arrived. I was doubly disconcerted to see Mrs. D, the previous reception teacher, in the front row of spectators.

I led my troop of children out onto the lawns, all attired in pretty dresses or short pants with bibs and braces, and they took their positions around the pole, waiting for the music to begin so they could show off their dancing skills. There was hardly a free space on the vicar's lawn as the crowd waited expectantly. I nodded nervously to the person manning the gramophone and there was a moment's pause before the air was filled with music, and the children began their complicated routine around the maypole.

The trouble began when one child dropped their ribbon, and someone else lunged forward to retrieve it, causing instant chaos in the pairs of dancers still trying to hold on to their ribbons while weaving in opposite directions. Some children were tripping over each other, others tried to valiantly push their way through the routine and continue undaunted, while the ribbons became a hideous tangled mess, weaving around the children's ankles and missing the pole altogether.

I picked the arm of the gramophone off the record and stopped the music while the children disentangled themselves from the ribbons and each other, and we trooped apologetically back into school. There was a light ripple of applause, probably from one or two of the parents, but the last thing I saw before I escaped was the face of Mrs. D., with an expression that seemed to say, "Oh yes, I may be retired, and you may be the new replacement, but I am still Queen of the Maypole—and don't you forget it."

The next week, the *Biddulph Chronicle* filled its centre spread with photos of the stalls and the crowds, and a couple of shots of the maypole dancers standing stationary around the pole, holding ribbons in their hands and smiling at the camera. The reports told of the usual high attendance, and the good weather that was enjoyed by all who attended, and it was generally agreed to have been a great success in every way. I never commented, but I believe that year saw an end to the merry gambolling around the maypole. The death knell had been struck.

But I had my own celebrations to prepare and plan for, as John and I had decided to get married sometime during my first year of teaching. We originally thought that June would be a wonderful month for a wedding, but because John was expecting an overseas posting, we brought it forward to the end of May. We chose the little chapel at the bottom of the hill from Mosslands as a venue because it had been an important part of my mum's life through the years, and we began to make inquiries about dates. It turned out that it wasn't registered for weddings, so the registration had to be applied for. This meant that we would be the first couple to be married there. The chapel stewards were delighted at the prospect, and Bill Mayer, a wonderful carpenter, was asked to design and make a new lectern, pulpit, and communion rail for the front of the chapel. Bill had married Winnie, Auntie Sarah's daughter, so it was like keeping it in the family.

We booked the Park Pavilion for the reception, along with their caterers, and asked a friend to make the wedding cake. The next important matter was my wedding dress. Mum and I decided to take a journey to Nottingham to buy a dress made out of Nottingham lace. It seemed like only a day or two previously that I had made the same journey on the way to Eaton Hall for my teacher training college interview, and it was a shock to realise that nearly three years had passed since then. John had been measured up for his wedding suit at Pedley's tailors in Congleton during one of his weekend visits, but he was unable to return to have a fitting till about a week before the wedding weekend. I was on pins as the weeks whizzed by, and I checked and rechecked the arrangements while still teaching and working hard at the school.

The morning of the wedding dawned bright and clear and was quite a leisurely affair at Mosslands. I had breakfast while a visiting hairdresser washed and curled my hair, and my chief bridesmaid— my best friend, Gwen, who had arrived the previous day—started to get herself ready. John's sister, Jenny, together with Bill and Winnie's little daughter, Kathleen, were the other two bridesmaids who would arrive later, already fully dressed and ready for the ceremony.

Meanwhile, chaos reigned at John's home. He had to dash to Pedley's tailor for a last-minute fitting and pick up his shoes from the Army & Navy Stores in town, while his mum sorted out the rest of his attire back home.

Nevertheless, at the appointed time, the congregation filled the church in their best bib and tuckers, and the wedding car delivered John to the church first, before returning to pick up me and Dad.

I felt like the belle of the ball as I linked my arm into Dad's and made my way into the church. The bridesmaids followed in pale blue dresses, with a trim of anemones, carrying matching bouquets. Mr. Caunter was the minister who led the procession into the beautifully refurbished church, which was packed full to the brim, and the service went flawlessly—apart from one moment of hilarity. When John knelt down at the new communion rail, the congregation was treated to the sight of a bright yellow sticky label on the soles of both his shoes, revealing that they had been recently purchased at the Army & Navy Stores. Our good friend Peter's loud guffaws could be heard ringing round the congregation, until the minister brought the merriment to a conclusion, saying, "It'll be your turn next, Peter!"

After the photographs, a wonderful wedding meal was served at the Pavilion. The wedding cake was cut, and everyone trooped outside to have a group photograph showing the crowd of friends and family who had attended. Among the bystanders was Yvonne, the little girl I had helped to settle into school, together with her mum, and several other parents from school—including Mrs. B. and Mrs. T., the wonderful dinner ladies!

At the end of that wonderful but exhausting day, we piled into John's dad's car with our suitcases to make the journey to Llangollen for the first night of our honeymoon. We were spending a week in Aberdaron on the Llŷn Peninsula in Wales but decided to split the journey at Llangollen. My going away outfit was a white shirtwaist dress, with a green duster coat and white high heel shoes. The shoes were quickly discarded as soon as we were en route.

It was a fabulous week. Mrs. Williams looked after us in the B&B as though we were her family, and we meandered through the Welsh country lanes at our leisure, stopping off to explore anything that piqued our interest. The proprietor of one old hall gave me a bunch of orange blossoms from one of his bushes to remind me of my wedding day, which astonished us, while the skipper of a small boat asked John if he was booking the trip for one-and-a-half adults, thinking that I was a young schoolgirl.

We wandered the beaches and gazed into rock pools. We walked along cliff paths and explored little seaside towns. We frequented the Copper Kettle cafe to enjoy plates of ham sandwiches and cream scones and innumerable pots of tea.

But all good things come to an end. John had to return to base to continue his engineering work and wait for his posting. I had to complete my probationary year of teaching and hopefully receive my letter of affirmation from the Education Authority. There was work waiting for us back home. The honeymoon was at an end! But our journey together had just begun, and, unbeknownst to us, just around the corner a tremendous adventure was waiting. New relationships, new home, new jobs, foreign climes, extended family ... but to begin with, we had to travel halfway across the world.

It is said that each journey begins with a single step. We had taken that step as we joined hands in front of the altar in the little chapel in Mossley, and now a whole new world waited for us, thousands of miles away. It would necessitate putting down the known and embracing the unknown, but we were undaunted. We had joined forces and were ready, hand in hand, to travel the future together.

CHAPTER ELEVEN

Off to Cyprus

The weeks after the wedding passed by quickly. John returned to Waddington to continue his course on the Vulcan Bomber Aircraft, coming home to Mosslands on Friday evenings, and returning on Sunday afternoons. I continued to work hard at school, preparing the children to move up into the next class while waiting to hear from the Education Office that I had passed my probationary year of teaching. It was just before the summer break that the welcome letter arrived, informing me that they were pleased to tell me that they had received a favourable report from the school, and that I was now a fully accredited teacher.

Several weeks later, John too received news. He had been posted to the Air Force base at Akrotiri, Cyprus, and he was to pack his bags and be ready for a speedy departure. There was a flurry of activity at his base camp, and it seemed no time at all before we had said our hurried goodbyes, and he had flown away. I was to follow later, when things had been sorted and arrangements had been made. By the end of that school year, I had handed in my resignation to the head and was busy arranging for packing cases to be delivered and collected, while at the same time saying my goodbyes to friends and family. My bedroom was full of belongings ready to be packed and sent by sea in the packing cases, and suitcases full of clothes I would be taking with me on my journey.

While I was busy at my end, John was arranging for entry permits and looking for suitable living quarters. He had decided we would be much happier away from the actual base, so he found a little bunga- low in nearby Limassol on a road called Agia Fyla.

There was so much to do—business to be settled in England and new arrangements to be made in Cyprus—and the weeks seemed to pass swiftly. I had a suit tailored at Pedley's, ready for the journey, in a lovely green material with metal buttons on the jacket.

At last, all had been packed, everything had been sorted, and I was ready to go! It was quite breathtaking to think that I was going to travel by myself to an island in the Mediterranean Sea, thousands of miles away. I had received instructions from the Air Force that I was flying first to Gatwick from Manchester, and then on to Cyprus. They advised me to bring an overnight bag, just in case we were delayed at any point. I didn't think that was very likely, so I filled my overnight holdall with shoes and other things I hadn't managed to squeeze into my larger cases.

Mum was upset at the thought of me flying so far away, and nervous about the long journey I was going to undertake by myself. There were tearful farewells as I set off from Mosslands to begin the first lap of my journey.

Everything was new and exciting for me, from checking in, to going through security and seeing the shops and cafes at the airport, to waiting at the gate, ready for my flight to arrive. This was not only my first solo flight … it was my first flight in an aeroplane, and I was full of apprehension. I saw the planes lined up in their bays outside the airport windows and wondered how they could possibly lift off the ground with their huge fuselages packed with hundreds of bulging suitcases and crowds of passengers. By the time I was due to board, I was really anxious. But the stewardesses were cool and calm and smilingly showed me the direction of my seat.

It's a very short flight from Manchester to Gatwick, but by the time we made our approach, heavy fog had blanketed the airport, and we had to circle and queue for a long time before being given permission to land. When we arrived, I was told we were spending the night in the air base there and flying on to Cyprus the next morning. I remembered my overnight bag full of shoes and wondered what I was going to do.

We were given a basic meal, then some young Air Force cadets showed us to our—again, very basic—rooms. Unsure what else to do, I admitted to one of them that the contents of my bag were not the usual articles found in an overnight bag. He thought it was hilarious and soon came to my aid with a pair of men's pyjamas, soap, and a flannel.

I don't think I slept a wink all night, and I was up and ready to go when a knock on the door warned it was time. After a breakfast of scrambled egg on toast, and pots of strong tea, we gathered in a large group, ready to board the flight. I noted that all the passengers were either Air Force personnel or young women who were going to join their husbands. We were told that we would be flying directly into the Air Force base at Akrotiri and not to the national airport.

The flight takes approximately four hours, but it seemed like an eternity. I couldn't believe that John was waiting for me at the other end. It had been a few months since he left, but it felt like a year, and my excitement and nerves knew no bounds. John had told me that take-offs and landings were the most dangerous moments of the flight (he was always very safety conscious). I hadn't felt comfortable with the take-off, as the plane lifted off the runway before gaining height and reaching the usual three thousand feet, and I braced myself as we came in to land, grabbing hold of the arms of my seat and closing my eyes tightly. But at last it came to a stop.

There were a few minutes before the seatbelts began to click, as one after another were released. A slow, slow shuffle down the aisle, clutching my carry-on bag. Down the steps of the plane—and then John was there, waiting on the tarmac at the bottom of the steps. I couldn't believe I'd arrived, and he was there in his civvies with an enormous smile on his face, ready for our first hug in months—a wonderful welcome to Cyprus, the "jewel of the Mediterranean," which was going to be our first home together.

John hurried us through the formalities as quickly as he was able, then we carried all my baggage into his waiting car, and we were off through the gates and checkpoints of Akrotiri base camp, and onto the Limassol Road.

I had noticed the heat as I stepped out of the plane. It was like stepping into an oven, but my reuniting with John, and all the forms and checks and officialdom we had to proceed through, had put it to the back of my mind. But as I climbed into John's waiting car, the force of it hit me. Off came the shoes and tights, and then the jacket, before we drove away with all the windows open, regardless of the wind blowing my hair every which way! We were both so wonderfully happy, and I couldn't wait to see the bungalow he had chosen as our new home. But first there was the journey!

It was the sight of groups of soldiers along the sides of the road, all carrying guns and pistols in their belts and peering into the car as we passed them, that began to alarm me. There were numerous checkpoints where we were stopped and the guards would ask John where we were heading, and where we'd come from, and checked his papers before they let us through. Every building we passed seemed to be daubed with large painted letters spelling out EOKA, or the Greek letters for some political party or organisation. Flags and banners decked windows and houses, declaring the residents' support and affiliation to one group or another.

I had known that the political situation in Cyprus was very unstable before I came, and newspapers had headlined the unrest there over the previous months. There was constant fighting between the Greek Cypriots, headed up by Archbishop Makarios, and the Turkish Cypriots, both parties wanting to lay claim to the island. To make matters even more dangerous, there was a movement of Greek Cypriot guerrillas, led by a man called Grivas, who called themselves "EOKA" and who wanted to reclaim the island back from British rule. Needless to say, it was a very torrid situation and was probably why John and his company had been posted there in the first place.

All these things were in my mind as I made that initial journey, especially when our car kept being flagged down by groups of armed soldiers, making me more eager than ever to arrive at our destination.

Then at last we were there, our car coming to a stop in front of a new bungalow on a little gravel road just off the main Agia Fyla. Wire fencing surrounded the house, covered with beautiful purple and white morning glory flowers, which cascaded over the fence and made it hard to see where the gate was. We made our way up the wide steps leading to an open porch and then through the large front doors into a cool reception room. The floor throughout the bungalow was covered with large, marble slab tiles, which were deliciously cold against my bare feet as I walked from room to room. There was a spacious kitchen, bathroom, living room, and bedroom, as well as the reception room, which could also be used as a dining area. I noticed that all the windows were covered by metal grilles and shutters, while safety bars were on the outsides of the doors.

There was very little furniture aside from the bare essentials, because John had been unable to afford little else after the rent. One thing I did notice in the kitchen was a luxury we had never enjoyed back home: a large refrigerator, standing in the corner. John proudly swung the fridge door open to reveal a cooked chicken and a watermelon, which I had never seen or tasted before. The chicken was delicious, but I was not so sure about all the seeds in the melon that had to be spat out before I could enjoy the refreshing succulence of the pink, juicy flesh.

Over the coming months, our furniture was augmented as the overseas packing cases arrived with my clothes and belongings. We used the packing cases as large bench tables, which looked great when covered with brightly covered material and garnished with pretty table lamps and bowls of fruit, fresh from the plantations. We would go to the orange and mandarin groves and buy large quantities of fruit, measured in okes, which tasted like nothing I'd ever had before. We'd buy them from huge crates full of fruit with some of the green leaves still attached, or we'd wander down the rows of trees and actually pick them off the branches, the air heavy with the scent of ripe fruit and heat and greenery.

From the moment we arrived in Agia Fyla, we were hailed as the new folk on the block, and we excited the curiosity of the locals down the road. There was Anou, a tiny dark-haired Cypriot lady, who seemed to have just one large front tooth and a nose that could sniff out every movement or happening on the road. Nothing was missed by her eagle eye, and nothing seemingly escaped the edge of her tongue. She would shout her comments to all and sundry as they passed her single-roomed, square, breeze block house, with its open firepit in the front yard. She would gesticulate frantically as she tried to make us understand her conversation, before eventually giving up and wandering away with a disgusted look on her wrinkled face.

Her neighbour and verbal sparring partner was a Greek lady called Kyriakou. The two ruled the roost up that gravel road, better than any police patrol ever could. Fortunately, they liked us and went out of their way to interfere on our behalf at every available opportunity!

Our immediate neighbours were an Air Force couple, Ken and Marie, while a Greek family lived in the opposite bungalow across the road. Over the bondu (a large, wild, open space) at the back of our bungalow lived another Air Force couple, Brock and Ruth, who we became quite friendly with. Brock was delightful, but Ruth, though pleasant, was extremely bossy, especially with her husband, who seemed to be subservient to her every command. On one occasion she told him sharply to "follow when he'd collected himself" as she flung her way out the door. I was shocked to see him just shrug his shoulders and meekly follow after her.

The bondu, full of dried grass and scrubby plants, separated two roads of houses and bungalows. Nobody seemed to walk across it but kept to the gravel roads instead, probably wary of lurking snakes or other scary wildlife hidden away. There was nothing of any note about the bondu area, until one morning, after a long hot spell, the autumn rains came. I opened my shutters as usual but this time was met with an amazing sight: the bondu was completely covered with a carpet of glorious anemones that had sprung up overnight. It was as though moments before I awoke, someone had thrown a counterpane of jewelled flowers across the dead barrenness of the bondu. As far as I could see, there were red and blue and purple and mauve blooms, opening their petals in the morning sunshine. A sight to take the breath away and last a lifetime in the memory.

Apart from the morning glory on our front fence, and a trailing gourd on the side wire netting, our garden was as devoid of blooms as the bondu in the hot summer. John tried planting a few things, but the only one that flourished was a huge castor oil plant, which produced lots of large leaves but no flowers. The garden came in very useful, though, as a space in which to hang up a long clothesline. It was wonderful to put out a line of washing and be able to fetch it about half an hour later, completely dry because of the hot sunshine.

Anou offered to wash my sheets and bedding, so she would come and collect them and carry the bundle across to her place. She had a large cauldron with a fire underneath, and she heaved the water inside before putting in my laundry. After the washing and rinsing was complete, she would wring out the sheets and throw them over the hedge around her garden, leaving them to dry in the sun before folding and carrying them back to my house. On one occasion, I had made up the bed with the freshly laundered sheets that Anou had just returned and tucked them into place, thinking how lovely it was to have fresh sheets smelling of sunshine and fresh air. That night as we climbed into bed, John got in and was just about to pull up the covers when he gave a yowl and shot out of bed, grabbing his foot and hopping about. It turned out that he'd had a sudden encounter with a thorn from Anou's hedge that had been caught in the sheet. He wasn't quite as keen about freshly laundered bedding after that, and always climbed in cautiously after the bed had been changed.

We sometimes had other unpleasant visitors from the garden that found their way into the house: enormous centipedes that trekked their way along the tiles with surprising speed, or gigantic, hairy spiders that seemed to turn and look as you came into the room. They were so big, you could actually see their eyes. We also had a snake in the garden once, but fortunately Ken from next door came around and dealt with that before it had a chance to come indoors.

I'm not surprised they all came in to seek shelter from the burning sun, because it was extremely hard to acclimatise to the heat. I would sometimes come inside and strip off my clothes to lie flat on the cold tiles in the corridors to find some relief. I soon understood how sensible the locals were to take a siesta in the middle of the day, when the heat was most intense, and then resume their activities as the temperature dropped a little.

We had some other unwelcome visitors who regularly invaded the kitchen, regardless of temperature. Cockroaches that usually went on their hunting expeditions during the night, under cover of darkness, and disappeared with amazing speed if a light was suddenly switched on. Ants, however, were not so shy, and would appear day or night if any tiny particle of food had been dropped on the kitchen counters. They would troop in in their columns, marching purposefully with military precision, left, right, left, right, until they arrived at their destination. They would then begin to remove the food particle by particle and weave their way back through the oncoming column, before disappearing through some crack or other.

The only creatures that seemed to actually disturb the locals were the flies. On the occasions when they invited me across to their homes to sample the ouzo (a potent drink, smelling and tasting of aniseed), or the lethal black Turkish coffee, I would sit for a while afterwards, as it was considered rude to leave before the coffee dregs had gone cold. I took the opportunity to have a look around, although not much could be seen in the small dark interior of their single-roomed homes. Basic bits of wooden homemade furniture stood about—a table, a couple of chairs, and the odd stool. The bed would be along one wall, and all the cooking and kitchen utensils were kept outside, where all the cooking took place. A single bulb hung from the darkened ceiling, and by its side a sticky fly paper dangled, thick with dead flies. I've no idea how long they left them there, but there must have been hundreds of flies that had been attracted to the bulb before getting irretrievably stuck to the paper. It was a grim sight that put me off accepting any further delicacies that were offered after the coffee drinking ceremony was complete.

I had plenty of time on my hands during the day to accept invitations to coffee and such like, although the number of visits I made to neighbouring houses were very few. John left the house early in the morning to drive to Akrotiri and begin his shift, because most workdays finished at lunchtime, due to the heat. I would see to all the chores in the house and still have time to spare, so when the opportunity of a part-time teaching job came up, I was eager to apply. It was at the army school of Berengaria, which catered to all the children of the service families in the area. My interview was successful, and I took up my post almost immediately. A taxi would pick me up first thing in the morning, at about 8:00 a.m., returning for my journey home at 12:00 p.m. The staff were pleasant, and most of the children were well behaved, but there was an atmosphere of arrogance and superiority that seemed to pervade the place. Teachers had the rank of officers, and the children's parents were mostly high-ranking army personnel, so it wasn't a very comfortable working atmosphere.

I would return home before John, so I would have a quick shower to freshen up. Then I'd lie on the floor tiles for a while to cool down before preparing a light lunch, ready for John to come home to. Afternoons and evenings were our free time, which we enjoyed immensely in spite of the heat. We would visit the zoo in Limassol, or, more often than not, make a trip to the beach, finding some shade by the rocks along the coast. Because of my fair complexion, I had to be particularly careful not to expose myself to the sun for too long. I would lather myself with sun lotion, but even while swimming in the sea I could be easily burned. I remember covering myself in towels while sitting on the sand after swimming and still ending up with blisters all over my shoulders.

We had to choose where to put all our belongings and the place to sit on the sand very carefully, because in no time at all we were often surrounded by young Greek youths, all smiling and trying to prac- tise their English. They often followed me into the water as I went to cool down and would swim underwater and bob up and down out of the waves. In the end we would have to move away to rid ourselves of their unwanted attention.

Evenings were the most delightful times. They were still warm, and as the shadows lengthened and the stars began to appear, we would venture out and wander through the twisted streets of Limassol, away from the main thoroughfares. Many of the locals, both Turks and Greeks, would be lolling on steps and benches around still-open shop doors, trying to encourage passers-by, especially foreigners, to enter and make a purchase, or even join them for coffee.

Turkish men in their baggy pantaloons, and women in long, floor-length black skirts, cotton scarves around their heads, would beckon, "Come, come," and point to the dark interiors of their tiny shops. Little groups of men, often playing games with tiles or cards, would be sitting around rickety little tables along the sides of the street, smoking or chewing tobacco. Donkeys would amble past, either carrying heavy panniers or pulling laden carts behind them.

Passing through the streets, we would wander into little town squares surrounded by houses, some with open doors revealing glimpses of inner courtyards with colourful mosaic walls and tiled floors. In the squares were numerous cafes, tables, and chairs spilling out onto the pavements. There would be the occasional kebab stand, skewers of lamb and vegetable on blackened spits producing wonderful, mouth-watering aromas. Music and singing, laughter and loud chatter would fill the air, and we would occasionally be persuaded to sit at one of the tables near the kebab stand and be served with skewers of hot meat and veg, accompanied by dishes of fresh tomatoes, cucumber, and cool yogurt, washed down by long glasses of cold juice or mineral water.

Toward the end of the evening, we would take our leave and wander into quieter, almost deserted streets, passing only the occasional stray dog roaming about, searching for morsels of food, or a somnolent cat perched high on a window ledge, waiting for the coast to clear before he began his nightly prowl. As we left the noise and activity behind, silence and darkness seemed to blend together, covering the streets with the tumbledown buildings and filling every crevice and space, hiding them from sight. Our last memory of the evening, as we climbed into our waiting car, was not of the noise, the busy cafes, the Greek music, or the laughter and chatter, but of the heavy fragrance-filled air, scented with jasmine and orange blossom, which seemed to grow in every available outdoor space and covered the old town in an aura of beauty.

We didn't always drive straight home but meandered along the coastal road, stopping the car to listen to the ocean and gaze in wonder at the night sky, or wander barefoot across the beach, enthralled by the Milky Way, a band of thickly clustered stars that arched across the heavens and gave off a glow one could read by. We'd eventually arrive home exhausted but happy, wondering what joys the next day would bring.

Sometimes at the weekend, when we had two full days to enjoy without having to go to work, we would decide to take a long walk along the coastline stretching from Limassol to Akrotiri camp. It was, for some reason, called "Ladies' Mile," and took a couple of hours to walk. The trail led long the sandy beach, around the rock pools and over low-lying promontories jutting into the ocean. Care had to be taken to time this journey well so that we were not over-taken or marooned by incoming tides. It was a long haul but a lovely experience, especially as we neared Akrotiri and looked forward to a well-earned meal in the mess.

There was a point, nearly at the end of our journey, when we usually stopped for a welcome break. It was near some cliff-like rocks around one of the bays, and there was frequently a group of young Air Force cadets in swimming gear who were attracted by the challenge of diving from the cliffs into the deep blue water of the bay beneath. It was a difficult undertaking that required a lot of courage, and they would stand looking down into the waves far below, trying to pluck up the courage to jump. We would sit nearby, taking a breather from our long walk, and watch them as they delib-erated before hurling themselves off the edge into the waves below. I remember watching one young man trying to pluck up courage as he paced to and fro along the edge while his companions encouraged him with a few raucous comments.

"Go on then, what yer waiting for?"

"Come on, don't keep prancing about!"

At long last, with a final look around, and one or two little mincing steps at the cliff edge, he took a deep breath, stretched out his arms, and flung himself into space. Immediately as his feet left the safety of the cliff side, a shout went up from the crowd of youths:

"Sharks! There's sharks in the water!"

I have never seen such a contorted body, arms and legs being flung in every direction, as the poor fellow looked as though he was trying to return to the safe perch he'd just left, while all the time he was hurling into the depths below. I don't think the point of impact could be described as a belly flop, or even a crash landing, because as soon as he felt the water, he was swimming to the edge of the bay as fast as his arms and legs would propel him, while the group at the top lay about on the grass, laughing uproariously.

Having enjoyed the break, we would finish our journey and head into the Air Force canteen to refresh ourselves with long cold drinks and a meal before embarking back home. If we were tired, we would take a taxi back to Limassol, being driven along the same road I had taken on that first day of my arrival. By now, there were certain land-marks I always looked for, which had become familiar to me. The first one lay on the coastal side of the road, along the horizon where the sea met the sky. It was a long, narrow stretch of swampland that was a favourite breeding ground for a huge flock of flamingos. When at rest, they lay unnoticed in the distance, but if disturbed, they rose like a vast pink cloud that lifted and swirled as far as the eye could see, before beginning to break up as the birds settled back into the watery reserve and disappeared from sight.

As we continued, we came to a T-junction, where the Akrotiri and Limassol roads met, and there on the corner, partially hidden by a grove of yellow mimosa trees, was a large, square stone build-ing: Kolossi Castle. I have since discovered that it had been built originally in the thirteenth century, before being reconstructed later in the 1400s. It was captured by Richard the Lionheart on one of his crusades, and had become the home of the Knights Templar. When we were travelling in our own car, we would occasionally stop to explore this fascinating relic from previous centuries, and wonder at the fighting and revelry that had gone on inside the stout, strong walls.

Such jaunts were wonderful, but the intense heat was exhausting, and sometimes in the long dry summer we would long for a shower of cool, refreshing rain. Memories stir of a heat-drenched afternoon when I huddled over a small radio that was broadcasting a cricket programme that had been halted due to rain. I sat with my ear pressed to the speaker, eyes closed, as I listened for the rain drumming on the pavilion roof, and I longed to be there. At other times, however, there was "water water everywhere," and we hurried inside for safety—the local Water Festival!

The Greeks and Turks who lived up our road seemed to get on well in spite of the unstable political situation on the island, but there were still occasions when the tensions spilled over, even in Agia Fyla, and one of those was the Water Festival. Hoses and watering cans, buckets and containers of all kinds were put to use, filled with water and thrown or squirted over everybody in sight. We were encouraged to join in, probably because they wanted to drench us, and I was handed buckets filled with water to join in the water fight. Both John and I ended up soaked, but so did everybody down the street, and after a while the hoses were squirted and the buckets were thrown a lot more purposefully as people lost their tempers and began to retaliate more forcefully. I retired speedily after hurling not only the water but the bucket at somebody. It felt as though the atmosphere was becoming a little too tense, and rather unfriendly, and I didn't want a bucket hurled back at me!

There was another occasion when I met with a less than friendly response from the nearby locals. I had called at Ruth's after returning from school one lunch time and gratefully accepted the offer of a cold drink.

"I'll get you my favourite and most refreshing drink," she said. "Just sit there and cool down while I pour it."

She brought a wonderful ice cold lime cordial drink from out of the kitchen, and I downed it gratefully, accepting a refill when offered. Altogether during the course of our conversation, while recovering a little from the heat in the shade of the balcony, I drank three tall glasses of Ruth's delicious drink—not realizing that she'd added vodka to the lime. I took my leave, feeling a little strange and lightheaded, and made my way back home along the rough gravel roads around the bondu. In spite of the strange fuzziness in my head, I felt remarkably cheerful and waved to everybody I passed in the street, calling out a greeting to them as I waved.

"Piso skylo," I called. "Piso skylo!"

It was only later that I understood the unfriendly responses to my unfortunate use of the Greek language, when I realised I had returned home shouting, "Scram, dogs, scram!" to all and sundry!

It was round about the end of May and the beginning of June in that first year that Anou began to give me some strange looks. She would study my face and look me up and down, all the while gesticulating excitedly and chattering away, before disappearing, cackling, into her yard. Soon after that I discovered I was pregnant, and if I could have understood her, I'm sure Anou was declaring to everybody down the street, "I told you so! I told you so!"

We were delighted and started to plan for the forthcoming event, but first of all there were clinics to attend in Limassol, doctor appointments to be made, and registrations to be attended to in the Force's hospital at Akrotiri. Apparently, it was a first class hospital with all the latest up-to-date equipment, and I wrote to Mum and Dad that I would be in safe hands, and they were not to worry.

Every fortnight, a special bus took all the Air Force ladies who were pregnant up to the clinics at Akrotiri hospital for their regular check-ups. It was commonly known as the "Blunder Bus" by Air Force personnel!

I finished my part-time teaching job and busied myself with my new plans of sorting out what we needed to buy, and finding out where to purchase baby things in Limassol. A friend of ours, Christine, and her husband, John, had announced a month or so previously that she was expecting a baby, so when we all got together for supper, Chris and I would have plenty to chatter about while the men disappeared to do their own thing. Chris told me of a Cypriot lady who was an excellent seamstress, so when John and I next went to town, I found one of the many material shops from which to make my purchases.

The following week I made my way along the unmade roads off Agia Fyla to visit the lady Chris had recommended, and she readily agreed to make up a couple of maternity dresses and wrap around skirts when I required them. I was able to wear my ordinary things for the first few months, but later I was fitted for my maternity dresses and skirts, which the lady sewed beautifully. One of the dresses was particularly smart, made of navy-blue linen with an inverted pleat down the front, and a little white Peter Pan collar. I had trouble with the wrap-around skirts at times, often leaving them behind when I stood up, and having to hastily retrieve them and fasten them back into place.

In the meantime, life went on in much the same vein as before. We went to the beaches, shopped in the town, made trips around the island, and prepared for another event: the arrival of John's younger sister, Jenny, who had decided to come and visit us. She arrived at the hottest time of the year, and we met her at the main Nicosia airport, where she joined us in arrivals, puffing and blowing with the heat. Before climbing into the car in the carpark, we covered the leather seat with a towel so she didn't burn herself. We had learned to take such precautions to avoid getting scorched. As soon as she climbed in, she started to take off as many clothes as she could, and we drove home with all the windows open, regardless of the dust that filled the car as a consequence.

She gazed out at the Mediterranean landscape as we sped by. The tarmac road, almost deserted, gleamed white in the heat of the sun. Scrubland lay on either side, brown and barren apart from the numerous olive trees, with their harvest of black and green fruit ready to yield the rich golden oil that is used so widely in the Mediterranean cuisine. Few cars travelled the road, but every now and then we would pass a heavily ladened donkey stumbling along, urged on by its owner and encouraged by a stick applied to its hind quarters. Above, a cloudless blue sky, and to the side, the turquoise ocean, undisturbed apart from the occasional sailing boat, or a cruise ship silhouetted on the horizon. Jenny would love cooling off in the clear blue waters or walking along the sandy beaches over the coming days as she tried to get accustomed to the heat.

Two weeks flew by, packed with sightseeing and visits to nearby villages where we sampled the local dishes: goat cheese with cucumber and tomatoes, fish fresh from the sea and sauteed in olive oil, dishes of fresh olives with chunks of homemade pita bread, and large bowls of salad, all washed down by ice cold orange juice or cans of fizzy lemon from the large chest freezers that adorned the outside of the some of the cafes. We made a long trip into the Troodos Mountains, their lower slopes covered in vineyards, while just below the snow-capped peaks lay forests of pine and fir. But in no time at all, the holiday was over, and we were speeding along the road to Nicosia on the return journey to the airport, and Jenny was making her way back to rainy Manchester, where she would have to find her thickest sweaters to adjust to the cold and wet of a typical English summer.

After Jenny's departure, we decided to use the next few months, while still uncluttered by carrycots and pushchairs, to explore as much of the island as we possibly could. Every time John had a few days' break, or an open weekend, we visited as many places as possible. We explored new beaches, visited historic sights, and drove miles to discover tiny villages that were full of character and tradition. We sometimes chanced upon village fêtes or festivals, where the people danced along the streets, fully regaled in national costume, banging their drums or playing wonderful Greek music on a variety of instruments. The streets would be overflowing with people who had obviously come from neighbouring villages, and we had to slowly edge our car forward, people banging on the top and sides, waving flags and smiling while greeting us in a good-natured way. I always found such encounters somewhat intimidating and was glad to come out at the other end of the village street unscathed, with the car still in one piece.

My unease was not entirely unwarranted, as not all the islanders were quite so welcoming! We would sometimes come across groups of men sitting around on their rickety old chairs on the pavement, who would stop their conversations as we approached and

scowlingly watch us as we passed by. Or women who would stop
their chatter and let their sewing lay unheeded on their laps as they
stared sharply until we had disappeared. Needless to say, we didn't
linger in such places.

We spent many hours admiring the interiors of the fabulous Greek
Orthodox churches, not only because they were cool shady areas
where we could sit and rest, but also because of their lavish decora-
tion and ornate wall hangings. Beautiful domed ceilings, supported
by majestic columns with their hanging candelabra; gold-laden altars
backed by enormous wooden reredoses, fretted and carved in minute
detail; row upon row of richly painted icons depicting numerous
saints and religious characters; candles and lamps burning on every
available surface, while the whole atmosphere was pervaded by the
heavy scent of incense, and age, and burning candles. We would owl-
ishly blink our eyes as we left the dark interiors and made our way
back out into the glaring noonday sun.

We travelled the length and breadth of the island, calling at or
passing through towns with wonderful Greek sounding names,
some familiar, others unknown: Famagusta, Kyrenia, Lefka, Paphos.
We heard the faithful being called to prayer from the minarets and
even ventured to scale the spiral stairs leading to the top to see the
fabulous view from the tiny balcony. We wandered around ancient
historical sites like Salamis, with broken columns and disintegrating
walls, but still displaying floors of intricately patterned mosaic tiles.
Revisiting Troodos, we would stop at one or other of the amazing
monasteries in the mountains, some even more elaborate than the
churches: Kykkos, Stavrovouni, Ayia Napa. Two in particular stand
out in my memory, one because it housed hundreds of stray cats,
the other because of corridors of small cupboards, each containing

a single skull. Apparently, they belonged to monks who had lived in the monastery hundreds of years previously.

But my favourite place on the whole of the island lay on the far northern tip: the historic harbour of Kyrenia, with its dozens of bobbing sailing boats, its tall, three-storey buildings crowding the harbour as if determined to step into the ocean, while its ancient square fort stood guard over the whole area, like a sentry on duty.

Near to Kyrenia was beautiful Bellapais village, and Saint Hilarion Castle, which sat on one of the mountain tops of the Kyrenia Range. Apparently, Lawrence Durrell made his home in Bellapais for several years, and wrote about life in Cyprus in his book, *Bitter Lemons*. I can imagine him retiring from the hustle and bustle of life to lose himself in such wonderful rural surroundings while he absorbed the essence of life on a Greek island, squeezing the juice out of each day to delight his readers with his findings.

One of the skills embodied in the culture was that of lace making, together with embroidery and thread drawing. It was a common sight to see women sitting outside their houses, bobbins and pins in their hands, as they skilfully created their intricate lace design to border and edge tablecloths and covers of all descriptions. I still am the proud owner of some of their handiwork from sixty years ago, and they grace my table on special occasions.

But slowly and surely the weeks and months passed by, and our long-haul adventures came to a halt as my delivery date drew near. The action started one evening when we had invited John and Christine and their new baby boy, Philip, for supper. We were playing a board game after finishing the meal and chattering away when my waters broke. Christine stopped throwing the dice, while John turned to my John and said with a grin, "It's your turn now!"

John, with his mind still on the game, said, "No, it isn't; it's Christine's."

The confusion only lasted a minute before action stations set in. The overnight bag (already packed) was grabbed from behind the settee, sandals and jackets were hastily thrown on, guests were dispatched, and we were in the car and heading along the Limassol-Akrotiri Road on the way to the hospital. It seemed an age, but in reality, it was thirty to forty minutes before we were at the hospital and I was being admitted by a lovely red-haired nurse. She showed me to a single room, where I waited for a midwife to come and examine me. She allowed John to come and say goodbye before he left, and on the way out he walked headfirst into a glass door at the entrance to the ward.

"It's always the same," the nurse laughed. "The husbands are always in a bigger flap than the wives, and they're not the ones with all the work to do!"

The "work" lasted for hours, but eventually Catherine Jane made her debut into the world. Her birth caused great delight and celebration, which rippled across the world to Mossley and Congleton, where both sets of parents were thrilled at the arrival of their first grandchild.

Beforehand we could never have prepared ourselves for the way such a tiny person could change a complete household overnight! Preparations, plans, routines, and life itself was turned upside down, but in a delightful way. Even day and night changed places in those early months. Feeds every few hours during the night, and naps in the day to try and recoup some lost sleep. Friends and family, and the neighbours down the street, expressed their delight at Cathy's arrival—except for Anou, who was rather disgruntled. All the way through my pregnancy, she had nodded her head and sagely pronounced that it was going to be a boy, and she was rather put out that her predictions were incorrect, looking at me as though I had made a mistake and not her!

Cathy was born on January 26, in the very early part of the Cypriot year, when the weather was mild and wet, with all the hot sunny weather to look forward to in the coming months. As the rain gave way to sunshine, she would nap outside in her pram, a sunshade protecting her from the direct glare, until her legs turned a lovely golden brown. Even my fair skin, which had blistered so easily when I first arrived, had developed a tan in the constant sunshine. But we were always careful not to stay too long in the noonday heat.

Other exciting news came from home too! Roy, who had finished his time in the army, had married his girlfriend, Eileen, earlier in the year. He was now heading off to Kenley Bible College to begin his training for ministry, while Eileen set up home in Broadhurst Avenue, Congleton. Everything would be different when we arrived back home. Mum and Dad's family at Mosslands would be depleted now that Roy and I had formed our own family units. Thoughts of home began to fill my mind, especially since John's posting would come to an end at the close of the year, and we would be heading back to England at the end of December, when Cathy was eleven months old. But ten months of sunshine still stretched ahead of us, and we made the most of them.

We resumed our jaunts around the island, this time with a car full of all the paraphernalia that accompanies a small baby. I remember revisiting the ruins at Salamis with Cathy in my arms. She was dressed in a little green gingham sunsuit I had made, with a sunhat covering her head. An older English couple stopped to admire her.

"Oh, she's beautiful!" the lady said. "Enjoy her while you can, my dear. In no time at all she'll be grown up, and you'll wonder where the years have gone."

I smiled back at her while thinking, *How silly. It'll be an age before she's grown; she can't even walk yet!* But looking back across the years gives a very different perspective than looking ahead, and as I remember her words, I realise how very true they were. Time does indeed fly!

Over the next few months, we made two new acquisitions to our family: a brand-new blue Volkswagen Beetle to help us on our travels, and a beautiful Alsatian puppy we called Shaun, both of which we planned to take home to England. When Dad heard of our plans to bring Shaun back with us, he said, "Well, if you bring an Alsatian dog into my home, I shall take my leave!" His threat was never realised, because he soon lost his fear, and they became the best of friends after we returned.

I recently found a letter that I had written home during this time, making plans for our return, and replying to Mum's questions about the things we would need:

"You ask what we would like you to get Cathy for Christmas," I wrote. "The very best thing possible would be a cot, and they're only about £6–7. Not a large, elaborate one, just an ordinary one, because remember that we shall be 'roamers' for quite a few years yet!"

October and November saw us busily making our arrangements for departure: rental leases to be terminated, packing cases to be packed and transited, arrangements made for the car, and kennels sorted for the dog, who would have to be put in quarantine for six months in Liverpool when we arrived. Mum sent a warm coat for Cathy, and I knitted cosy woollen jumpers, bonnets, and leggings in which she would face her first English winter.

At last, all was ready, and we took our leave, waving sad farewells to all our neighbours and friends as we made our last journey along the Limassol-Akrotiri road, past the grove of mimosa trees and Kolossi Castle, past the pink flamingos in the coastal swamp and on to the air base.

The aeroplane lifted off from a sun-drenched island in the Mediterranean and landed under the gun-metal skies of a bitterly cold Manchester, knee-deep in snow and ice. We made the last leg of our journey by train, arriving at Stoke Station late in the afternoon, and I remember warming my hands at a burning brazier on the platform while shivering with cold. But a very warm welcome awaited us in Congleton, where families and friends were anticipating our arrival.

We had left as a fledgeling married couple, and we were arriving home a family unit (though not yet complete!) and, as I'd told Mum in my letter, we were not yet ready to settle. We would indeed be "roamers" for the next few years—years that would fill our lives with joys, tears, adventures, and even some surprises.

CHAPTER TWELVE

The Baby Boom Years

That homecoming year of 1962 could well have been renamed the "baby boom" year. Before leaving for Cyprus, my doctor had predicted that I would come home with "three bambinos."

"It's the hot climate that does it!" he joked.

As it turned out, I came home with one and a half, as I was already six months pregnant with Sally Ann. But Roy and Eileen were to join the ranks of burgeoning families first, and within a month of us arriving home, John Mark was born on January 11. Roy had completed his course at Kenley Bible College and was back home at Broadhurst Avenue with Eileen when John made his appearance, so they began married life together as they celebrated his birth.

Mum and Dad's lives were suddenly full of busy activity. We had arrived home from Cyprus with Cathy and another baby on the way (who arrived two and a half months later), while cousin John swelled the little family at Broadhurst Avenue. The empty nest at Mosslands was now full to overflowing, especially as we were living with Mum and Dad until we found a place to go to. When Roy and Eileen came to visit, the place was full of carrycots and toys, blankets and hand-washable nappies, top up feeding bottles and dummies. Joyous times of chatter and laughter against a background of rattling teacups and the clink of tea plates as Mum bustled in and out of the kitchen, while Dad surveyed the scene from his rocking chair and calmly smoked his cigarettes.

In the middle of all the activity, there was more excitement in those first few months when the car arrived from Cyprus and we had our own transport. When Shaun arrived, she had to be in quarantine for six months, and we went to visit her a couple of times, feeling desperately sad to leave her at the end of the visiting time. When we finally took her home to Mosslands, she soon became a part of the extended family, even making friends with Dad.

Sally was born at Congleton War Memorial Hospital, under the eagle eye of a martinet called Sister King, who ruled the place with military precision. I remember her walking down the corridor toward the ward I was in, and as she neared my bed, she declared, "If Baby McLellan isn't born by the time I come back on duty, I shall see what's to be done!"

I think it was fear that precipitated her arrival in the night that followed, and by the dawn, our little family had grown to four.

We were delighted but also aware of the difficulties our increased numbers posed for Mum and Dad. Cathy was in a small box room that overlooked the golf links, and an extra cot had to be squeezed into our front bedroom. John's parents came to the rescue by buying a newly built house in Highcroft Avenue, halfway between Mossley and Congleton, and renting it out to us.

We had very little furniture but plenty of space there, and we were able to spread out to our hearts' content, each of the babies having a room of their own. The huge downside of this was that John was only home for the weekends. He was back at Waddington RAF base Monday to Friday, and home with the family from Friday nights until Sunday evenings.

Going from being surrounded by family to coping with the babies on my own was really difficult. Mum often turned up in the evenings, and she would busy herself at the sink, washing nappies that had been soaking in the Milton bucket overnight, only coming to sit and have a cuppa when the day's load had been dealt with. It was a wonderful help, and I appreciated the company. Jenny, who was at college in Stockport, also visited, as John's dad's chemist shop was just at the bottom of the hill.

John's dad was respected throughout the town for the potions he made up in his little dispensary, and local doctors tended to be put out when some of their patients asked them to prescribe "some of that ointment Mr. McLellan gave me last time!" Such requests sent them out of the surgery with a flea in their ear. The chemist shop was on the ground floor of a three-storey house between the Albion pub and Mrs. Hassell's furniture shop. Keith Hassell lived with his mum and was John's best friend before he was married. Behind John's dad's chemist shop was a living room, a tiny back room where they ate their meals, and a kitchen. The back room, though really small, was where most of the family life and activities happened. Mrs. McLellan was a wonderful cook, and the table was often garnished with the most delicious of foods: stews, salads, puddings, and baking of all sorts were always available, no matter what time anybody dropped by.

Two other members of the McLellan family squeezed into that tiny room. Granny Hornsby, well into her eighties, invariably occupied the armchair in front of the fire. She always seemed as though she'd stepped straight out of the bath—immaculately clean, pink cheeks and faded blue eyes, topped by a crown of thick, snow-white hair. She would sit quietly, smiling, while knitting endless little garments—usually white vests for the babies—often letting the ball of wool drop from her lap and roll under the table.

Sitting by her feet was the final family member: the most irascible, feisty little dog called Scamp. Everybody had been bitten at one time or another by him, and he sat by Granny's feet as though daring her to move. When her feet shuffled even an inch, he would growl, stand up with legs akimbo and head down, threatening her with dire consequences if she touched him. "Mother, keep your feet still!" was a cry often heard ringing around the kitchen. Granny would sit, unphased, still smiling, while the knitting needles continued to click, and the growling would eventually stop—though the watchful glare continued to monitor any movement from her old slippers.

I would often pop into the McLellans' for a cuppa when I'd walked the babies downtown to do some shopping, before I faced pushing the pram up the steep hill back to Highcroft.

I loved the house, but it was lonely during the week on my own with the children, and I lived for the weekends, hardly able to wait for Friday to come round. John would arrive in the middle of the evening, always carrying something in his hand to greet me: a small bunch of harebells he'd picked as he came over the Cloud near the end of his journey, or a rose picked off somebody's bush that was trailing over the hedge.

Weekends were wonderful but so fleeting, and in no time at all, Sunday evenings would flash around. Sad farewells, and another lonely week stretching ahead.

Roy had his own ideas as to how to alleviate my loneliness. He would often call in his little car to invite me to attend some meeting or another. While in Cyprus, John and I had not attended church at all. I don't recall ever seeing or hearing of an English church, or a Christian meeting anywhere in Limassol. Nothing except for the Russian Orthodox Church, which was quite literally Greek to us! Roy and his friend George, both freshly out of Bible college, were all set to evangelize the world, and Roy made a start with rekindling my commitment. They had undertaken several ventures, and at this time they were attending and leading meetings in the cottage of an old gentleman named Mr. Smith on Mow Cop. It was a tiny collier cottage, with typical furnishings that seemed to overcrowd the room: large square table, sideboard, and two or three chairs. Peg rugs were on the tiled floor, and a fire was always roaring in the old range. Once Mr. Smith was settled in his armchair, there was little space for visitors, but amazingly every meeting would see five or six folks cram into the room, some half squeezed in the doorway that led into the scullery at the back of the cottage.

The meetings I attended were prayer meetings for the blessing of the Holy Spirit. The passion and fervency, together with the volume, could have resurrected William Clowes and Hugh Bourne, who would have totally identified with such a gathering. The only way I can describe receiving that wonderful blessing is to liken it to standing underneath a shower and being bathed in liquid gold. It was a wonderful experience, and as we travelled home afterwards, I stared up at a sky full of a myriad of stars and felt I was almost transported into their midst. Needless to say, I shared the exciting experience with John, and at the very next opportunity, he too visited Mr. Smith's to receive prayer and the same blessing. Looking back over six decades, I would point to that night, in that miner's cottage, as the beginning of a lifelong commitment to the Church and Christian living. It was one of those epiphany moments when the light went on, and everything seemed to fall into place.

The first thing we both decided to sort out was to bring to an end our family separation. We needed to be together, and the girls needed to have their daddy home not just at weekends, but for bath times and bedtimes and stories at tucking-up times! So the lovely house at Highcroft was left behind, and we moved nearer to John's Air Force base and rented a married-quarter cottage in the village of Marston, in Lincolnshire.

It was a typical rural village: a church, a pub, two shops, a couple of farms, with one street that circled the village and joined up all the cottages, all surrounded by lush green fields. A bus lumbered its way along the street two or three times a day, linking the village to the town of Grantham, or to neighbouring market towns a few miles away. I had turned the clock back and returned near to the haunts of my college days. Retford, Worksop, Ollerten, and the rest all lay nearby.

Our cottage was on a corner at the far end of the village, opposite the pub, the school, and Green's shop. Buses stopped outside the front window, where lace curtains had been hung to deter curious passengers from gazing into our front room. The family next door were Colin and Jean and their two children, Peter and Carol, who were some years older than our two little ones. On the other side lived a man named Fred and his sister, who were not very welcoming at all and found every opportunity to grumble and complain. We lived in Marston for about three years but were always considered foreigners, while Jean from next door joked that she only came from the next village over but was still not accepted as a real member of the Marston community. Jean became a really good friend, and we often popped into each other's houses to share a biscuit and a cup of tea, chatting about children and babies and all manner of things.

Although John worked shifts, it was wonderful to be together as a family, and even when he was on nights, I still had my two girls for company and the knowledge that a knock on the dividing wall would bring Jean round from next door to see what the trouble was.

It was unfortunate that while we were living in this farming community Sally developed foot and mouth disease. Her feet, hands, and throat were covered in painful blisters, and she could hardly swallow. Waves of shock and horror travelled around the village, stopping all conversation when we called at the village shop, and bringing baleful glares from our neighbour, Fred. Fred was particularly concerned because he had a herd of cattle that he kept in a couple of fields down a lane near the corner, and he was obviously terrified that Sally was going to contaminate them. People would stand and silently gaze at us as we made our way round the village, as though we were carriers of the plague. I grew impatient with being ostracised, especially when visiting the shop, and advised Sally to stand and "moo" loudly if anyone stared at her. She never did of course, and eventually the blisters disappeared, along with the unspoken hostilities.

Cathy started to school while we were living down there, and I was horrified to discover that the segregation of a close-knit farming community pervaded even the reception class of the village school. The building was directly opposite our cottage, and I used to anxiously wait for playtimes and watch the children come out of their classes onto the playground. Cathy was always the last one to appear, and she would stand alone in a corner, eating her snack. All the children played their games of kick and skipping and hopscotch while totally ignoring her, and it broke my heart. I was always anxious for 3:15 p.m. to come, when school finished, and I would be waiting for her at the school gate, ready to take her home and make a fuss of her to compensate for the misery of her school day. I thought of the hours I'd spent walking round the playground of Biddulph North School to settle Yvonne into the reception class there and was angry that any teacher could ignore such treatment of a new little girl.

During the day, when John was at work and Cathy was at school, I would wander round the village with Sally and Shaun and explore some of the country lanes that lay between fields full of cows pulling the lush green grass, or thoughtfully ruminating under the shade of the trees. The hedgerows were bursting with lacy-headed parsley, red campion, and stitchwork, and the air was full of the drone of insects and birdsong. I rarely met anyone to disturb my wanderings, unless an old tractor bumbled up the road, its thick tyres bouncing over the ruts. We would sometimes pop into the shop for a treat or have a wander round the churchyard and look at the epitaphs on the grave-stones. Some villagers had lived to a grand old age, while some of the tiny graves gave evidence of very young children, or tiny infants, that had departed far too soon. We would lift the heavy metal handle of the church door and edge it slowly open to enter the musty semi-darkness and take a quick look round before escaping again into the sunshine and retracing our steps out of the churchyard and around the corner of the pub to wait for Cathy at the school gates. I would wait to see her face light up as she saw us, and Sally would jig up and down with excitement as she handed a treat or newly-discovered treasure to Cathy before we crossed the road and returned home.

On pleasant summer evenings, after John had returned home from work and we'd had a meal, we would all climb into the car and go for a drive to discover neighbouring villages and hamlets that lay scattered around. One of our favourite destinations was a sort of bird sanctuary that stretched over several fields, with hundreds of birds descending or circling over the swampy ground. We always kept the car windows partially closed there, even though we loved to listen to the birds, because the air didn't smell so sweet. When I mentioned the nearby bird sanctuary to Jean, she collapsed into fits of giggles.

"I'm not surprised you keep the windows closed," she said. "That's no sanctuary—it's the local sewage works."

That explained the number of rats that were frequently seen around the village. They were huge things that crossed the streets and darted in and out of ditches, some meeting their end under the tyres of passing cars. I hated them and was petrified when they actually found a way into the attic space that ran along our two cottages. Colin next door worked on one of the local farms and was totally used to dealing with rodents, but we were horrified. John put poison up in the attic but later discovered that the rats had covered it up by dragging chunks of mortar and debris across the wooden boards and hiding it.

I could hear them running around over my head while I was lying in bed, but when they started to gnaw chunks of the ceiling away, and several holes appeared, we'd had enough. The end came swiftly and indeed miraculously. One night when John was on night shifts, I was in floods of tears at the thought of being in a rat-infested house with my little girls.

"You can't leave us," I cried. "I daren't stay here with those rats ripping up the ceiling."

The girls were tucked up in bed, so John and I knelt down on the hearth and prayed that God would clear the house of vermin, and that they would never return. John left for work, and I very nervously climbed the stairs to go to bed. I think I lay awake most of the night, just listening, but I never heard one sound. Not even a scratch. When John arrived home the next morning, I was overjoyed to tell him that the prayer had worked. What's more, we were never troubled again; they never returned!

Another matter we prayed about was which church to attend. We chose not to go to the local Church of England church in the village but discovered a lively and very friendly Pentecostal church in Grantham. The minister was Pastor Mann, a gentle person who greeted us warmly and introduced us to his young wife, Shirley, and their little girl, Dawn. Over the coming months, we became good friends with the family, and were often invited for a meal with them after the morning service. It was while visiting their house that we met Mike and Rosy, another young couple who became lifelong friends, even when they later emigrated to Australia, where Mike pastored a church in Melbourne.

With Pastor Mann's blessing, John and I started to work with some of the gangs of youths in the town. We would ask Jean to babysit, and drive into Grantham to talk to gangs hanging round the street corners. We always paid a visit to the police station to tell them what we were doing and make them aware of our work with young people. Looking back, it was quite dangerous; some of them carried knives, or combs that could cause a horrid jagged wound, and they were often very threatening, even to us, but they also listened, and some of them became friendly. One gang leader, named Dick, considered himself my personal bodyguard and would even select the dustbin I could sit on.

"Get off there," he would snarl at anyone who happened to choose that spot for a perch. "That's *her* dustbin."

Wanting to give them a treat, we invited them over to Marston for supper one day, with home baked apple pie and cream. We wondered if they would arrive, but we needn't have worried. At about seven o'clock, there was a roar of several motorbikes careening into the village and coming to a screeching halt in front of our cottage. A couple dozen leather-clad youths squeezed their way into our small living room and kitchen, laughing and pulling cans of beer out of their jacket pockets. John banned the beer immediately, not wanting to deal with a drunken brawl as the evening progressed, and I fed them with slices of homemade pie. We didn't notice initially that they were disappearing in groups of two or three during the course of the evening, and at around ten o'clock we waved them off at the gate, not realising that anything was amiss.

It was the next morning that a furious Fred filled us in on some happenings of the previous night that we had been unaware of. They had, in their small groups, marauded around the village, scrumping apples from the gardens of the houses, breaking gates and fences, and causing damage to Fred's greenhouse. We were appalled and apologised to all and sundry, vowing not to be so trusting in the future.

It was while we were in Marston that the Baby Boom years continued. Diane Lesley (who has always been called Lesley, rather than Diane) was born in Grantham Hospital on April 3, 1964, completing our trio of beautiful girls. In Congleton two months later, Karen Joy arrived to join the family at Broadhurst Avenue. In the space of three years, Mum and Dad welcomed five grandchildren, with John the only boy amongst four girls. The house was crowded when we all arrived for a visit, the downstairs ringing with shouts and laughter as children ran hither and thither, while upstairs the youngest babies would be having a nap or crying for a feed, while six adults talked and busied themselves in the kitchen or took a breather over a cup of tea. I can imagine Mum and Dad closing the door after waving goodbye to the last visitor and sinking down on the settee or rocking chair in sheer exhaustion, happy to see everybody but glad to see us go ... till next time!

While living in Marston, we often visited Congleton at weekends, loving to return home with the car piled high with children, carrycot, luggage, and dog to spend time with family. The children all enjoyed getting together enormously. Cathy and John were the ringleaders and organisers of all the games, while Sally, Karen, and Lesley joined the ranks that followed as they grew older and were allowed to join in. The weekends flew by, and in no time at all, we would be repacking the car to return to Marston for John to go back to work, and Cathy to resume her classes in school.

Jean from next door loved spending time with our family and often came round with Carol and Peter so that all the children could play together. Her two were quite a lot older than my girls, but they liked to look after them and play with them while Jean and I would chat. I think she enjoyed having somebody to share things with, because her husband was the "silent type" who didn't talk much, and she often grumbled about him and his constant visits to the pub in the evenings. She was interested in our regular visits to the church in Grantham and was amazed when we had the youth over for supper, not understanding why we would want to spend time with them, let alone entertain them for supper. After many discussions and lots of questions, she eventually came with us to church and made her own decision to become a Christian, a choice that still stands to this day. I've kept in touch with her over the years, and we sometimes phone each other for a catch up. She divorced Colin after we left Marston, and Peter and Carol are now grown up with families of their own. She has remarried and lives happily with her husband in Newark, where she is an active member of her local Salvation Army Citadel.

During those last years of our stay in Marston, Roy, together with some of his friends, had taken on two major building projects. First of all, after holding meetings in Mr. Smith's cottage, they decided to build a church on Mow Cop, on the opposite corner to St. Thomas' Church of England. They bought a Nissen Hut and started to dig footings and foundations, before adding the hut and the rest of the necessary construction. I remember helping to secure the roof covering during one of our weekend visits. With that building nearing completion, he started to build a bungalow for his family on the banks of Mow Cop, within striking distance of the Castle. All the building work for both church and bungalow was done after finishing full-time work. It was heavy and laborious and must have left them exhausted, as day after day found them working from early morning till late at night. The results, however, were well worth all the effort. The bungalow provided a lovely home for his growing family, while the church was hugely successful throughout the coming years, seeing the congregation grow into a thriving community under Roy's ministry.

As John's time in the Air Force began to come to an end, we decided to move back to Congleton. My long-suffering parents agreed for us to go back to Mosslands yet again, although it would be more difficult this time, with another cot to squeeze into the bedroom to accommodate Lesley. John would work at Waddington during the week and just return at weekends. Our "roaming" had not taken us to many different destinations, but we had certainly totted up the miles, driving to and fro between Lincolnshire and Cheshire.

Even though the lack of space presented some difficulties, I'm sure Mum and Dad loved having us there. I remember Mum brushing the girls' hair one at a time as we got ready to go out.

"Cathy Jane," she would say, "with hair like a raven's wing. Sally with her blue eyes and hair like a golden sheaf of corn. And Lesley, with hair like a burnished chestnut."

They were indeed beautiful, and she was so proud of them, as she was of all her grandchildren.

I was delighted when John's RAF time finally came to an end, as all the travelling did as well, but we were unaware of what a horrible year lay ahead. Queen Elizabeth said that 1992 was her Annus Horribilis, but ours was definitely 1967. Turbulent and tragic times awaited us as we settled back in Congleton.

The year 1967 also brought to an end the Baby Boom years for both of our families. Two additions, one to each family, would be the highlights of the year. Two bright stars in an otherwise black sky.

For the first time, John was out of work and looking for jobs, something he had never had to do before, having joined the RAF as an apprentice as soon as he left school. The work he was trained to do—aircraft engineering—was very specific, a skill that wasn't required in the majority of jobs, even engineering jobs. So although he made lots of applications to various companies, he wasn't even called for an interview. He became very disheartened and wandered about the house at a loose end, wondering if he should have left the Air Force and the job security it provided.

Cathy was at school during the day. She had started Mossley Primary School when we returned to Congleton, but even so, the house was extremely cramped and busy. We tried to largely restrict ourselves to one room downstairs, so as not to encroach on the privacy of Mum and Dad, and on rainy days it was sometimes unbearable. Too many people, too much paraphernalia, too little space when the miserable grey weather outside seemed to pervade the atmosphere inside.

To make everything much worse, the children went down, one by one, with chicken pox. On top of an already difficult situation, we now had miserable children, irritated by the itchy rash, crying with frustration, unable to sleep, and irritable throughout the day. Sally suffered most of all, the rash covering every nook and cranny of her body, even down her throat, in her ears, and surrounding her eyes. Poor little thing was traumatised! The only thing we could do to alleviate her condition was to give her cool baths, dose her with calpol, and cover her night and day with calamine lotion. It seemed to go on forever; one would be sick for three weeks, then the next one would start, followed three weeks later by the last one to catch it. The chicken pox ran its course for approximately nine weeks, which meant being cooped up inside for all that time. The household was nearly driven mad, but at last it was over, and our spirits were lifted as we celebrated the birth of Julia May, the final addition to Roy and Eileen's family. Our celebrations, however, were short lived.

Mum was working at this time at Radway Green R.O.F., in Alsager. She worked full-time during the week and spent a lot of the weekend catching up on jobs and preparing for the coming week. One Sunday morning, we were all getting ready to go to the Mow Cop church. Mum decided to come with us and do the rest of her jobs when she got back home. We piled into the Beetle, with John driving. I was in the front seat with Lesley on my knee (there were no seatbelt regulations at that time), while Mum, Cathy, and Sally were travelling in the back. We had only driven along Leek Road and turned down Moss Road—a very short distance—when a car pulled out of a side road, causing an almighty crash. The other car was tipped upside down, while our car was a complete write-off.

I was hurled into the windscreen, injuring my neck and jaw; Lesley was badly cut on her face and chin; John had a cracked skull and several broken ribs; the two girls in the back suffered shock and multiple bruises; while Mum was catapulted through the windscreen before being flung backwards again. She was dreadfully injured, with horrendous damage to her face and head. The first thing I remember on regaining consciousness was lying on the grass verge at the side of the road, being attended by two paramedics. My dad's face appeared in my clouded vision, and I asked, "Is it a dream, Dad?"

"It's no dream," he replied. "It's a nightmare."

I will pass quickly over the next two or three days, only to say that all three girls recovered well (although Lesley was still pulling shards of glass out of her chin for several decades), and John was able to walk away from the crash. Mum and I were in worse condition and were taken to hospital. I was soon released, but Mum died as a result of her injuries ten days later.

More than fifty years have passed, and I still think, along with other things, of those little jobs that Mum fussed about that she had to do when she came back from church. So important to her, yet nobody ever knew what they were, and nobody ever missed them not being done. How important it is that we prioritise the right things and not get hung up on insignificant details.

I was five months pregnant when the crash took place, and everyone was concerned in case the baby had suffered injury. So when David John made his appearance on July 19, we were all ecstatic that he was completely healthy. A wonderful little boy completed our family and increased the number of grandsons to two! Heartbreakingly, Mum never saw him, and never knew.

David's birth not only brought us delight but also brought the events of the Annus Horribilis to an end. John got a job at nearby Manchester Airport, and our family started on the road to recovery as we began to adjust to the awful reality that Mum was no longer with us.

As a life ends, a chapter closes. But just as we can turn the pages back and retrace the story, so we can look back over lives no longer with us and relive the memories. As I look back over Mum's life, I can say with the Apostle Paul: Mum, "I thank God for every memory of you!"

CHAPTER THIRTEEN

Settling Down
(1967)

Those first few months after Mum died were difficult. The whole household had changed. Yes, there was more room, and things were less crowded, but there was a gaping hole in our lives that couldn't be filled, no matter how much activity we squeezed into our days. Dad was grief stricken, and he would spend hours just lying on his bed, fully clothed, or sitting at his organ playing his favourite hymns to while away the hours. But little by little, the situation began to ease as the weeks went by, and the laughter and activity of the children began to replace the tears and heaviness.

In those early months, Dad made the decision to sell Mosslands and move into a smaller property in Congleton town. Of course, we decided to buy it. Over the years it had been a magnet in our lives, constantly pulling us back, and it seemed the most natural thing in the world to make it our permanent "forever home." We felt our roaming days were over for the time being; John had a steady job at the airport, and the two oldest girls were now in school, so we decided to pitch our tent and drive in the tent pegs, establishing a secure base for the children to grow and thrive in.

Before Dad moved out, while he was still looking for a suitable property, he became a superhero, averting a potential disaster. He was babysitting one night while John and I went to a meeting in the Mow Cop church. We left the girls ready for bed, and David had had his feed and was tucked up in his carrycot in the front room downstairs so Dad could keep his eye on him. After the girls had gone to bed, Dad settled down to watch TV, checking on the baby every so often. On one of his visits to the front room, he thought he could smell smoke, but seeing nothing amiss went back out and shut the door behind him. I don't know if it was some sixth sense that alerted him, but it wasn't long before he decided to recheck, and on opening the door was horrified to see a low pall of smoke filling the far end of the room, near to the empty fireplace. He snatched up the carrycot and rushed out of the room before phoning for the fire engine. In no time at all, the Congleton fire engine was racing up the hill, bells and sirens clanging, and three or four firemen were unwinding their hoses to direct their jet into our front room.

There was no fire in the grate at the time, but it seems that previous fires had set alight a joist that ran underneath the hearth and started a slow burning fire that had been smouldering for some time. Imagine our surprise and horror to arrive home to be met with a fire engine at the gate, firemen rewinding their hoses, and the room that had recently housed the baby inches deep in water. When they had pulled back the carpet, they had discovered several scorched floorboards, as well as the slow burning joist. Obviously building regulations had not been adhered to when the house was built, and the discovery that night, along with Dad's rapid response, had averted a major house fire. We were more than thankful!

Dad eventually found a little terraced house in Holford Street, Congleton, which suited him well. It was in the centre of town and near to a little cafe in the adjoining street, where he would go for breakfast. He also decided to attend the URC church, which was just a few yards up the street, where he would once again refresh his skills at conducting and training a pensioners' choir.

Meanwhile, we started to make a few alterations at Mosslands, the first being to put an extension at the back and install a new kitchen. The person we chose to do the job was a marvellous character named Freddy, who came from Mow Cop. He was an undertaker by trade but was a wonderful carpenter as well as a builder. He was small in stature, with a ruddy complexion, and a pair of national health glasses perched on his nose. He was a typical "man from Mow," entrenched in the old ways, dogmatic, with opinions set in stone: unchanging, unflappable, and always right! But we got on well with him, and he became very fond of the children—and of me! He regularly arrived carrying a bunch of roses for me, which he'd picked from the garden. "Here you go, Miss Jean," he would say as he gave them to me. "A rose for a rose!"

He brought a packed lunch wrapped in foil, and at lunchtime he would quietly remove his dentures and place them carefully in his handkerchief before tucking them into his pocket and getting to work on his sandwiches.

He did a great job sorting out problems and working out how to manage the lifting of heavy lintels and beams on his own, sometimes calling John to help: "Just get a hold of the end of this, John, and give us a hand."

Eventually, all the necessary building work was completed, and I was quite sad to see our new friend disappear—although he did reappear on odd occasions to bring me more roses, as well as a dozen brown eggs that his hens had laid.

A quiet gentleman named Frank installed our new kitchen and laid the floor tires. He was a craftsman and carried out each task meticulously, with very little conversation, only stopping work to have a cup of tea or coffee when offered. It took two or three weeks to install and finish all the remaining tasks, which included the outside drainage. We spent those weeks climbing over furniture in the living room, searching for cutlery, and balancing trays on our knees, while doing only the most basic of cooking, and eating the simplest of meals. Visits to the chippie at High Town became more frequent, and the children were of course delighted.

Completion of the job brought great relief to all, and we celebrated by throwing a "new kitchen" party, to which both Freddy and Frank were invited. Only Frank and his wife accepted, however, Freddy eschewing such social gatherings as unnecessary and frivolous, and not fitting into his staunch Primitive Methodist roots.

John had settled quickly into his job at the airport, used to working on aircrafts, and once more enjoying the camaraderie of working with men of like minds and with a similar skill set, many of whom had also served in the Air Force. He was given overalls to work in, and one day he presented me with a pair that needed a new zipper, asking if I could repair them. Knowing my limited sewing ability, I was a little nervous but cheerfully accepted the challenge. I searched for a zipper in my work basket but couldn't find one that was suitable. Then I had a brilliant idea, one that would make the task much simpler and didn't even require a zipper. I cut two lengths of Velcro and sewed them into the overalls, congratulating myself on my ingenuity and a job well done! Unfortunately, John didn't agree with me. He arrived home the next day and immediately took off the overalls.

"You can get that Velcro stuff right off. I brought the whole of the men's toilets to a standstill today," he said. "Every time I pulled it apart, it made such a loud tearing noise that everybody fell about laughing!"

John was not amused, but I'm afraid I thought it was hilarious, and I disappeared upstairs to hide my laughter so as not to provoke him to any further frustration.

When David was just eighteen months old, we decided it was necessary for me to get a teaching post in order to help out with the family finances. With four children, and quite a large house to maintain, I began to inquire about vacancies in the local area. I soon discovered that there was a job at Biddulph North, which was now known as Biddulph St. Lawrence. I was delighted when I was successful with my application, and I started to make arrangements for the children. As John worked shifts, some weeks were easier than others to manage, as he would be at home to help with the childcare. At this point, Cathy was at full-time school, but Sally and Lesley were still pre-school, and David was just a baby. A friend from the church at Mow Cop said she would look after the girls, and I enrolled David in a Congleton nursery. And so began what I later called "the crazy time."

We would all have to be up very early to get ready, have breakfast, and get Cathy ready for school. Then I would take the two girls and David to catch a bus down to Congleton, and dash David into the nursery before catching another bus up to Mow Cop. David hated being left, and I would invariably leave him screaming and tearfully make my way with the two girls to do the next leg of the journey. Barbara, our friend, would be waiting at the Mow Cop bus stop, and she would take them off the bus while I stayed on to make the return journey back to Congleton, getting off in Gillow Heath, and running the rest of the way to Biddulph St. Lawrence, where I would teach all day before doing the whole thing again in reverse. It was an absolute nightmare, and as I look back, I wonder how on earth I had the energy and stamina to survive. Fortunately, the situation didn't last long; I only stayed at St. Lawrence for seven months, leaving at the end of term. Sally was in school when the new term began, and I started work at Knypersley First and made more convenient arrangements for Lesley. I still had to leave David in the nursery, but by then he had thankfully settled in.

But it wasn't all hard graft, work, and busyness. We had our fun times too, and lots of them! We loved doing things as a family, and John liked nothing better than loading us all in the car, together with the dog, and taking us on a mystery tour. We explored Macclesfield Forest and Tittesworth Reservoir, picked bilberries on the Cloud and Congleton Edge, popped up to Mow Cop and climbed the slopes of the castle—calling in at Roy and Eileen's for a cuppa—and went further afield into the Derbyshire Hills. Living so close to Congleton Edge, the children would disappear for hours up the fields and along the old railway lines, or stay closer to home in the fields nearby. They sometimes spent time exploring Auntie Jessie's garden, just as I had done as a child, picking raspberries from the canes, or gathering bunches of forget-me-nots by the stream, or sweet peas off the climbing trellises.

I remember a mum from Copperhill Road stopping us one day as we were about to set off on one of our explorations. "The McLellan family has their name on a bronze plaque around Copperhill," she said. "You always seem to be out doing things together!"

We also enjoyed certain traditions throughout the week. Friday night was a special time, as we celebrated the end of a working week. Tea was always tomato or vegetable soup with a packet of crisps, followed by a Kit Kat bar of chocolate. Then the children, older ones looking after the younger ones, would go to the garage at the bottom of the hill with some pocket money to buy sweets. Friday night was also the night when Dad turned up to sit a while, have a cuppa, and smoke his cigarette. I hadn't the heart to tell him that I wasn't very happy for him to be smoking around the children, so I would fetch something for him to put his ash in without saying a word. The children remember that he always called in at Woolworths before getting on the bus to come up, and he arrived with one of his pockets bulging with pick 'n' mix sweets!

Even in later years, Dad depended on the bus for transport. He took driving lessons, and entered for several tests, but was never successful, so he eventually gave up the idea. I was relieved, because I think he would have been a very erratic driver.

Sunday was another highlight. After a busy day of church and Sunday school, tea was a really special occasion. We called it a "picky bit" tea, when there were sandwiches and home baked cakes, together with a plate of kunzle cakes from the shop. I baked a lot in those days when I had the opportunity, and the family all enjoyed the results, but the bought cakes were the specialty. It reminded me of the vests that Granny Hornsby so lovingly knitted, but how delighted Cathy was when I bought the first brand new vests from the shop. Now she could be like all the other girls in P.E.!

After tea, when the table was cleared and the dishes washed, the children were allowed to watch an hour of TV. There was always a children's classic showing on Sunday afternoon, and they sat, entranced, watching Black Beauty and Ginger on their coal rounds, or gambolling in the fields. I think there were still vestiges of traditions that had come down through three generations of keeping Sunday, the Sabbath, as a day apart, and not indulging in such things as TV or games. That's probably what made that hour of TV so special; it was a guilty pleasure, a stolen treat, and the children loved it.

As I think of family times, a mention has to be made of our pets. We always had animals as part of our family, right from the days when we were in Cyprus. Shaun was our first, and she became a much-loved part of us. Even Dad thought the world of her, and he, along with the rest of us, was heartbroken when she eventually died of leukaemia.

Tog, the black cat, held a unique place in our affections because he was the only cat we ever had. He lived, fully active, to the grand old age of seventeen.

Cleo, a beautiful English Setter, came next, with her white and black silky coat and plumey tail. She was tragically killed, being knocked down by a car when John was taking her for an evening stroll up Boundary Lane. The whole family was heartbroken, especially John, and the children were allowed the next day off school because they were so upset. We took them up to Webberley's Stationary shop in Hanley and bought them pencil crayons and scrapbooks to assuage their grief a little.

We had a second Cleo, an identical English Setter, immediately afterwards. While we still had Cleo, Lesley fell passionately in love with a tiny basset hound pup that we spotted in a pet shop in Hanley. I think we had gone into the shop to buy some tropical fish to add to John's tanks, and Lesley insisted on taking a closer look at the pup. As soon as she held it, she desperately wanted it, and as we were fascinated too, Gussy came home with us! Knowing that she would grow into a long sausage-like dog, we thought of calling her Rhubarb, but thought the neighbours would think it strange if we stood at the back door shouting, "Rhubarb, Rhubarb!" as we called her in at night. So we decided that Gussy was more appropriate. She was stubborn, determined, and virtually untrainable, but gorgeous. A real Gorgeous Gussy!

Kate followed, a wonderful Giant Schnauzer we bought from a breeder in Surrey. The owners invited us down to interview us, and we were vetted before they would accept a cheque from us and hand her into our care. She was well worth all the care taken, and we adored her for many years.

I can understand those special corners in the grounds of large estates or stately homes that are reserved for the graves of the family pets, the headstones telling that Timmy or Bobby or Jasper lies there. We unfortunately don't have such reminders and can only rely on the well-worn photos and cherished memories.

After leaving St. Lawrence, I had taken on a Grade A post of responsibility at Knypersley First, where I worked with children who were from deprived circumstances and in need of compensatory education. Again I was teaching a reception class and thoroughly enjoying it, particularly the aspect of helping children with physical or educational limitations. One of my students, Alan, struggled in many ways and almost required one-on-one help, but there were others who needed my attention too. I remember a little girl named Ruth who came into class one morning clutching one of her eyes and was obviously in pain. I looked at it several times during the first session and eventually realised that one of her pupils had been damaged. I notified the head, Mr. Rees, and Ruth's mother was instructed to come and collect her to take her to the hospital.

It turned out that Ruth had prepared herself some breakfast that morning, unsupervised, and had somehow poked a knife into her eye and blinded herself. One little girl trying to cope on her own who lost her sight and was impaired for the rest of her life.

Alan's difficulties were not physical, but he struggled immensely with the smallest of tasks. It took him weeks to learn how to write his name, and we worked on scrapbooks together, cutting out tractors and cars to colour in and trace his name underneath. He was my shadow, and I loved him, encouraging his mum when she came in upset because of his limitations. Halfway through the year, a special school opened nearby, and Alan was transferred. A month or so later, his mum appeared at my classroom door in floods of tears, begging me to take him back.

"He hates it," she said, "and has learned nothing since he's been there. He screams in the morning and wants to come back into your class."

He had started to read before he left me but had since regressed because he was so upset. But of course I could do nothing about it. I've met him in recent years, always recognising his booming voice: "Mrs. McLellan, do you remember me?" Of course I do, Alan, you're one of the many that I will never forget!

David left the nursery in 1971 and joined his three sisters in the old building of Mossley School at the end of Leek Road. I had grown tired of travelling back and forth on the bus, so I had driving lessons with a driving instructor named Albert. He was extremely patient, but I could tell from his use of endearments how bad my mistakes were.

I clipped the kerb while reversing: "Come on, love, let's do that again."

I indicated right and turned left: "Oh, honey, no, no, no."

I started to drive the wrong way up a one-way street: "SWEETHEART, SWEETHEART, STOP!"

Amazingly, I passed my test the first time! That day, at 3:15 p.m., I set out on my own for the very first time in our blue Beetle and went to meet the children from school. I couldn't wait to see their faces when they spotted me at the school gate, and a look of realisation dawned when they discovered it wasn't Dad behind the wheel, but me. They ran and clambered excitedly into the car: "You did it! You passed your test! Wow, Mum!"

It made such a difference, making my life so much easier. I enjoyed the independence of being able to go from A to B without all the fuss of waiting at the bus stops, especially on cold, wet days. We covered many miles in those days, to and from school, work, and church, as well as visits to friends and families. The Beetle soldiered on, eventually nearly losing the panels in the stairwell of the passenger seat, but even then, we continued to drive it.

Church was going well, and the congregation had grown considerably. Roy was a great pastor, well loved by his flock, and gave wonderful Bible studies that were riveting and left his congregation almost speechless, not wanting to talk about ordinary things when he had finished speaking. My piano skills had improved somewhat from my debut at then-Biddulph North Primary, and I was the church pianist for some time. I remember playing the piano to accompany my three girls, who were singing at a special service at Congleton. They came out to the front and stood there while I took my place at the piano: dark, golden, and chestnut hair shining above the rosy cheeks of three little girls, while their sweet voices trilled out over the congregation, "There's not a friend like the good Lord Jesus. No not one, no not one!" they sang, while a few tears were wiped away. Applause followed them as they made their way back to their seats.

It was right at the beginning of our time at Mow Cop Pentecostal Church that Cathy, at a very tender age, made her own commitment to become a Christian. She had responded to Roy's appeal at the end of one of the services by putting her hand up, but Roy hadn't noticed, and she came home really upset. Both John and I talked to her and said it didn't matter that Roy hadn't noticed, because Mr. God had, and that if she'd meant it, she was now a Christian. Cathy, however, was inconsolable, so after talking to Roy, we said she could go out to the front of the church at the next service. When the time came, she sat beside me and put on her bonnet and gloves and buttoned up her coat in readiness to make her stand. When Roy made his appeal, she got up and made her way down to the front to stand alone while Roy prayed for her. Looking back, that one instance epitomizes Cathy's character: determined, even stubborn, but as straight as a die, and courageous enough to make a stand, even if she stands alone.

There were lighter sides to church life, like the occasions when we set out across the hill to conduct open air services on the castle slopes. A group of about ten would set off, one of the men carrying the piano accordion, which was extremely heavy, and which was used to accompany the singing. When we arrived at the chosen spot on the hillside, they would hand me the accordion, but it was so heavy that when we started to sing and the instrument was fully extended, I couldn't squeeze it together again. Gordon and Bill would be stationed on either side to give me a hand before we could continue. It must have been hilarious to watch.

"Years I spent in vanity and pride"—push, push, push—"Caring not my Lord was crucified"—squeeze, squeeze, squeeze—"Knowing not it was for me he died"—push, squeeze, push—"On Calvary."

Mrs. Gibson, my neighbour, accompanied us one Sunday afternoon to give her testimony. The microphone was handed to her so that her voice could wing its way down the slopes and ring out across the Cheshire Plain. As she stood with the mic in her hand, she seemed to freeze with fright. Her intention was to say how wonderful the whole church experience was, but all she could manage was, "Oh ... I can't describe it... it's ... it's absolutely *vile!*" The mic was hastily retrieved from her numb fingers, and we tried to continue with an ear-splitting series of chords from the accordion.

The whole congregation was heartbroken when Roy accepted a pastorate in Mansfield. When he left and took his family to fresh fields, we were like sheep without a shepherd, or a ship without a rudder. We struggled along until Pastor Duckinfield was appointed to carry on the work. But it was no easy task to fill Roy's shoes, and the church floundered for a while.

By this time, John had learned to ride a motorbike, and as with all new interests, he was absorbed in it. He started with a 250cc, but after he'd passed his test, he bought a Honda CX 500, with all the necessary extra equipment—which included a crash helmet for me to ride pillion!

The first time he took me out on it, we drove up a very steep hill nearby called Blackie Bank, then round a few country lanes, before heading into Macclesfield town. I had dressed for the part, wrapping a silk scarf round my neck to blow in the breeze. I had never imagined the force of the wind rushing by as we picked up speed, and I bent into the corners as John had instructed. We had only come to the bottom of the hill before climbing the steeper slopes when the scarf was ripped off my neck and floated away into the hedge somewhere. I was hanging on for grim life, head down, and arms holding John's leather-clad body as tightly as I could. I kept my eyes closed and my teeth gritted for the rest of the journey. When we arrived in Macclesfield, I couldn't stand up straight when John stopped the bike and I alighted. We stood for quite some time with the bike stabilised at the edge of the pavement while we stood gazing into a hardware store, and I tried to straighten my legs and back. I was a bit more hesitant to take my place on the bike for the return journey, but eventually I climbed on, and we made our way home.

I had ridden pillion several times when we decided to visit Roy and Eileen and family in Mansfield. We left the children with Dad prepared to keep an eye on them and set off. It was a lovely journey: straight roads, blue skies, and sunshine on the way there. But the return journey was a nightmare. The weather had deteriorated, the wind was blowing, and rain was pouring down as we drove onto the busy motorways. Spray covered us as we passed other vehicles, and when we overtook a lorry, there was a horrible feeling of being sucked into the sides of it. I rode with my head tucked behind John's shoulder, but every time I raised my head, the visor was ripped back by the wind, and I felt as though it was taking my head off. I was really scared and hung on with my eyes closed until we exited the M6 at Sandbach and travelled the rest of the way home on quieter roads, away from all the heavy traffic. It was my Waterloo: I never rode pillion again. John, however, continued to enjoy the experience and travelled to and from the airport daily.

I remember calling him one day when it had snowed heavily, and I was scared of him riding in the snow. It took a long time to reach him, as he was working on the tarmac. When he was told I was calling, he dashed through the airport hangars, thinking there was an emergency at home.

"What's the matter?" he said. Hearing the panic in his voice I hesitated.

"John … how are you going to get home on the bike in the snow?"

There was a long pause before he answered. "I'm going to cock my leg over the bike, switch on the ignition, and ride it. How do you *think* I'm going to get home?"

The phone went dead, and I was left to anxiously wait for him to arrive safely home later that evening.

It's only in recent years that I learned that when John had his 250cc bike, he encouraged David to ride it. He showed him how to handle it and took him to empty car parks to learn how to ride around. Knowing John, he would have insisted that he wore a safety helmet, but nevertheless, I still wouldn't have agreed to it (he was only about fifteen). But what the eye doesn't see, the heart doesn't grieve about, and so they both got away with their adventures.

Something else we weren't aware of was the growing friendship of Dad with one of his Holford Street neighbours. Violet lived at Number 1, two doors away from Dad, and I think she must have been delighted when he moved in, because she very quickly made over-tures of friendship. Dad was still grieving the loss of Mum and was looking for something to fill the void, so the popping in for a cup of tea, and the calling by for a chat became more frequent. It was when John and I had dropped in to visit one afternoon, and I was making a cup of tea in the kitchen, that Violet also made an appearance and was invited to join us. As I handed round the cups, Dad said, out of the blue, "Well, aren't you going to congratulate us?" We looked at them in astonished silence while Dad continued. "We're engaged to be married!" To say you could have knocked us down with a feather was an understatement. We were totally gobsmacked but covered our astonishment with smiles, hugs, and congratulations.

It is said that those who marry in haste will repent in leisure, and I think that Dad looked back at the brief period of independence after Mum died with regret that he hadn't hung onto it for a longer period of time. Nevertheless, let us just say that life may not have been a bed of roses, but Dad made the best of it. He took the hard with the soft, and the rough with the smooth, continuing to find solace in his choirs, his organ, and his music, while still managing to smile and remain the cheerful chappie he had always been.

CHAPTER FOURTEEN

High Days and Holidays

Before the children of my memory tumble out of childhood and run helter skelter into adult years, I want to pause a while to recall the high days and holidays, fun days and family days that are lost to time but wonderfully preserved in the treasure troves of yesteryear.

Be under no illusions: our family had its fair share of disagreements and fall outs, noise and squabbles. But I am sweeping all of those times under the carpet and concentrating on the good times. Who wants to dwell on the downside anyway? Everybody knows about those times. Instead, let me talk about our special times: our treats and outings and magical moments.

Christmas was wonderful, starting weeks before December 25 with secret shopping and planning, mysterious packages and parcels, and goings-on behind closed doors. Excitement mounted with each passing day, and letters were written to Santa Claus and posted up the chimney, the charred remains from the flames watched carefully to see that they made their escape in the smoke and disappeared up the sooty chimney pot.

By Christmas Eve, excitement had always reached a crescendo that could hardly be contained, but one occasion stands out from the rest in my memory as the best of all times! Instead of our regular evening, John and I decided to take the children on a mystery tour. So everyone piled into the car, full of questions, wondering where we could possibly be going on Christmas Eve when it was dark and they were usually settling into bedtime routines. We had only just begun the journey when John said, "Look … look on the windshield!" There were big, fat snowflakes landing on the window before being swept away by the wipers. A roar came from the back seat: "It's snowing! It's snowing and it's Christmas Eve!"

We made our way through the tree-lined country roads, past Eaton Church with its black and white timbered structure, through the villages where the roads were already completely covered by snow, and on to our destination: the cinema, where there was a special Christmas showing of *101 Dalmatians*.

What excitement as they edged along the rows to their plush covered seats, hugging their treat-sweets and drinks tightly, while waiting for the red curtain to rise. They adored the puppies and all the dogs who came to help them, and not even Cruella de Vil could take away the excitement of the occasion—although Lesley pinched my arm so hard I nearly cried out!

We stepped out of the cinema afterwards into a winter wonderland. The snow lay thick on the roads, and we had to sweep it from the car before making our precarious journey home, where hot pork pies and fizzy pops awaited us. Four very tired children made their way up the stairs that night. Lesley and David had to be carried, so overcome by exhaustion were they. But stars still shone in all their eyes until the very last minute before their heavy eyelids finally closed.

But it wasn't the end of the day for John and me. The rest of our night was spent with last minute wrapping of presents and stockings, setting out the mince pie and carrots on the hearth for Santa and the reindeer, and sprinkling glitter on the stairs— evidence in the morning that Santa had climbed up to hang the stockings at the foot of each bed! And if any of them had listened carefully, or stirred in their slumbers, they might even have heard the tinkling of bells that could only have come from Santa's sleigh as it flew from the rooftop and disappeared into the snowy night. Christmas Eve magic that has passed down through the children into the traditions of their families, and hopefully will go on through the years.

Christmas Day had a feel all its own, and it started very early. John and I had a rule that no one was allowed to go downstairs before everybody was awake. The very early risers had to stay in bed but could delve into the delights found in the stocking at the foot of their bed: little toys, sweets, and mandarin oranges were all tipped onto the covers, while every heel and toe were examined to make sure nothing had been missed.

Then the fun started in earnest. Whoever's turn it was (and they always remembered from the previous year) crept down the stairs first and had a quick look around before running back to announce, "He's been! Santa's been!"

This news had everybody tumbling downstairs and running into the living room to find out which pile of presents was theirs. They took turns at opening them one by one, so that everyone could share the delight: dolls, trains, books, crayons, little sewing machine, a blue work basket—all met with "Oohs" and "Aahs" of joy and wonder as they were revealed. When the very last piece of wrapping paper had been collected, and all the presents had been stacked in their respective piles, cups of tea and pieces of toast were on offer, just to last them till the wonderful Christmas lunch was ready.

Already the kitchen would be filled with the delicious smell of slow-roasting turkey, placed in the oven on very low heat the previous night, before John and I had wearily climbed to bed. John was in charge of lunch, and a cordon bleu chef could not have produced a finer spread! A huge bronze-skinned turkey took pride of place, surrounded by all the trimmings: John's own stuffing, made with added mushrooms and onions, potatoes mashed in lashings of milk and butter, crisp roasted potatoes, baby sprouts, buttered carrots, and thick delicious gravy with added extras from the chef's secret recipe. The pudding that followed was covered in beautiful white sauce, with an added spoonful of cream. The plate of mince pies was usually left untouched until later, as everybody declared themselves "full to bursting" as they climbed down from the table to return to their presents and a—hopefully—quiet afternoon as they played or read to their hearts' content.

We didn't have a traditional Christmas tree. Instead, we had our own unique festive branch that adorned the chimney breast above the fire. It made its mysterious appearance in the week before Christmas. Under cover of darkness, John and Cathy would disappear, only to return a couple of hours later carrying a large tree branch, which was left outside to be dealt with the following day. Having been sprayed and painted white, it would be brought inside and carefully positioned above the fireplace before being beautifully decorated. Hung with baubles, festooned in tinsel and tiny garlands, and covered in sparkling lights, it was truly a sight to behold! John was so creative and artistic that the completed branch was a work of art. A feast for the senses.

Nobody ever asked where John and Cathy had found the branch every year, but years later I heard tales of two shadowy figures seen disappearing through gates and scaling the walls into the garden of Old Mossley Hall before reappearing, carrying a strange, unwieldy object on their shoulders, which they heaved onto the roof rack of a waiting car.

I wonder if perhaps John might have been the original proto-type for Mary Norton's *The Borrowers*! Rosebuds and honeysuckle, or a sprig of orange blossom; a strangely shaped pebble, or a tiny branch of larch cones—all would appear on my kitchen counter, where I would find them when I first woke. I loved each discovery, but the creme de la creme was the Christmas branch that adorned our fireplace.

Christmas tea was a measured affair of roast ham, salad, turkey and stuffing, trifle, and tiny slivers of Christmas cake and crumbly mince pies. But appetites had been sated at the lunch table, and much was put away to be appreciated at a later date.

The day reached its conclusion as we gathered to savour the last moments around the fire. The children were back in pyjamas, dress-ing gowns, and slippers, clutching the best and most loved presents of the day, and sharing about their "favourite bit of Christmas" that year. Sitting there with the lights off, just the twinkly lights on the branch illuminating all the sparkly decorations, and the firelight making eyes sparkle and cheeks glow, we bade a wistful farewell to yet another Christmas as it made its way into memories of Christmas Past.

John's culinary skills were not limited to particular seasons. Just as I was applauded for my scones and apple pies, John was well known for his roasts (always accompanied by his stuffing if appropriate), his mushroom soup, which was always bursting with flavour, and his homemade bread. August or September would see us setting off with our jars and containers to collect the ripe blackberries, which would be carried home and turned into blackberry jam or bramble jelly (often strained in a clean silk stocking) and ladled onto thick slices of John's delicious fresh bread. Summer would see buckets of elderflowers, collected along the old railway lines, being turned into cordial, and flat tins of treacle toffee would be produced on Bonfire Night.

Moving away from home, there is a consensus of opinion among the children that two holidays stand out from the rest, and we shared both of them with Roy and Eileen and the cousins.

The first was our trip down to Devon, when we stayed in a Christian boarding house in Ilfracombe. The accommodation was good, and the food was appetising, but the main attraction was the wonderful coastline. There were miles of golden sands where we could find a great spot, set out all our belongings, and stay for the whole day. There were bays and inlets we would explore, rocks to climb, treasures to collect from the beach, and rockpools. Then there was the sea to paddle, swim, and sail on. Sandcastles to build and games like quoits and beach tennis to play together. A little further round the coast was the Woolacombe sands, where the sea came in in huge breakers, and the children tried to jump over or dive into them.

One day, we visited this beach later in the evening, when the light was beginning to fade, and the daring ones amongst us still went in to brave the crashing water. We stayed until the light had gone and darkness began to spread over the waters, and as we sat along the beach to listen to the roar of the breakers, we saw the most amazing sight. As the waves rushed in and reared up before crashing down in a froth of white foam, a mysterious blue light could be seen along the crest of certain waves. We watched in awed silence, thinking of how the children had paddled and played in this sea during the day, and were struck by the sheer power of this night ocean that was crashing all around us and emitting this mysterious blue light. We didn't stay long but gathered our things and made a hasty retreat to the safety and warmth of our boarding house.

After breakfast one day, the landlord appeared to ask if anyone wanted to go walking. He organised walks once a week and graded them according to how strenuous they were. Several people agreed to join him but preferred to do an easy route. When we heard that the walk would be easy, and the destination was the Bedruthan steps that led down to the ocean, we decided to join the group.

We set off in high spirits, envisaging a gentle ramble through the Devon countryside, ending with a beach picnic, which the children would enjoy. Two very elderly ladies were in the party with their walking boots and trekking poles, so we were confident that the walk would not be too difficult for the children. How very wrong we were. We walked for miles over hills and down dales, climbing over stiles and fording streams, puffing up steep inclines and stubbing our toes on gravel covered tracks. I began to be a little apprehensive when the two elderly ladies behind us were struggling to make their way over one of the stiles, and I heard one of them gasp, "Oh God, help me. Please help me."

"Not far now!" called our leader at the front of the party. "Bedruthan steps just around the corner."

Just around the corner turned out to be a long stretch of road, where we followed him along the verge in single file before arriving at a gate leading down to the beach via an enormous stairway of steep, stone steps. We made our way precariously down, holding tightly to the younger children in case they lost their footing and tumbled into the depths below. Eventually we landed on the soft sand of the cove, where we sank, exhausted, to get our breath back. Our spirits lifted as we were handed drinks and packed lunches, but I remember looking round as I munched my sandwiches, wondering where the easy exit was from this cove. I couldn't even imagine that we would have to go back the way we'd come and climb up that enormous flight of steps! But that's exactly what we had to do.

Eileen and I couldn't believe it. We gasped as we were told that our "easy" walk had come to an end, and we were catching the bus home. All we had to do was climb the steps, and the bus stop was just at the top. We struggled and gasped our way upwards, stopping frequently to catch our breath and muster strength to keep on climbing. At one point near the top, Eileen, who was a step or two behind me, gasped, "Leave me here, Jean! You go on, but leave me here to die."

I looked in a guidebook recently to see the description of the Bedruthan steps. "There are 150 steps," it read. "It is a difficult climb down (and back up again), and there is suspected damage sustained to a lower section of the steps." If only we'd known before we went. I think we would have preferred a leisurely afternoon on the beach. Nevertheless, that holiday stands out in all the children's memories as an amazing time. And apart from that death-defying ramble, so it was!

For the next favourite holiday of the children, we travelled north, up into the Scottish Highlands, exploring the wonderful coastline en route. Both our families now had caravans, much to the delight of all the children, so the week before we set off, we packed all that we would need for the two-week holiday, excitement mounting as each day passed. It was the ideal way of travelling and holidaying with a family because we would drive through the day, stopping for breaks whenever it was convenient, then hitch up for the night, waking refreshed to tackle the next leg of the journey. The children loved being together, and there was much swapping about in the cars each time we came to a halt, or in the caravans as we settled down for the night.

There was great excitement as we crossed the border from England to Scotland and took a welcome break in Gretna Green. Gretna Green is two miles over the border and is famous for being the place where English couples go to get married. Apparently in the 1700s, English law forbade couples to marry without their parents' permission if they were under twenty-one, so many fled across the Scottish border to Gretna Green, where no such restrictions existed. We only stayed long enough to refresh ourselves with cups of tea and sandwiches before we were on the road again, as our sites were set further north, up in the Scottish Highlands.

The first destination on our list was the lovely seaside fishing town of Oban, with its picturesque harbour full of fishing boats. Most of the boats were real fishing traders, with small crews of fishermen who took their craft out in all weather to make a living from the haul of fish they managed to catch from their expeditions. We saw boats returning and unloading boxes of ice-covered fish, which would be taken as quickly as possible to sell in local fish markets or sent speedily down to London hotels. The rest of the vessels in the harbour were mostly pleasure craft, which were privately owned, but there was a sprinkling of boats ready to take eager tourists for a short sail along the wonderful coastal waters.

Whenever we visited ports or harbours, John would spend ages just standing and gazing at the different craft. He would point out the clinker built boats and explain how the struts overlapped each other to make them sea-worthy. He studied the sails and the rigging, taking in each detail as he leaned over the harbour. For weeks afterwards, he would be obsessed with the thought of owning a little boat of his own and sailing off on jaunts around the coast. But eventually other things would crowd out the daydreams, and he would forget them till our next seaside visit.

We stayed a couple of nights in Oban, walking round the harbour walls and visiting the quaint little shops full of souvenirs and trinkets to tempt the tourists. But the third morning saw us packed and heading on our northward journey toward Kinlochleven. After travelling miles along the coastal road, the weather began to take a turn for the worst, and it became clear from the lowering clouds and the sea mist rolling in that a storm was brewing. We decided to strike camp in Glencoe, seven miles away from Kinlochleven, as the sky darkened, and the wind began to blow. We found a site on the edge of Loch Leven and made preparations for an overnight stay.

All around us, people were preparing for the fast-approaching storm, some trying to pitch tents as the wind strengthened, making it difficult to manage the flapping tarpaulins. Roy and John, together with John and Cathy, went to help the families who were battling the elements, while Eileen and I were inside the caravans preparing a meal for both families and handing out mugs of tea to the people outside. We shut the caravan doors and huddled inside as the sky turned black and huge raindrops pelted on the windows and the top of the caravans.

Glencoe, on the edge of the Loch and surrounded on three sides by mountains, seemed to hold the storm, as if trapped in an earthen bowl. The thunder echoed round in a continuous roar, while the lightning filled the whole valley with a sulphurous light. The children loved it, pressing their noses against the caravan windows to gaze at the vivid flashes and listen to the thunderous roars, while I hated it but kept my fears to myself. Glencoe is well known for the massacre that took place there in the 1700s, when the McDonald Clan were slaughtered in their beds as they slept by Robert Campbell and his men. I imagined that the noise of the storm that night would even have outdone the noise of that dreadful massacre all those years ago.

We stayed an extra day in Glencoe, and in the evening, the men and boys took their dinghy out on the Loch. In just a few minutes of pushing off from the side, they disappeared from sight as an almighty cloud of black midges descended on them. They returned quite quickly, covered in red itchy bites all over their bodies, and had to be daubed all over with calamine lotion to relieve their discomfort.

The next morning saw us heading up the valley to Kinlochleven to a beautiful caravan site at the edge of the water. The storm had cleared the air, and the weather turned sunny and warm. We decided to stay for a few days and explore all that the area had to offer. There was plenty to do right there on the caravan site, as we were parked by the side of the Loch. The caravans were set out in a horseshoe shape facing the water and the beach, and the children only had to step down from the caravan steps, and they were on the sand. Out came the buckets and spades, deck chairs and windbreaks. On went the swimming costumes and trunks, and the children were set for the day. Great fun was had with the rubber dinghy, but great care had to be taken not to drift out too far if the wind was blowing. Roy and John both discovered this as they were nearly swept out when they got caught in a strong current. Fortunately, they realised what was happening, and managed to get back to the shore by paddling furiously.

The dinghy also came in useful for fishing, and they caught quite a few mackerel, which were delicious when cooked on the barbeque in the evenings, with a fresh salad and chunks of French bread. With their appetite whetted for fishing, John and Roy decided to sign up for a morning's fishing in Oban, and they planned to take John and David along with them. The boat was setting off early, so plans were made the previous evening so that all would be ready for the morning. As planned, John and David got up in our caravan before the day had started, while it was still quite dark, and crept about as quietly as they possibly could so as not to disturb the rest of us. The same thing was happening in Roy's caravan. Clothes were quietly slipped on, breakfast was skipped, and doors were carefully eased open to release four shadowy characters out of the two caravans, who then tiptoed to one of the cars. Four people slithered onto the car seats, and the doors were gently pulled to. At last, all was ready for take-off, and the key was placed in the ignition and carefully turned.

That moment, it was as though all hell had been let loose. The car horn blared out with a deafening roar, its claxon shrieking across the slumbering caravaners still in their beds. The noise came to a sudden halt as John switched the engine off in a rush. A moment later he tried again, and once more the horn screamed over the caravan park. As several doors flew open to see whatever was going on, John put his foot down on the accelerator to make a rapid exit, the horn continuing to blare out all the way round the site until they disappeared through the gates.

The caravan park seemed to spring to life. Doors were opened, and pyjama-clad figures appeared rubbing their eyes, while small groups were gathering to wonder who the silly idiots could be that had awakened all at such an early hour. Our two caravans stayed silent. Our blinds remained closed, and the doors remained shut, as if to deny the fact that we were connected in any way with the aforementioned idiots. Inside our caravans, two very different scenarios were playing out: I was rolling about on the bunk, hysterically laughing, while the children peered through the blinds. In the other caravan, Eileen was in floods of tears, mortified at how things had gone so wrong, and dreading confronting the rest of the angry holidaymakers who had had such a rude awakening.

On their return, Roy and John went to each of the caravans to apologise for the incident and explain that the car horn had jammed, but that all had been rectified, and it certainly wouldn't happen again. Fortunately, they'd had a good morning's fishing and came home with several juicy mackerel, which we all enjoyed at our evening barbeque.

After several days of action-packed fun and frolic, we packed up and set off to see how far up the coast we could travel in the time we had left. It was a difficult route, up mountain sides and down into valleys, our cars struggling to pull the caravans behind them at times. We briefly visited Fort William and made our way as far as Mallaig, from where we could look across the waters to the Isle of Skye. By this stage of our holiday, we didn't have enough money to board the ferry to visit the Scottish island. It was time to retrace our steps and make the journey home, all agreeing that it had been a marvellous holiday, and one that would be recounted many times when the families came together over the coming years—especially the story of the car horn.

Those two holidays were the ones that came top of the children's lists of favourite summertime jaunts, but there were so many more. One of my favourite memories is the journey we took up the Northumberland Coast, stopping at Alnwick Castle before taking a boat to visit Lindisfarne on Holy Island and walking along the causeway when the tide was out. Visiting the beautiful stretch of sand along the beach at Beadnell and calling at Whitby (a favourite watering hole of Queen Victoria), which is famous for its jet. Learning about Grace Darling in Bamburgh, who was just seventeen when she helped rescue fishermen who were shipwrecked in a terrible storm. That holiday reached its climax with a visit to the Edinburgh Tattoo, where we saw soldiers climbing up the sides of the floodlit castle, and all the different troops in their wonderful uniform and brightly coloured kilts marching in formation, led by the bands and the mascot goat.

We visited McLellan Castle in Kirkcudbright and stayed in a little stone cottage. One thing we all remember is that Cathy ended up with a sheep tick on the back of her neck after one of our long walks over the hills, and I had to pull it out with tweezers!

We took the caravan to Colley Mill, which is just outside Congleton, and parked it under the twenty arches by the stream. We were so close to home that John went to pick up a tin opener that we'd forgotten and was back in the caravan in about half an hour.

We took a large tent and camped in Edale and other Derbyshire sites, venturing out in the middle of the night to wade through wet grass to go to the toilet block. You may gather that I wasn't overly keen on the camping holidays, but the children loved them.

I'm surprised the Florida holidays didn't come tops for the children, when we visited Disney World twice in one year, travelling first class one journey on John's staff ticket from the airport. Memories flood thick and fast: lost luggage from the flight, when we had to walk around in sweltering heat in our travel clothes for two days; arriving at the Holiday Inn, where John refused the offered "roll-up" (an extra fold-up bed) from hotel staff, saying he'd already hired a car; the breathtaking sights and shows in the marvellous Magic Kingdom of Disney World; David eating dozens of bags of fresh oranges and mandarins; tropical rain that avalanched out of the sky but dried up almost instantaneously in the heat of the sun. I could go on and on! We took lots of photographs and put together a leather-bound album when we got home, which David would browse through every Sunday afternoon and relive the holiday.

I feel privileged to look back into those precious childhood years to catch glimpses—brief cameo shots—of the characters of my four children. Looking at them now, all grown, with children and even some grandchildren of their own, I see the full-formed picture, the fully developed characters, and I am proud.

Cathy, at barely eighteen months old, fetching and carrying things for me as I bathed Sally in the baby bath on the hearth, and later holding the hands of the younger ones as she led them to play up Congleton Edge, promising to take good care of them all. She is now a lay reader and key worker in her local Church of England church, helping and counselling, leading and caring for numerous parishioners.

Sally coming downstairs in her pyjamas, with a Bible in her hand, after I'd had a meltdown while putting them to bed and left the room by slamming the door behind me. "Look, Mum," she said, "I know you know this, but can I read it to you?" And she read me the "love" chapter in 1 Corithians 13, before hugging me and climbing the stairs again. Now she has four children and four grandchildren of her own; she's a homemaker who loves to cook and feed and look after people, and who adores her family, extending care and love at every opportunity.

Lesley, a born worrier, who had to be reassured over so many little issues, coming downstairs when she couldn't sleep because of something that was happening at school. Still a worrier but conquering her own doubts and fears to become a passionate defender of the weak and champion of justice, with a passion for mission and the red dirt roads of Africa.

And David, the only boy and baby of the family, loved and spoiled by everybody, whose reception teacher said, "I only have to look at his big blue eyes, and I can't be cross with him," when I went to inquire about his reading progress. I look at him now, father of a family that he adores and of whom he is so proud. A brilliant worker, reliable and responsible. As a little boy, given much love; as an adult, he gives care and love— not only to his family, but to friends who need a helping hand or a word of encouragement.

Yes, I am indeed proud!

CHAPTER FIFTEEN

Growing Up

After Roy left Mow Cop, the church never seemed the same. The new pastor arrived with his lovely family, but it seemed like the heart had been ripped out of the fellowship. We found solace in the wonderful friendships we had built within the congregation, especially with some people who seemed like family. There was Vernon, the music and choir man, and his wife, Mave, and Gordon and Mary and their two children, David and Irene. Many a Sunday evening found us hunkered down in Mary's stone cottage at the top of Woodcocks' Bank. The children would disappear to another room to play under the supervision of Irene while we would talk and laugh until the cows came home. When it was late and folks started to think about leaving, Gordon would start to make chips in his own particular way. Each chip was so fat that only three or four would be enough to make up a portion: hot and succulent, steamy and delicious. As soon as the smell of cooking chips started to come from the kitchen, the children would reappear as if by magic, determined not to miss Uncle Gordon's wonderful chips. Several mugs of tea later, we would gather everybody together, perhaps retrieving one or other from a comfortable sofa where they'd fallen asleep, and we'd pile into the car to make our way home through the mists of early morning. Wonderful times, wonderful friends, wonderful memories!

It is often said that people from Mow Cop, as well as people from Biddulph Moor, on the neighbouring hill, are a breed unto themselves. The reason given for the eccentricities of people from Biddulph Moor is that they are descendants of the Huguenots, but no such reason is found for the inhabitants from Mow Cop, though our good friend Mary was a prime example. Totally uninhibited in mode of dress or manner of speech, she knew no boundaries. Hair tied back in a ponytail, and still wearing her slippers, she would arrive at the church unaware of the glances from other people. If she was playing the piano, she would make her way to the front and take her place on the piano stool to bang out the choruses and ripple up and down the chords in her own flamboyant way. She was highly intelligent and could be sarcastic on occasion, giving her opinion freely and without reserve. But she was generous to a fault and unswerving in her loyalty as a friend.

She was good friends with a local artist named Jack, who had painted her many times. He painted in oils, and much of his work was abstract and obscure, but he became quite famous, and nowadays, his work sells for many hundreds of pounds. Lots of his canvases adorned Mary's cottage, but I don't know what became of them, although they would certainly be quite valuable these days.

Some time later, we left the Mow Cop church, and after spending a few months in a small church in Congleton, we settled in Mossley

Church of England church, because John had the notion of becoming a reader there. Although the reader idea was short-lived, our stay in Mossley Church was much longer lasting, and we were happy there for several years and made many wonderful friendships.

By this time, the girls were in their teens and going to the Secondary and Grammar schools in Congleton, while Dave would leave Mossley Primary and attend Box Lane Boys' School soon afterwards. I was still teaching at Knypersley First School, just outside Biddulph, but as I was now driving, the short distance to travel presented no problems.

When David was twelve or thirteen, he became interested in running, so John took him along to a club in Macclesfield, the Macclesfield Harriers, where a man named Arthur was the main coach. At first John was just the taxi service, driving David to and from the training sessions, but after a while, he became interested in running himself. Many a weekend would see them driving to different racetracks and circuits around the area, and many evenings would be spent collecting aspiring runners to group together and run ever increasing distances around the country lanes.

After two or three years, in spite of much success, David lost interest, but John was truly hooked and decided to start coaching. He took course after course over the months, working out the practical issues on the circuit at Macclesfield and returning to his coaching textbooks to tackle the exams. Everything John did, he became completely involved in, whether work or leisure, and his involvement in running became an obsession. He entered and ran several marathons and half marathons, while he coached several young adults—Anne and Jill being two of them—to achieve success on many racetracks and meetings around the country. John pursued his coaching until he successfully reached International Level, by which time he was regular coach of an ardent group of runners, who often turned up at our house and became almost part of the family.

Similarly, out of the blue, John decided to take up pottery. He joined a G.C.S.E class at Macclesfield College and passed the exam, progressing successfully to A Level and becoming great friends with Robbie and Jane, who taught the course. He built a shed in the back garden where he could do his pottery, and homemade kilns appeared, from which he produced raku pottery, sending plumes of smoke across the neighbouring gardens. A small kiln was bought and housed in the shed, and pots of all shapes and sizes began to appear: slab pots and turned pots; pots decorated in the style of the Swiss sculptor, Giacometti, with his stylised figures; delicate porcelain pots and large ornamental garden pots; beautiful pots with ferns and grasses pressed into the clay before firing. All shapes and sizes, some large and heavy, others almost translucent in their delicacy, all flowed out of that little garden shed and took pride of place on shelves and dressers and graced the gardens of many friends and relatives.

Meanwhile, the girls were growing up and beginning to make their own mark on the world. We had encouraged them to take up an instrument to play, and each one of them had chosen a different one. Cathy chose the clarinet, Sally the guitar, and Lesley the flute. None of them had shown any real aptitude for the piano, and after a year or so, the chore of practising their chosen instruments became too onerous, and music lessons died a death.

Cathy and Sally began to show an interest in pursuing nursing when they left school, while Lesley began to head in another direction. As a little girl, Lesley had lacked confidence, but this had grown throughout the primary years. I remember the way she needed to be reassured and would wander down out of the bedroom when she was worried about something at night, but in the last year at

Mossley, she won both the speech and music prizes, following in Cathy's footsteps. She also began to perform in a country music club, singing duets with her best friend, Liz. Liz would play the guitar, and they would sing duets together, becoming a very popular item on the club's itinerary.

Lesley and Liz had been friends from the reception class and were inseparable throughout their school years. All their spare time was spent together, in and out of each other's houses, having sleepovers, playing music, and singing together; they were the best of pals. Liz had younger twin brothers, Phil and John, who occasionally played with David, although David's best pal, Geoff, lived further up Boundary Lane, at the village shop. It's amazing how strong the ties of friendship are that are built in childhood, many of them lasting a lifetime. Geoff, for instance, became a chef and started his career on a cruise ship, moving to Australia, Thailand, and Canada, then back to Australia, and he and David still catch up with each other occasionally to share any news and wish each other well.

John and I established many lifelong friendships over the years. There was Isobel, married to Hugh, who was a member of Mossley Church. Isobel was a fiery Scot who taught Biology at a high school in Newcastle, and she was a force to be reckoned with. She used to coach Lesley in Biology for a little while but took a great liking to Sally. I think the girls were scared of her forcefulness, but that didn't deter Isobel. I remember Sally telling the tale of going to the toilet while visiting one day and admiring a beautiful impatiens plant on the windowsill. "Ah yes," said Isobel, "it grows well because of the ammonia, you know," as she gave Sally a mischievous wink!

Another wonderful lady was Brenda and her four boys, who were part of the youth group that used to meet in our house. Brenda was married to Vic, an ophthalmic specialist, and she suffered with M.S.

One day, walking home from church with John, she asked him if he'd pop in for a coffee and pray for her. He did, and she's been in remission ever since, and she still leads a full and active life, forty plus years later.

Anna Lisa was a Dutch lady whose husband was a geologist who worked in the South African diamond mines. She lived in Astbury Land Ends with her two children, Mark and Yvonne, while her husband, Roy, was working away.

Lesley also spent a lot of time with other friends of ours, Steve and Chris, especially when the babies started to arrive. She would get off the bus on her way home from school and call at their house to play with Paul, the baby, while she chatted with Chris. John and I spent a lot of time with Chris and Steve too. Chris was a great cook and a wonderful hostess. We ate many meals together and enjoyed hours of friendship and fun that lasted into the early hours. When Steve felt called to leave Mossley Church and establish a new church fellowship in Congleton, we joined forces with him and became some of the founding members of New Life Church, which is now a large, flourishing, and well-respected church. In recent years, Steve has been awarded an MBE for his services to the town. Mighty oaks from little acorns *do* grow!

John and I were always busy. John still worked at the airport, and I was still teaching at Knypersley, and there was always something going on with church or family or youth group. However, despite our busyness, we still found time to go away together for an occasional weekend. We had a wonderful mini break in Amsterdam one time, when we visited Anne Frank's house, sailed along the canals, and went to see the fabulous tulips in the Keukenhof Gardens. It was wonderful to wander aimlessly beside the water and pop into one of their many cafes to enjoy hot waffles and maple sauce. One street we wandered down gave us an almighty shock and sent us beating a hasty retreat. It was the windows on the ground floor that provided the surprise. The curtains were drawn back, and a light was shining on the windowsill, while a scantily clad young girl would be sitting on a chair, in full view of the road. We were like innocents abroad and couldn't understand what they were doing at all. It was only when a young woman appeared from a doorway and openly propositioned John that the penny dropped! We had wandered into the infamous Red Light District of Amsterdam, from which we departed as fast as our legs could carry us.

The Welsh town of Hay-on-Wye provided no such shocking surprises, although it did have its mishaps and unexpected—even scary—moments. We had decided to set off roundabout teatime on Friday, when John came home from work, so I decided to take Gussy for a walk up the old railway in the afternoon. I collected a lovely bouquet of wildflowers as I walked, which I put in one of John's large slab pot vases to adorn a corner of the hall. The children, now old enough to manage on their own, were left with numerous instructions, and we set off on our weekend break. A B&B had been booked, the route had been pencilled in on the map, the bags were packed in the boot of the car, the weather was good, and we were excited to be setting off to explore Wye and the surrounding area, which was completely new to us.

As soon as we arrived at the B&B, which we had booked for a single night, we discovered our first mistake. We had left one of the bags at home, failing to notice it as we made our quick departure. The bag had all my clothes in it, including toiletries, underwear, and everything I needed for the next two days. We decided we would make the best of it and not let it spoil our short break, so we had a quick freshen up and headed into the little town to find somewhere to have a meal. It was a lovely evening, and after eating, we left the car to wander round the quaint streets for a while before returning to our lodgings for a good night's sleep, in order to make an early start the next day.

After a good breakfast, we packed our bags into the car and set off to explore the town and surrounding area. Hay-on-Wye is a beautiful little town just over the Welsh-English border in Powys. The church of St. Mary's has stood guard over the area since the twelfth century and lies to the west of the town, virtually looking out across a loop of the River Wye. Built of stone, St. Mary's is quite a small church, consisting of a nave and chancel, with a tower at the west end, which houses only one bell. If unimpressed by the outward appearance, just push the large oaken door at the main entrance and peep inside at the interior. We loved it! A stone slabbed nave leads down to the chancel that houses an ornate altar, bedecked with tall golden candlesticks and covered with a beautiful altar cloth. Much care over the years has added a rich patina to the old wooden pews, which lay bathed in the multicoloured glow from the stained glass of the windows, while plaques and commemorations on the walls give witness to parishioners of note who have graced St. Mary's over the centuries. We sat for a while to soak up the atmosphere, sensing the deep peacefulness that comes from centuries of worship and prayer.

After a while, we made our way out of the old church, and found ourselves in the bright sunshine of the old town, with its grey stone buildings and higgledy piggledy streets. Some of the shops, with their bullseye, small-paned windows, had stepped entrances leading up to the shop doors. I half expected to meet Isaac Peabody (from *The Dean's Watch*, by Elizabeth Goudge) bending over his candle as he mended his clocks and watches—but that was not to be.

A mixture of ancient and modern rub shoulders throughout the town. Townsfolk and tourists alike busy themselves in a flurry of modern day living in an ancient setting of stone buildings and antiquated streets. Shops full of books hot off the press sit cheek by jowl with proprietors of old bikes and baskets, antiques and paraphernalia of all sorts. But our delight lay mostly in the many book shops throughout the town. Hay-on-Wye is famous for its bookshops—twenty in all—and the thousands upon thousands of books found there. An old cinema has been converted into a book shop and boasts that it contains a million books of every genre. We browsed titles to our hearts' content, reviving ourselves in several of the many delightful cafes that are to be found on every corner.

We explored and ambled and refreshed ourselves throughout the day before returning to the car and heading out of town to begin the search for somewhere to spend the night. We were confident there would be no problem, because the whole area caters for tourists, and it wasn't the height of the season. But after one or two vain attempts to find a bed for the night, we were less optimistic.

Eventually, we lighted upon a beautiful little cottage with a board outside declaring "Lodgings Available," and we gratefully made our way up the garden path.

"Oh, I'm so sorry," said the lady who opened the door. "I've just taken the last booking, and I've not had a chance to change the notice!"

We made our way down the path again, thinking how nice it would have been to spend a night in such a picturesque little cottage, when she shouted to us from the doorway: "Just a minute," she said. "You can have my daughter's room. She's away at college at the moment."

We returned, delighted, and she showed us up an old, well-polished, wooden staircase to a lovely old room under the eaves. *What luck,* we thought as we went to find a nice eating place before returning to the cottage for the night. Our day had been a busy one, and we soon fell asleep in the old four poster bed, with its comfortable mattress and plump feather pillows. I wakened in the early hours while it was still dark and made my way over creaking wooden boards to the bathroom, which lay across a landing with a silled window that looked out across the garden. I hadn't switched the light on, not wanting to disturb anyone, but the moonlight was enough for me to slowly edge my way back to bed over the creaking landing.

After a goodnight's sleep, we were enjoying a full English breakfast when the landlady asked if we'd slept well.

"Oh, it was great," we said. "Very comfortable bed. We had a wonderful night!"

"Did you hear or see anything in the night?" she asked.

I stopped eating, an uneasy sensation beginning to creep up my back.

"No," I said, wondering where the conversation was heading. She sat down at a spare chair at the table as she explained that a small child haunted the landing upstairs, who sat on the windowsill crying and wringing her hands in the middle of the night. I was horrified as I thought of my moonlit journey to the bathroom over the landing and past the window.

"Would you have taken the room if you had known?" asked the lady.

It makes me shiver as I think about it now, and if I had known at the time, I certainly wouldn't have slept a wink, and would probably have hightailed it down that cottage garden path quicker than a bolt from the blue!

We had a last look round the town before we started to make our way home in a leisurely fashion, calling at a village fête en route, where

I bought a huge fuchsia to cheer up my kitchen window. Upon arriving home, all had been well, apart from Gussy, who had had several bouts of diarrhoea, which Lesley had had to deal with. She didn't look ill; her coat was shiny, her appetite was good, her nose was wet and cold. We were puzzled, until we discovered that she had been found eating the wildflowers that I had put in the hall before leaving on our journey, some of which we realised to be valerian, a drug that grows in the wild. Poor Gussy had unwittingly become a drug addict during our absence!

Refreshed by our short break, I returned to work and my normal school routine. Knypersley was a traditional and well-respected primary school (known as a First School, after the Comprehensive System had been brought in) under the headship of Mr. Rees, an austere Welshman. Mrs. Rees was also on the staff, along with Beryl, Elaine, Glenys, Gill, Steph, and several others. The staff were friendly, and there was a good atmosphere throughout the school, probably because the children knew exactly what was expected of them under the strict but fair regime of Mr. Rees' leadership. The main part of the school, a grey stone building, sat on the corner, by the Knypersley traffic lights, but a new infant section had been added on the side of the playground at the top of the field. It was in this new building that I was then teaching a first-year class, along with Steph, who now taught reception, and Gill, who had the second-year infants. The staff "family" was augmented by Margaret, the secretary, and Pat and Dorothy, the TAs. Margaret and Dorothy had been at the school for many years. They knew all the parents and grandparents and were invaluable to the smooth running of the school. Many problems were solved, and many disasters averted, because of the wise counsel and swift action of these two redoubtable ladies.

Life in school, for both staff and children, runs along well regulated lines of timetables and schedules, punctuated by bells and break times, but highlights stand out from the routine, like bright stars on a dark night. These incidents are almost invariably connected to the children, and more often than not, the naughty ones!

One such character was Ellis, a beautiful little boy who attracted trouble like a honey pot attracts insects. With dark hair and big brown eyes, he could charm the birds off the trees, but with his volatile temperament, he could be a ticking time bomb. He was the bane of the dinner ladies' lives, and other members of staff hated the odd occasion when he was left under their supervision. I felt I had the measure of him, but there was more than one occasion when he completely took the wind out of my sails! One playtime, a brawl broke out in the boys' toilets. Voices were shouting, and doors were banging, and when I went in to see what was going on, there were fists flying in every direction. I pulled the two boys apart and made them stand by the door.

"What's going on here?" I demanded. "Who started this?"

One of them, of course, was Ellis, who stood by the toilet wall looking dishevelled but highly indignant. He turned his face to me and said, "Mrs. McLellan, you've been telling us that God made *everything*, and *he*," he said, glaring at his opponent, "*he* has just squashed one of God's little creatures under his foot!"

It's hard to keep a straight face on such occasions, but I managed to warn them of the consequences of settling disagreements—even disagreements over squashed insects—with fists instead of words.

On another occasion, I met a dinner lady coming out of my classroom as I was returning from lunch.

"I've put Ellis in your classroom, Mrs. McLellan," she said. "He's been an absolute nightmare all through the playtime. We can't do anything with him!"

I apologised to her and said I would deal with him.

Right, I thought. *I'll read him the riot act.*

I went into the classroom, where Ellis sat waiting for me.

"Come and stand by my desk," I said. He came and stood meekly in front of me. I bent down so that my face was level with his, so I could give emphasis to what I was saying. I spoke firmly and warned him of what would happen if he continued to behave in such a way. After a lengthy reprimand, I stood up and looked down at him, thinking that I'd really got through to him and put a stop to his lunchtime escapades. He looked up at me with his big, innocent, brown eyes.

"Mrs. McLellan," he said curiously. "Have you got a mint in your mouth? I can smell mints while you're talking."

"Go and line up outside with the other children," I said firmly as I pushed my after-dinner mint to the side of my mouth. "And make sure you stand quietly!"

I had to wait a while to compose myself before I could call them in to begin the afternoon session!

A lot can be learned just by watching children—the way they play and interact with others, what they do when they think they are on their own, their reactions to different situations—and many tell-tale signs are given as to the characters they will become. I often thought of the children in my class when our house was invaded by the youngsters from the youth group, or the youth gangs who often hung out with us. I knew the parents of the young people in the church group, but the gangs were an unknown entity. Many had left home because they couldn't get on with their parents, and some were on the streets, while others "sofa surfed" with friends. Many of them weren't so many years older than the children I taught, and I wondered about the influences that had brought them to the place they found themselves in. Some were rough and well-versed in the ways of the world, but others seemed young and vulnerable. I remember one young girl from Manchester, with her long skirts and fringed jackets, who had such a sweet demeanour. She had left home to live rough on the streets with a disreputable young lad. Drink, drugs, and violence were their way of life, but as we spent time with them, talking and listening to them, we discovered the characters they really were … or wanted to be. They seemed to love being included in the family and got on famously with our children, although we were careful not to leave them unsupervised.

One night, John offered one young man a bed for the night because of some difficulty he found himself in, forgetting that he was on night shift at the airport. It was a good job I insisted that John take the night off and stay home, because we later realised that the lad had a knife in his haversack.

Oh, the influences that steer and guide our lives! Although I have been a teacher for many years, I am of the opinion that the greatest influences are found outside the classroom as we learn to handle the building bricks of life itself. I remember answering a question in the General Paper of my A Levels, asking which was the greatest factor affecting growth and development of character: heredity or environment. It's certain that we pass things on to our children from our gene pools, but I believe the environment in which we nurture our children has a tremendous effect on the people they become.

At this stage of our family, some of the children were ready to fly the nest, while the others would follow in quick succession. At such a crossroads, they had to decide what subjects they wanted to continue studying, what careers they wanted to choose, and where they wanted to go to pursue their choices. They all flew in different directions, but they all chose caring professions, and they all became caring people.

Let's jump the nest and follow them as they pursue their different ways. Fasten your seat belts—it may sometimes be a bumpy ride. Let's go!

CHAPTER SIXTEEN

A Necklace of Diamonds

Whenever the family gets together, a common refrain is always heard: "The very best times we had were when we cousins were all together." It didn't matter where they were, be it in the house, garden, up the hills, on holiday, travelling in car or caravan— wherever it was, they were happy in each other's company. So I shall give this chapter over to them, to let them tell me something of their own stories. And as they tell, I'll thread them together into a necklace of diamonds, for that indeed is what they have turned out to be.

***

I remember the last Sunday before Cathy left home, and I prayed for her as I watched her make her way down the church to take communion. I asked that God would guide and protect her as she began to journey on her own, and looking back, I think he's done a remarkable job.

She left in September of 1979 to start her nurse's training in St. Helier, Jersey. People used to ask me why she had chosen to go all the way to Jersey, and I used to reply, "Because she's got the common sense to make such a good choice." But it turned out that she hadn't just made a random choice. Apparently, she made about ten applications to various training hospitals, and prayed that the right one would respond. Out of all the hospitals she wrote to, only one responded, and that was Jersey. So her choice was made easy, and she went through the one open door. It seems that the choice was made for her.

John took her to the airport, and while they waited in the departure lounge, he bought her a clock cube so that she wouldn't be late for her classes. A lady stopped to offer words of encouragement, because she was in tears at the thought of leaving and flying so far away: "Don't worry, dear; flying's quite safe these days."

She found herself on the first floor of the Nurses' Home accommodation, in a sparsely furnished and basic little room. That first evening, she was invited to go to the pub by a group of student nurses along her corridor, but she refused, choosing instead to stay and unpack. Another student had also elected to stay in her room that night, and later the two met up along the corridor and introduced themselves. Her name was Ann, and the two became the very best of friends throughout their stay in Jersey. In fact, we became quite friendly with Ann's family, who lived in Cumbria, and went to visit them on one occasion. (That stands out in my memory as the first time I ever drove on the motorway!)

John and I visited Cathy about six weeks after her arrival there to see where she was living and how she was coping, and she did a tour of the lovely island with us. John returned to the island just before Christmas that first year. We reckoned that she might be homesick, having her first Christmas away from home. John stayed in a B&B, and late one evening, he and Cathy undertook a mysterious sortie, visiting places I know not but returning with a familiar object over their shoulders: a large tree branch! It was hung and secured in her room, and a delightful time was spent as they decorated it, hanging cascades of baubles and glitter, ornaments, and tinsel over every available surface. John's special Christmas branch had made its debut in Jersey, much to the envy and admiration of the other students.

Cathy and Ann each had a 25cc moped to take them around the island on their days off. They became familiar with the coastal route, with its inlets and bays, and explored the hidden coves and unspoiled beaches. The little moped was replaced at some point by a humble bicycle because Cathy had somehow managed to crash the moped. She gives no details—nor did I ask for any, choosing to remain ignorant of the facts that are now shrouded in the mists of time! A year later, both girls moved out of the Nurses' Home to rent rooms in one of the local B&Bs, and it was around that time that she remembers being shocked at the news of John Lennon's death. A much happier memory was seeing the filming of *Bergerac*, with the celebrated John Nettles taking the lead.

In her second year, she joined me on a trip to Israel with Roy, Eileen, and cousins John, Karen, and Julia. My John had chosen not to go, so he stayed home with Lesley and David. Many marvellous experiences stay in the memory from that trip. We visited Jerusalem, Bethlehem, and Jericho, but Cathy's favourite things were the trip to Masada, with its fascinating story of the siege that was held there, and swimming in the Dead Sea, noticing the gun patrol boats in the distance. One of my favourite moments was breaking bread on the shores of Galilee, with the water gently lapping at our feet.

On the successful completion of her training, Cathy decided to stay in Jersey and joined a nursing agency who allocated various jobs on different parts of the island. One of the jobs was working for a Mrs. C. and her husband, the Colonel, who took a liking to her and engaged her full-time. The Colonel and his wife lived in a beautiful bungalow with an extensive landscaped garden. So that Cathy could take the best care of Mrs. C., they offered her their car to journey back and forth on a daily basis. Days followed a regular pattern: coffee was served by the maid, Nancy, at 10:00 a.m., martinis at 1:00 p.m., and cucumber sandwiches (no doubt minus the crusts) at 3:00 p.m. The main meal was in the evening, after Cathy had left to return to her lodgings. This interlude lasted approximately six months but was brought to an end when Mrs. C. suffered another stroke. She was taken into hospital and consequently into care, after which time Cathy lost touch with the family.

It seems strange that even though she wasn't in the habit of drinking alcohol, she met Richard, her husband to be, in a pub. Apparently, she enjoyed playing bar billiards and was quite good at the game. It was during one of her billiards sessions that she met him. At the time, Richard was an assistant chef at the Chelsea Hotel and used to join the group of nurses over the billiard table with his friends. Their relationship developed from opponent to buddy to companion when they started to date and go out as a couple.

When the relationship became serious and marriage was on the horizon, they both decided to come home to England. They both stayed at Mosslands for a while before Richard went to stay at Steve and Chris's until they were married. Once again, Biddulph Road was the chosen wedding venue, with the reception meal at Moody

Hall in Congleton, followed by a honeymoon in our friend Peter's cottage in Norfolk. Cathy took up a nursing post at Congleton War Memorial Hospital, while Richard had a job at Morley's Mill, and they made their first home at Severan Close, Biddulph.

Their first baby, Michael, was born in 1988, with Emma Jane following in 1992. Cathy was hospitalised for several months during her third pregnancy because of persistent problems with ovarian cysts, and Ben's birth was difficult for both mum and baby. Fortunately, all was well in the end, and Cathy and Richard's family was complete— that is, until the grandchildren started to arrive. To date, Michael has two delightful little girls, Emily and Charlotte, while Emma and her husband, Aaron, have a wonderful little boy named Leo. Who knows what names will still be added to the list? Ben is still at home, but no doubt he will be adding names to the family lists in the not-too-distant future.

Over later years, Cathy has become really involved in the church life of St. Lawrence, in Biddulph. She spent two years studying for her Bishop's Certificate, which was a precursor to her Lay Readers course, then spent three years in getting her post-graduate certificate for Leadership and Renewal at Cliff College. She was awarded her certification for Lay Readership at a wonderful ceremony in Lichfield Cathedral, led by the bishop. She now leads and preaches on a regular basis in her church and frequently officiates at funerals.

But apart from that, Cathy is a wonderful carer, not only to the church congregation, but to anyone, at any time, who needs help. She is definitely one of my main supports and encouragers. The little girl born in the sunshine and raised in the rain has yielded a bountiful harvest not only in her own life, but in the lives of all who are privileged to know her.

***

Isn't it amazing how the course of our lives hangs on the slender thread of choices made and risks taken. One decision, even a conversation, can become a pivotal crossroad that determines our future. So it was with cousin John! He claims no particular aptitude or even interest in engineering or transport, but because his Uncle Clive was connected to the British Road Service, it was suggested that John should start training as an apprentice mechanic. He began his HGV apprenticeship in Coventry, and when the family moved to Milton Keynes, he continued in the same trade. After working with nuts and bolts for some time, he chose to take a sideways step, moving away from just the mechanical side of things into sales and marketing, first with Scania and then with DAF trucks.

John claims that he has only ever had one ambition in life, and that was to be self-employed so that he could be independent and the master of his own destiny. That ambition has definitely been realised, as John has been a self-employed truck dealer for the past twenty-five years.

I smile as John emphasises the point that he struggles with authority, and my mind wings back over the years to the time that John was a pupil at Woodcocks' Well School. Apparently, he and some friends had made their way after school to play in the churchyard of St. Luke's Church, which stands opposite to the school building. I don't know if it was one of the winged angels that sat atop one of the gravestones, but something had caught their eye as a great target for throwing practice. I can imagine them collecting their little piles of stones and taking turns to aim. "Go on, John," I can hear them say. "See if you can get its nose!" Someone, perhaps a shocked minister or the sexton, discovered the little band, and they were speedily sent packing, and the head was informed of the sacrilegious goings on.

Imagine the embarrassment of Roy (the local pastor) and Eileen as they were called into the school for an audience with the headmaster!

I don't think that was John's first brush with authority, and it certainly wouldn't be the last, but I imagine it has stayed finely-etched in Roy's mind as he, a minister, had to sit and listen to the report of his son's desecration of church property. John lays no claims to many gifts or talents, except for one. He claims that he has talked his way through life—that he has "the gift of the gab"—and I do pause to wonder if that was one of the occasions when he had to put it to use!

That very same gift came in useful when he spotted a pretty young girl in the church congregation and began to woo her. Nicola was several years younger than John, but he was not deterred, and he was determined that she was the girl for him. His persistence paid off and came to fruition when, at the respective ages of twenty-four and eighteen, they were married. They were together for fifteen years and had two lovely children, Connor and Casey. Connor not only looks like John, but he too carves his own unconventional channel through life, while Casey looks like her mum and is as pretty as a picture.

John describes the next chapter of his life as a roller coaster, with "big ups and big downs." His business fell on hard times, and he had to start to rebuild all over again, and then his marriage came to an end. But better times were to come. There was a pot of gold at the end of this rainbow, and that pot of gold came in the form of a lovely young girl called Lou who, after a time of courtship, became John's wife. They went on to have two children, Gracie and Albert.

John becomes philosophical as he comments on marriage: "The most important thing," he says, "is that you are compatible with each other. It's even more important than love. You need to 'get' each other. And Lou 'gets' me!" He continues, saying, "Lou is the best thing that's happened to me. Not a day goes by without us laughing together about something. For thirty-one years there have been children in my house—first Connor and Casey, and now Gracie and Albert, and I love it."

Commenting on how important his Christian upbringing was, he said it was "foundational," and it had to become not something passed down from his parents, but a personal experience.

John has had another passion in his life that has been there since he was ten years old: football! He's a great football supporter, but not of just any old team! It struck me as he chatted that if he was split open, like a stick of rock, instead of writing entwined down the centre, John would have a claret and blue scarf in the middle of his being. He's an ardent Aston Villa supporter. A Chosen One!

But as I listen to him, one quality or passion evidences itself more than any other: he's a family man. He loves tracking down his family roots from long ago; he loves revisiting and reminiscing haunts and tales of yesteryears. He loves sitting round with family and digging up past memories and retelling old tales. That's why his heart lifts as he returns home at the end of the day and rounds the corner of their street to see Lou's car sitting in front of their door: Lou and the kids are home! That's why the end of summer days finds him in his allotment, across from their house, sitting on an old garden chair with a cuppa in his hand and a cigar in his mouth. The day is at an end, the family's home; he's complete!

***

Right from an early age, Sally has always been a wonderful storyteller. Every night as they were growing up, with all the bedtime routines complete and the bedroom door closed on the outside world, the bedroom would become the "Land of Make Believe." She would bewitch the others as she began to weave her tales of imagination and mystery, creating colourful characters and events that would often stretch over many nights. So vivid were her creations that on occasions, Lesley would be terrified and fly downstairs for reassurance, whereupon the story time would be brought to an end for that evening, with the bedroom door left open and a light on the landing.

When she reached the Sixth Form and was ready to make her career choices, her English teacher pleaded with her to go to university and study English. But Sally had set her heart on nursing, reckoning that she could still pursue her love of books and stories and storytelling along the way.

Consequently, in 1980, she successfully applied to the Manchester Royal Infirmary to start her nurse's training. The car was loaded up with cases and various belongings, and John and I drove her to the nurses' lodgings, which would be her home for the next year or so. It was a typical box-like student's room, bare and plain and unattractive, but as we were leaving, Sally said, "Tell Nelly-Bun (Lesley) that it's just like Anne of Green Gables' bedroom!" We had left Lesley sobbing over Sally's departure, and Sally wanted to send her reassurance that she was going to be fine. After all, isn't everything just fine in Avonlea?

Sally settled well into her new surroundings and made two really good friends: Evelyn, who became her flat mate, and Cath Latham, who would be instrumental in determining the next years of Sally's life. Evelyn was a hilarious character who brought much fun and laughter into their relationship, but Cath was responsible for introducing Sally to her prospective husband-to-be. Cath was going out with Pete Latham, and when she introduced Sally to Pete's brother, Tony, they clicked immediately, and so a relationship was begun that would grow steadily over the next few years.

Like Cathy, Sally had a 125cc motorbike to enable her to journey to and fro, and she would regularly turn up at Mosslands, clad in her leathers and crash helmet, to spend the weekend with us, much to Lesley's delight. During these flying visits, she would regale us with hilarious tales of exploits that had happened to both her and her friend Evelyn. I think they were well known to the police for constantly reporting their bikes stolen (before the motorbike arrived on the scene) when in fact they had left them somewhere—in front of a shop, or in the hospital parking lot.

Sally remembers being sent to the theatre for a "long weight," which she thought was a piece of equipment. She was told to sit on a chair outside the theatre, and she waited there for at least an hour before somebody took pity on her and her *long wait* and sent her back to the ward. I suppose all newbies and probationers are treated in a similar way, regardless of their profession!

When Cathy returned home from Jersey with Richard and made arrangements for her wedding, she asked Sally, Lesley, and young Joanne, the daughter of Chris and Steve, to be her bridesmaids. Sally came home with Tony for the grand day, and when they were on their way back to Manchester, Tony asked her to marry him. So another McLellan wedding was planned for the not so distant future. Yet again, Biddulph Road hosted the wedding, and a lovely reception took place at Holly Lodge Hotel in Holmes Chapel, with a caravan holiday in Wales to follow. Evelyn was of course invited to the wedding but, true to style, went to the wrong church and hitched a lift in the wedding car, arriving at the same time as John and bride Sally!

When we looked at the wedding photographs, we spotted that Gussy had managed to worm her way, unnoticed, into quite a few of them, obviously determined not to be overlooked on such an auspicious occasion. I don't know if it was spite, but when Sally and Tony were on honeymoon, Gussy discovered the tiara among the wedding clothes that Sally had left at our house, and she demolished it. "That's what I think of that!" seemed to be her comment on the whole affair.

When Sally qualified as a nurse, she decided to buy her own little house and settle in Manchester, as she'd grown to love the city and the hustle and bustle of life there. So when she and Tony married, they already had a home in which to set up family life. Sally became pregnant in that first year of marriage, and we were all hugely excited when she discovered she was having twins, but devastated when she lost one of the babies. Daniel John, strong and healthy, and with a wonderful cap of red hair, was born in 1987, much to everyone's great relief and joy! They moved to Burnage (still in Manchester) in 1988, and Jenny arrived a year later with her shock of golden curls. Laura and Sophie were to follow over the next seven years, after which Sally's lovely family was complete.

In 2001, she decided to move into Biddulph, buying a house across the road from Cathy and Richard, while at the same time she made the move from working in hospitals to care homes. A very clever career move as it turned out to be! She studied and took Open University courses, majoring in dementia care. Taking an overview, Sally is somewhat of an enigma, a person of many facets (like a diamond!), and a character of many qualities. She ranges from a slightly ditzy blonde, to a fabulous homemaker, to a highly quali-fied professional.

As a homemaker she is second to none, as I discovered when Cathy, Lesley, and I recently spent a weekend with her when she was staying in Wiltshire. Flowers by the bedsides, chocolates on the pillows, trays of tea at regular intervals served in the finest bone china , fabulous roast dinners, plumped up cushions on the chairs, and slippers by the fire. She is the complete hostess!

Professionally, she has taken over care homes on the brink of closure and elevated them to an OFSTED standard of excellence. She is nationally acknowledged to be a leader in dementia care and training and has recently commissioned a new home from its foundations to its completion, hired the staff, installed the training programmes, and awaits its grand opening in a week's time from my writing this.

But though she has received accolades and prestigious awards for her professional achievements, those who know her know her as Sally the homemaker, the mum who adores her four children and her four grandchildren: Alex, Dominic, Gracie, and Reuben. The mum and gran who is never so happy as when she has them all over for a sleepover, when they all listen to her stories as she cuddles them in her big bed, or when she's in the kitchen with her apron on and all the family comes round to enjoy her cordon bleu roast dinners and fabulous puddings, and the laden table has to be extended to accommodate as many as possible to sit around it.

All in all, the little girl whose grandma used to brush her hair, "golden as a sheaf of corn," has achieved many things. But in Sally's book, the finest is her role as Mum and Nanny.

***

Two books changed the course of Lesley's life: *The Cross and the Switchblade*, and *Run Baby Run*, by David Wilkerson and Nikki Cruz respectively, in which they told of their work with gangs of young people on the streets of New York. Previously, she had always wanted to be a teacher and follow in my footsteps, but she was captivated by the stories of danger and adventure and decided she wanted to work with young offenders as a social worker.

It was during this time in between high school and university that she made another major life-changing decision. She decided to go down to London to take part in a six-week course on evangelism at Ichthus Christian Centre. It was on this course that she met a handsome young Canadian by the name of David Wiebe, and when the course was finished and David returned home, they began to correspond.

Before making an application to Hatfield Poly (later renamed as the University of North London) to study social work, she was given the opportunity to take a year out of her studies and go to Pakistan as a nanny for a wealthy couple, Anwar and Anita, and their three children. "Don't bring any clothes; you don't need luggage," they told her. "We'll buy you a new wardrobe when you arrive!" It was a massive undertaking at the tender age of eighteen, to fly across the world and live with people she didn't know, and we were all really sad to say goodbye at the airport, knowing that if everything went as planned, she would be gone for a year.

She arrived in sweltering heat (forty degrees Fahrenheit) after a long journey and was delayed through customs when one of the officials tried to steal her passport. Fortunately, a senior supervisor intervened, and Lesley made her way out of the airport, thankful that Anita was there to meet her, and glad she didn't have to collect any suitcases. Anita led her to a chauffeur-driven, hugely impressive car, and she gratefully sank into the air-conditioned interior, trying to catch a glimpse of a new continent through the darkened windows as they sped along the busy roads.

Their destination was a huge villa within a gated compound, the iron gates automatically sliding open for the car to pass through, and

Anita and Lesley made their way inside the cool, capacious entrance hall. The villa consisted of three distinct blocks, linked by corridors. One block was for the three children, one for Anwar and Anita, while Lesley was given the complete run of the third, which contained everything she could possibly want.

Anwar was the organizer of all the sports equipment for the Pakistani Cricket team and frequently hosted Imran Khan and his English wife, who was friends with Princess Diana. Over the coming months, Lesley saw many wonderful things and visited many places, including the Taj Mahal, Peshawar, and other well-known landmarks. She was given tea by the soldiers on the Afghanistan border guarding the Khyber Pass. These fully armed soldiers were nomadic and lived in tents. They were known as the "beautiful people," tall with startling blue eyes.

She remembers another memorable experience when she was left in charge of villa, children, and servants while Anwar and Anita went away on a visit. As soon as the couple had taken their leave, the servants took total advantage of the situation; they didn't turn up for work, didn't do their jobs, didn't obey any instructions from Lesley at all. She was left to cook and clean and look after the children … but worse was still to come. Anita sent word that an important visitor was due to arrive, and Lesley was to entertain him and cook a meal for him. The visitor turned out to be the Ambassador of Denmark, who arrived with all his entourage. Lesley was overwhelmed, but the Ambassador was the nicest man, courteous and interested in all things English, and they ate together and chatted throughout his stay. Some time after she arrived back home to England, a large parcel arrived from Denmark. It was from the Ambassador himself and was full of Danish food and delicacies in appreciation of the wonderful way she had entertained him on his visit to the villa.

After such an extraordinary year out, life in the UK must have seemed very boring as Lesley prepared to start her four-year university course for social work. Before leaving for university, she worked for a while at a residential school for juvenile offenders to gain a little experience and decided to change from probation work to family-based social work.

Lesley left home after Ichthus to begin her studies at Hatfield. She lived with university friends over the next three years, after which she went to board with Roy and Eileen for the last twelve months before taking her finals. She had passed her driving test at this point and had become the proud owner of a dilapidated old "banger," which made many trips up and down the M6 as she came home to visit for weekends.

In between the third and final year, David phoned and invited her to visit him in Canada, to be part of a team at a children's summer camp together. Because of John's staff privileges at Manchester Airport, he was able to get her a ticket for £20, and off she went on her travels again, this time to British Columbia, Canada. "East is East, but West is best" must be a true saying, because when she returned from Canada, she was wearing an engagement ring on her finger, and a lifelong partnership had begun with David, the "handsome young Canadian!"

During the last year of her studies, she travelled to and fro across the Atlantic, making six trips in the twelve months. So regular a traveller was she that she aroused the suspicion of the Canadian customs officers, who hauled her into their offices on one of her journeys, suspecting her of drug trafficking.

As soon as her four-year course at Hatfield was successfully completed and she had obtained her degree in Social Work, David flew over to England, and John and I finally met him—two weeks before they were married!

It was a low-cost wedding, but nevertheless beautiful. Lesley wore Sally's dress and didn't even plan on having a wedding cake, deciding it wasn't necessary. Karen stepped in and gave her the top layer of her wedding cake, which she had planned to save to celebrate the birth of her first baby, according to tradition. After a lovely reception in a Wilmslow Hotel, they disappeared for a honeymoon in Cornwall to feast on cream teas and cornish pasties ... and put on several pounds in weight! And then they left to begin their married life in Canada in 1987!

That first year was a difficult one, and Lesley found it hard. Canada wasn't just one of her travel destinations; she now had to hang her travelling boots up for the foreseeable future. This was her new home, and she was dreadfully homesick for England. They had an apartment in a city called New Westminster, and Lesley spent many hours alone, as David worked shifts. John and I visited in the first month, as did two other friends, Gordon and Julie, and gradually, as the weeks ticked by, she began to settle.

Starting work as a social worker in one of the city children's homes filled her empty days, and bit by bit she began to find her way around, and things became more familiar. Although the road and traffic systems were different from the UK, Lesley passed the Canadian driving test and drove a bus—often filled with children belonging to the children's home.

It was to be three more years before they came back to visit the UK, and that was to be a bittersweet experience that I will touch on later. Upon returning to Canada after that visit, the promise of great joy awaited them as they discovered that Lesley was pregnant. Erin Mae made her appearance in August 1991, followed by Megan

Elizabeth three years later, and Joshua John in 1997. One would have thought that the family was complete, but no, in 2006, the whole family travelled to Ethiopia, where two delightful siblings awaited them: Ayana Kalkidan, born in 2004, and her baby brother, Moses Ermias, born in 2006, were adopted into the Wiebe family with great rejoicing. Now the family was well and truly complete!

But "them boots were made for walkin'," and this time all the family were going to start journeying. Many places, many destinations, many sights—until the voice of Africa began once more to call, and the family pulled up sticks and left Canada in 2009 to begin work in South Africa, then Uganda, before eventually landing in Zimbabwe.

There a huge work was undertaken to come alongside local organisations to work with orphans and vulnerable children in the surrounding areas. This work has since grown and been responsible for nurturing and nourishing families, for sponsoring and educating children, and for saving many lives. The family returned to Canada in 2014.

I hesitate here, pen suspended in mid-air, as I am loath to leave Lesley and her family's story in the suburbs of Vancouver. I am convinced that the blue skies and red dirt roads have made an indelible impression upon the hearts of Lesley and David, and possibly other family members. Only God knows when the call will come; only God knows when the times are ready, so I'll leave it with him. In the words of the psalmist: "But I trust in you, O Lord. I say, 'You are my God. My times are in your hands.'"

**

Before I launch into cousin Karen's teenage years and the career choices she made, I want to reflect on a couple of significant things from her childhood that give a preview of the person she was going to be in later life.

I think that the position children find themselves in in a family can have an influence on their characters, and Karen was a middle child. She always had an older brother to look up to or try to keep up with, and this probably consolidated the fact that she was a tomboy. She often played with John and his friends and was determined she wouldn't be left behind or outdone in any of the games or activities they took part in. Living as they did on Mow Cop—virtually on the summit of Mow Cop—rock climbing became one of their main activities and the catalyst for many challenges and dares. Being a tomboy myself in childhood, I identify with how she felt: no rock would be too sheer to climb, no toe-hold too small to cling onto, no gap too wide to jump, no challenge too difficult to accept. Even the fact that the rock face disappeared at one point in a sheer drop into what was known locally as the "sugar well" didn't daunt them, and they became as daring and sure-footed as mountain goats. Those rock faces and hair-raising drops became a training ground for the competitive young lady Karen was growing into.

As Roy reminisces about his children, he remembers Karen as "a collector of all things small." Her pockets were always full of bits and bobs of things: buttons and string, pebbles and shells, bits of broken pot or shiny marbles. She treasured each little finding, and when her pockets were bulging, she would find "safe" places to hide them, one of the favourite places being underneath her pillow or stuffed into her dolls' pram when she was smaller. I smile as I write, my mind going to a book I read many years ago by the wonderful author Elizabeth Goudge. In her book, *Scent of Water*, she describes the visit of a little girl named Mary to see her grandmother. While visiting, she made a wonderful discovery: a glass display dome full of "small things"—miniature treasures, "fairy things of silver and gold, jade, pinchbeck, glass, ebony and ivory, all so small that only the eyes of a child could fully perceive their glory." Karen no longer collects bits and bobs, but she is still a treasurer of small things in the form of the many young children in her care, both in her professional and family life.

When Karen was sixteen or seventeen, her family moved to Coventry, where she took a job in a travel agency. It was at this time that she also met a young man, Steve Edwards, who was to play a major part in her future. When the family relocated to Milton Keynes, the travel agency transferred her to one of their branches there. When she moved, Steve also decided to chance his luck and follow her, staying with her brother, John. It was a move that bore fruit, because the courtship continued, and on a cold, snowy day in 1985, they were married. It was so cold, she remembers that the guests were huddled in thick coats and scarves, the gathering resembling a football crowd rather than a church congregation. The only concession she herself made for the cold was to wear thermal insoles in her shoes to ward off frostbite in her toes!

After the wedding, they stayed in Milton Keynes, and two years later, Emily was born, bringing much delight. Two years afterwards, the joy was doubled when, on Karen's birthday, into the world came Lucy in 1989, and the little family was wonderfully complete.

It was a little family that was about to undergo seismic changes, though, as Steve decided to become a teacher and, after much deliberation, left Milton Keynes to start his training at Sheffield University. Karen and her two little girls went to stay for three months with Roy and Eileen, who had since moved from Milton Keynes up to Congleton, before following Steve and setting up home in Heeley, Sheffield. Greater and more traumatic events were to follow, because when Emily was four and just starting school, Steve decided to leave the family to plough his own furrow.

It is said that every cloud has a silver lining, and this family break up, in spite of the pain, was the catalyst that Karen needed to fulfil an almost subconscious desire to continue her own education. Her thirtieth birthday found her entrenched in her own studies at university, where she too was training to be a teacher, confounding her own self-doubts as to her ability, or lack of it!

Her first teaching job after successfully completing her training was in a difficult catchment area. She then moved on to teach in a multicultural school in the city centre. "I'm still there," she says, "and I absolutely love it!"

The little girl who picked up things that nobody else wanted and treasured them has now become a fine teacher, a champion of special needs children, a supporter of the underprivileged, *and* a proud grandma! Emily, married to Sami, is now mum to Maria, Owain, and Noor, while Lucy has three lovely boys: Khalid, Kai, and Junior.

But mention has to be made of yet another achievement! Her love of a challenge and her competitive streak that were honed on the rock face at Mow Cop now find fulfilment on the running track. She loves to run and compete in races, even completing a gruelling London Marathon in April of 2016. During her training, she sustained an injury and had to attend a running rehabilitation training centre, where she had to sit with her feet in bags of ice—no thermal insoles allowed this time! But regardless, she determined her way through, continued her running, entered the race, and proudly picked up her medal. In all sorts of ways, and against the odds, Karen is a winner!

***

Being the youngest of the family, Julia was used to all the love and attention that goes with being "the baby," loved and adored by all. As a result, she was confident, outgoing, and sociable, and as she grew up, she was extremely popular—a great member of any social group. She always loved singing and music, and in her early teens began to take an interest in playing the piano. She had a few lessons but soon discovered that she had the wonderful ability to play by ear. Because of this innate musicality, she soon became a lovely pianist, often leading worship in church services and youth meetings. Most young people have no idea what they want to do when they leave school, but Julia was in no doubt: she wanted to work with children. They were a magnet to her. In Sunday School, church, or youth group, not only was she attracted to children, but they were attracted to her, a veritable Pied Piper. They were probably drawn to her because of her sunny disposition and outgoing friendliness.

So as soon as it was time for her to make decisions concerning her career, she elected to begin training as a nursery supervisor, attending college to take her N.N.E.B. After spending a few months as a nanny for her Auntie Sylvia, Julia found a position in the Early Learning Centre as an assistant manager in the creche before accepting a job working in the nursery attached to a school, where she was in charge of the four to five age group, which she loved. Not only did she love the children, and the age group, but she loved school life in general, fitting into the routines and schedules like a hand in a glove, becoming an invaluable member of the school staff.

Apart from her musical ability and gregarious nature, Julia has a special quality, a distinct single-mindedness! From an early age, she knew what she wanted, so her decisions have been straightforward, uncluttered by distractions, and unhindered by indecision. This same quality was evident when she met a charming young man called

David. She was only sixteen when she met him, but they met often in church and social gatherings, and the friendship grew and matured.

At this time, Roy and many other families, including the young people, were joining together to build and establish the "Christian Centre" in Milton Keynes. Every opportunity was taken not only to labour on and build the church, but also to fund it. Young and old alike felt a responsibility to contribute in every way to seeing the vision of a Church Centre realised. At this time, Julia had a Saturday morning job in a Christian bookshop, and though she earned very little, she too made her contribution to the church funds.

I should imagine that even before the church doors opened, the congregation were in complete unity of heart and mind, because they had worked so hard together toward a common goal. It was in such an environment that David and Julia's friendship grew and blossomed, coming to fruition when they married in the Centre when Julia was twenty years old, and David nineteen.

Although the occasion was tinged with sadness because David's dad had recently died, it was a wonderful day of celebration. The weather was clement, the bride was beautiful on the arm of her smart groom, and the reception that followed in the Wayfarer at Willen Lake was splendid. They honeymooned in Tenby, Pembrokeshire, a Welsh seaside coastal town, before returning to Milton Keynes to begin married life together.

Here Julia makes special mention of the importance of making the right choice of a partner, and of having a good foundation on which to build a secure family. It was into this secure base that, over the course of the next seven years, three bonny boys were born. Ben made his appearance first in 1990, Jack two years later, in 1992, with Tom following in 1994.

Julia now turned her attention to building her family, making her house into a home, and putting all her energy into being a great mum. She chose not to return to work while her boys were young, regarding them as more important than any financial contribution she could make.

While David spent his working days as a Project Manager, dealing with finance at Canary Wharf, Julia made a celebration of home and family life. Birthdays and Christmas time would find the place festooned with seasonal decor, while the rafters would ring with fun and noise when all the cousins congregated to join in the festivities. Christmas especially held a special place in Julia's heart, and consequently in that of the whole family.

One of her boys mentioned to me that she has the innate ability to make people feel at home, and I can vouch for that, as I have personally experienced that open-armed welcome when I've had the privilege of visiting the family.

Julia and David stayed happily in Milton Keynes until the boys had flown and started to find their own way in life. Jack is now married to Luisa, while Ben is in a relationship with a young lady named Davi, and Tom is building a career as an engineer with Tesla.

End of story, one would have thought—but absolutely not! In 2017, when Julia was fifty years old, she and David moved to Shropshire, near North Wales, renting a large house in Ellesmere, before deciding to make their stay permanent and moving into a lovely property on St. John's Hill. Same couple, family flown, new beginnings! How exciting!

I pause here because I'm going to hand over to Jack, to allow him to comment on his take on the mum and homemaker that Julia has become over the years. Here's Jack:

"My mum, more than anything, loves family time, especially at Christmas. Christmas is a special time for every family, and of course is a time when we are thankful for what God has provided. Growing up, my mum has always had that magic touch of being able to make us feel at home. At Christmas, and all through the year, she makes the home come alive with seasonal flowers and decorations. She has always been creative like that! I will always remember those family gatherings, when all the cousins would come together in the Gooderham household. She loves Christmas so much, as the time for giving and sharing. She even used to watch the Christmas channel all year round (she may still do). It's a tradition we will all continue with our future children, and the magic of 'do you believe' will always be alive."

***

After leaving school, David joined a Youth Training Scheme in Sandbach. I don't know if he was aiming to follow in his father's footsteps, but he initially decided to study engineering, before very quickly changing his mind and enrolling on the Office Course. This wasn't a random choice. There was a method to his madness, because his eye had alighted upon young Tina, a lovely young brunette who was enrolled on the Secretarial Course. It may have been a casual "Shall we meet in the park?" or even a proper date, but it inspired David to conjure up a clever and daring plan. Lesley's then boy-friend, Tim, had left his motorbike in a shed near to our house, and David decided to "borrow" it on the quiet, meet Tina in the park, and then replace it in the shed without anyone knowing.

It was a smooth ride out to Sandbach, but things were soon going to become very bumpy indeed. As David and Tina were chatting, they were spotted by a gang of youths, one of whom also had designs on Tina. When David left the park, they began to chase him off their territory. He ran as fast as he could to where he'd parked his bike, leapt on, and made a rapid exit. Halfway home, a red light signified that the bike had run out of oil, and it chugged the rest of the way home on a wing and a prayer. That hairy scary ride heralded the beginning of a relationship for Dave and Tina, but the death knell of the bike.

I think Dave must have impressed himself with his driving skills, because on completing the YTS, he decided to take up driving as a career, but this time on four wheels. He worked for a short time in Congleton before buying himself a van and driving for another company. At twenty-one, he passed his HGV Class 1 and became a driver at the Co-op, a job that lasted for the next ten years, before he started his own company. During this time, Tina, making the most of her YTS training, had become a legal secretary, working for some time at a bank in Nantwich.

Although David was a very quiet little boy who was quite shy, he has grown up to be fun-loving and gregarious. Like John, he is a passionate football supporter (but a supporter of Manchester United), and he loves attending matches with a group of his friends—especially the away matches, when he will be away from home for the full day. He's also a keen member of a local snooker team and practises every week with another group of friends. Tina says that neither of them like to be the centre of attention, and Dave would say he is still shy, but when the family gets together, we can have the most uproarious times. Sally, with her storytelling, and David with his sense of humour and wit, can set the rafters ringing with merriment.

Lesley remembers a couple of occasions (out of countless examples) when David turned up at a fancy-dress party. The first one was at Lesley's friend Liz's house. After most people had arrived, there was a knock at the door. It was opened to reveal David standing on the doorstep in a white overall, with a large stick in one hand. He was invited into the gathering and asked what he'd come as. He stood up straight, banged the stick on the ground, and said, "Forensics. Special Branch." At which point the whole room fell about laughing. Tina was with him on the second occasion, when they turned up at a party as two crows: black shorts, black t-shirts, black pumps, and bright yellow tights. Lesley remembers Tina looking quite glam, but the sight of David in yellow tights, flapping his arms as if about to take off, still gives her hysterics.

David, at the age of fifty-three, still lives in Mosslands, the same house where he was born. I think he gets very comfortably established and doesn't see the need for change. So it was with his courtship. They had been courting for nine-and-a-half years when Tina, obviously becoming a little impatient, said, "Shall we get engaged soon, then?" Dave reacted well to the "prod," and they went shopping in Hanley to make the necessary purchase of a ring. Christmas Eve, 1993, found them on the top of Mow Cop, overlooking the Cheshire Plain, sparkling with a myriad of lights, where Dave asked Tina if she would marry him.

Such a romantic engagement warranted a suitable follow up, and sure enough, they surprised us all by electing to combine wedding and honeymoon on the tropical island of Jamaica in 1994. Tina was allowed an extra case in which to transport her dress, which was a beautiful confection of lace, beads, and pearls, covering a large skirt with flowing train. They stayed in a hotel, where their room opened out onto the beach, and they were married in the Shaw Park Botanical Gardens. A wedding table with champagne and cake was set out in the gardens, and Tina's brother, Terry, and his wife, Katrina, made up the wedding party. Photographs were taken in the gardens and on the beach, Tina trying to keep her train off the sand.

A fabulous week followed as they shopped in the town, sauntered in the markets, and visited the Blue Mountains and Dunn's River Falls, where they climbed up the waterfall. David was also thrilled to visit Bob Marley's former home and recording studios, and he still enjoys listening to his music while driving around in his car. Snorkelling and swimming and jet-skiing completed a wonderful honeymoon before they returned to Congleton to set up home at Mosslands. They have just celebrated their twenty-fifth wedding anniversary at the time of my writing.

Their son, Kyle, who was born in 1996, has a degree in Accountancy and Marketing at Lancaster University. Alicia, born in 1999, and in a relationship with Ed, currently works at Reginox in Congleton, where she follows a similar course to her mum, doing sales administration and PA work.

Between them, Dave and Tina have produced a lovely family and established a beautiful home. Apart from the odd day off, David gets up early each morning to drive around the country with his delivery job, while Tina has put all her designer skills into creating a lovely family base. Sewing curtains and covers (and fancy-dress costumes for the children when they were in school), decorating rooms and arranging flowers and ornaments, with the ability to put everything in just the right place for maximum effect. When David arrives home—often after popping into the gym—he loves to disappear into the kitchen and concoct the most delicious dishes, which the family enjoy all together around the large dining room table.

But Mosslands, the home that has been in the family for the last three generations, holds a secret high up in the rafters. Somewhere up there, in a corner of some old box or package tucked away in a dusty corner, is a tiny object the size of a thumbnail. A little nutmeg, picked up off the ground in Shawpark Botanical Gardens, hidden in Tina's pocket, and flown thousands of miles to be kept as a memento of a wonderful day of celebration in August 1994, when their story together really began!

***

These are my seven diamonds, strung throughout the course of my life. Real diamonds are graded by four Cs: carat, colour, cut, and clarity. But I grade my special necklace by other criteria. Each one is a caring, honest, reliable, loving, and genuine character, all of them stating that they appreciate the Christian values that have become the foundation and yardstick of their lives. "Special Branches" indeed—straight and true!

CHAPTER SEVENTEEN

When All This is Over

The year 1987 saw the last of the girls fly the nest when Lesley married David Wiebe from British Columbia. Long, painful farewells were thankfully avoided because our car engine was acting up when we drove them to the airport. Keeping the car running while we said our hasty farewells, we dropped them near to the International Departures, and set off on our return journey before the engine cut out.

Now only David remained at home, staying with us during the week and spending weekends at Tina's, where he had his own room, and Tina's mum, Ivy, to cook his meals and do any necessary washing for him. Their relationship was progressing, and David was obviously content with the situation, feeling comfortable at home as well as at Tina's. No wonder he took so long to "pop the question" and needed a nudge from Tina!

Round about this time, my John took the opportunity of an offer for early retirement from the airport. He was beginning to suffer from back problems, so when the opportunity arose to stop working, he took it. The only thing that upset him was that I was still teaching at Knypersley First, and he didn't like the idea that he was retired, and I was still working. "I never intended it to be like this," he used to say, but life often doesn't happen in the way we plan, as we were to discover over the next few years.

When the summer holidays arrived that year, and I finished school, we flew over to visit Lesley and David in British Columbia. We discovered Canada to be a truly beautiful country and visited many breathtaking places. We drove up to Whistler Ski Resort and rode the gondola up the snow-covered, pine-clad mountain slopes, amazed to see a big brown bear and her two cubs lumbering through the snow beneath the gondola. We caught the ferry to Victoria, on Vancouver Island, and explored the island, visiting the beautiful Butchart Gardens. We picnicked in Stanley Park and shopped in Granville Island and Lonsdale Quay. Henry and Agnes, David's parents, prepared the most amazing picnics, veritable feasts, which we enjoyed on the beaches and up the mountain slopes. We met all of David's family and began friendships that would grow throughout the coming years. The three weeks flew by, and we returned home after a memorable holiday, delighted not only with the time we had spent together, but also thrilled to realise that Lesley had found not only a great husband, but also a very good friend and soulmate in David.

Returning home, John spent most of his time creating his pottery in the garden shed, or on the running circuits, training his keen young athletes. If I was home and the weather was nice, we would drive for miles around the countryside. One of our very favourite places was Bakewell, a little Derbyshire town near to Chatsworth, the stately home of the Duke and Duchess of Devonshire. It is reported that the Duke can frequently be seen in the little town, popping into the shops or visiting his local barber. Bakewell, with its world-famous tarts, is a beautiful little place. It's a magnet for visitors who love to amble through the street markets every Monday, or saunter along the banks of the River Derwent that meanders through the town, feeding the many ducks and waterfowl that lazily paddle its waters, awaiting the bread and seeds thrown in by the visitors.

Frequently, John and I wouldn't have a destination in mind. We would climb into the car and set off, driving in whichever direction took our fancy—often ending up in unknown areas but having enjoyed the ride and the beautiful landscape en route. "Stop, stop!" I'd shout, and John would stop the car while I would get out and pick harebells, dog daisies, knapweed, and scabious from the verges and take them home to fill one of John's vases. Such thoughts "fill up my senses," as the song says, as I daydream through yesterday's memories.

Cathy, so like John in many ways, took me on the Bakewell run just recently, and we wandered along an old disused railway track, picking flowers, watching the butterflies and bumble bees, while Pip, my dog, explored the odd rabbit hole and lost herself in the tall grass along the hedge banks.

Back in 1988, John and I also made a trip to the Isle of Wight, where his sister, Jenny, had gone to live. We crossed on the ferry and then drove our car round the lovely rural countryside, stopping whenever the fancy took us—perhaps for tea and cakes at some charming little tea shop, or touring the shops in the seaside villages. The main attraction, however, was exploring the summer residence of Queen Victoria and Prince Albert: Osborne House, with its breathtaking gardens and private beach. Wandering through its grand rooms and imagining the royal princes and princesses, nine in all, playing in the corridors and passages. I should think the little princesses would have had dozens of dolls, because Queen Victoria herself was reputed to have loved her many dolls when she was just a girl.

A couple of years later, I joined a group visiting Oberammergau, Bavaria, in the south of Germany. John didn't want to go, so I went with a group of friends. We travelled by coach through Europe, stopping in various countries along the way, the most spectacular being Austria with its picture postcard scenery and wonderful chalets. But though the journey was great, the destination was definitely the cherry on the cake.

Oberammergau is the home of the world-famous Passion Plays. They began in 1634, when the villagers prayed that if God spared them from the plague that was raging through the continent, they would perform a Passion Play, telling of the Passover and Easter events in the life of Christ, every ten years. Not one villager was lost to the plague, and they have been true to their vow over the centuries; 120 performers from virtually every house in the village take part in the fabulous event, and though it is in German, it is a breathtaking and emotional event from start to finish. It's strange to wander round the shops in the village and be served by "Judas," or spot "Mary" walking down the street. We stayed in the house of the "innkeeper" and his wife, and it seemed that we were actually living the experience ourselves.

After my solo journey to Germany, John and I had one more trip to make together—but that one would be in very different circumstances, a little ways down the road.

Meanwhile, John continued to pursue his running and coaching, as well as his pottery, and life seemed to tick along in its normal pattern ... but not quite. John began to have days when he felt unwell. He would be in pain, with occasional bouts of sickness, and the attacks become more regular.

During this time, I started to walk a lot. I would take the dogs up the old railway, enjoying the scenery, identifying the wildflowers along the hedge banks, occasionally praying, and loving the freedom of just walking alone, lost in my surroundings, in a world of my own. It was during these times that I felt God begin to speak to me. I became engrossed with the Twenty-Third Psalm:

> The Lord is my Shepherd, I shall not want. He makes me lie down in green pastures, He leads me beside still waters, He restores my soul. He guides me in paths of righteousness for his name's sake. Even though I walk through the valley of the shadow of death, I will fear no evil, for you are with me. Your rod and your staff comfort me. You prepare a table for me in the presence of my enemies. You anoint my head with oil - my cup overflows. Surely goodness and mercy shall follow me all the days of my life, and I will dwell in the house of the Lord forever.

(New International Version)

I sensed the comfort and reassurance of knowing that this God of all glory would meet my every need. That he would guide me into pleasant pastures and bring me peace and restoration when I needed it. I skipped over the bit about the valley of the shadow of death, because I felt it didn't relate to me, and went to the rod and the staff. What did that mean? Was I going to be disciplined? The more I pondered and thought about that phrase, the surer I became that the rod was for guidance, and the staff was for food—"the staff of life" always applied to bread. Food to strengthen us. While the "table" spoke again of provision even in difficult times, and the "oil" for the presence and blessing of the Holy Spirit.

Over the many weeks that I mulled over those verses, they became interwoven into my mind and imagination ... an integral part of me. Not only did I know the words off by heart, but I saw all the scenes and pictures in my mind's eye and would return to them at any time of the night or day, whenever my mind was at rest.

During the summer of 1990, John's attacks of pain and sickness happened more frequently. Our concerns turned to real anxiety when he discovered a lump in his stomach, and the doctor made John an appointment for a CT scan, which confirmed our fears when it showed an unidentifiable mass. Another appointment was made, this time for exploratory surgery. The date for the surgery was December 4, and John went to the hospital the day before so that all would be ready for the operation.

I decided to fill my day with as much activity as possible, being told not to ring the hospital until after 6:00 p.m. As it was nearing Christmas, I set about making mince pies—batch after batch after batch throughout the long, long day. Through interminably slow-moving hours, when the fingers on the clock didn't seem to move and time stood still. I rang the hospital as soon as the clock struck 6:00 p.m., and my heart stood still as I was told, "Oh, we can't tell you anything over the phone. Go to see the Sister on duty when you arrive. And are you bringing a family member with you?"

David drove there, and Sally and Roy came with us. I don't know if Cathy had rearranged her shifts, but, amazingly, she was on duty in the ward where John was, and she stayed with him during the night after we left.

Once there, we were given the news: John was terminal, and they gave him just three months to live.

We were on the way home from the hospital that night, David driving, and Roy and Sally in the back seat, all of us stunned into silence. As we came to the Flower Pot pub on the outskirts of the town, I looked up at the sky. Myriads of stars were clustered thickly as far as my eye could see, and it was at that moment that I became aware of a thought that was dominating everything else. It was as though it was written in the stars, striding across the night sky, filling my mind and consciousness: "When all this is over," it declared, "you're going to reap a harvest." I tried to shut it out. I didn't want to know. But still it blazed across my mind like a flashing neon sign.

"When all this is over, you're going to reap a harvest."

The months that followed were a helter skelter of appointments, scans, visits to Christie's, the marvellous cancer hospital in Manchester, chemotherapy, and urgent trips to the hospitals when infections set in and we had to send for the ambulance. I was given a leave of absence from school, where the staff and governors were really supportive and encouraging, so I was able to be at home with John twenty-four-seven. After recovering from his operation, he continued his athletics coaching and pottery, while I continued my walking on a daily basis. As I walked, I found my mind filled with words and phrases that I would string together and rearrange: strands of poetry, descriptions of things I saw around me. When I returned home, I would write them down.

This is one of them:

Faith Notes

Lord, sometimes my days stretch out like grey tracks
Mud underfoot, mist overhead.
Straightened on every hand by the blackness of bare trees.

Hopeless
Shadow-filled
Twilight days.

And then from somewhere deep within, the Spirit song.
Not played with notes of circumstance or outward evidence
But a quiet song of stirring hope.
Faith notes—striding ahead into the murky future and bringing
Certainty—sureness.

And with the awakening of faith
Comes an enhancement of natural sight.
The same bare branches now sport raindrops of crystal,
And tiny, hardly revealed buds herald
Spring growth
New life
Scarlet rose hips quicken the senses
And a solitary birdsong
Soars through the grey mist.

Lord, fill my days with your Spirit song.
Quicken my innermost being with the sure and certain knowledge
That all my paths are known by you.
My life is in your hands.
My hope is sure.

In later years I have tried to capture my thoughts and feelings in poetic form but have never really succeeded in the same way. I have come to realise that that was a cathartic experience for that time, and that set of circumstances, to enable me to make sense of the tumult of my thoughts and emotions. I also wrote a daily diary at the same time, which achieved a similar goal.

It was around that time on one Sunday morning that an ordinary service in New Life Church became, for me, totally extraordinary. I can't remember exactly when it happened in the course of the meeting, but at some point, someone stood up and read out the Twenty-Third Psalm. All the thoughts and meditations that had come to me as I spent hours walking up the old railway came flooding back, and as it was read aloud, the whole scene rolled out before my mind's eye.

I saw the shepherd walking along an old mountain track, rod and staff in his hands. I was walking beside him—his little lamb, staying close by his side. At one point I looked up at his face and asked, "Where is John?" He turned his head, and I saw that John, another little lamb, had been picked up, and the shepherd was carrying him on his shoulders. We came to a bend in the road, and there was a sheepfold. The shepherd unhooked John from around his shoulders, opened the door of the pen, and gently laid John inside the safety of the fold, closing the door behind him. Using his staff, he directed me on down the road and away from the sheep pen. I thought I was totally on my own and without help, but no ... he had placed a lamp in my hand and a mantle around my shoulders. Provision for the onward journey.

It was so vivid to me that I not only knew the outcome of the journey, but I also knew that as we walked through the valley of the shadow of death, there would be no need to fear, because we would have the necessary provisions, even for the darkest parts of the road.

Sometime during the next few months, Lesley and David visited from Canada. We were restricted as to what we could do and how far we could travel in the car, but it was wonderful to have them stay. We talked a lot, pottered about a bit, and drank innumerable pots of tea before a painful parting at the airport brought the wonderful interlude to an end.

During those months, I occupied myself in various ways when I had time to spare. We had a small greenhouse, and I grew salads—lettuce, radish, spring onions, and baby carrots. On my railway walks, I gathered bundles of elderflowers to bring home and soak in clean plastic buckets full of water, sugar, and sparkling lemon juice. The lids were then firmly placed on the buckets, and they were stored away for three weeks in a cool place. At the end of the allotted time, when the lids were lifted and the heads of elderflower were discarded, a beautiful, aromatic scent filled the kitchen. After sieving the liquid, and bottling and cooling it in the fridge, just a mouthful was all that was required to shout "summer" to all the senses.

I even tried my hand at dandelion wine, picking the fresh young flower heads, discarding every trace of greenery, and filling my basket with just the yellow petals. Great care had to be taken to take every little bit of leaf and stem away to avoid a bitter brew, or so I was told, and the job was slow and tedious. I followed all the wine-making processes carefully, but I'm afraid the end result was still a bitter brew, and nobody could drink it—unlike the elderflower cordial that was imbibed at an alarming rate, and much appreciated by young and old alike!

By sheer grit and determination, John continued to do his coaching, his loyal young athletes always ready to work at his side and lend a hand when necessary. Anne, one of his young runners, had obviously shared the situation with her mum in Ireland, and she invited us to go over to stay in her family home for a few days, promising that it would be very relaxing and restful. John expressed an interest in going, so arrangements were made for flights, and travel when we got there. Looking back at the photographs, I really don't know how

John managed to do it, but do it he did. True to her word, Anne and her mum gave us a wonderfully restful few days, lavishing care on us and seeing to John's every need. They were wonderful hostesses, but I know how difficult John found it, and we were both hugely relieved to get home.

In the middle of ever-deepening shadows, a bright light appeared. On August 10, 1991, over in British Columbia, Canada, a new little life joined our family in the form of Erin Mae Wiebe. Wonderful news that lifted our spirits and gladdened our hearts. The doctor advised me to make a short visit over to see her. "You need to have a break," he said, and John agreed with him and urged me to go. The doctor said he would be on call if he was needed. Dave and Cathy (with Sally just an hour away), Roy and Eileen, and a good friend, Alastair, were all at hand, and so with a mixture of trepidation and excitement, I set off. John even insisted on driving me to the airport.

Deuteronomy talks of finding honey in the flinty rock, and that's exactly what baby Erin was to me at that time: a glorious, if brief, sweetness in an extremely hard time. My "Honeypot."

Three wonderful days before the call came: "Jean," said Alastair, "I think you'd better come home."

And so that is what I did. An unbelievably stressful journey landed me back at Mosslands in time for us to say our goodbyes before John quietly slipped away. It was September 2, 1991.

Excerpt of *These Strange Ashes* by Elisabeth Elliot

"It is in our acceptance of what is given that God gives Himself... Each separate experience of individual stripping we may learn to accept as a fragment of the suffering Christ bore when He took it all... This grief, this sorrow, this total loss that empties my hands and breaks my heart, I may, if I will, accept, and by accepting it, I find in my hands something to offer.

And so I give it back to Him, who in mysterious exchange gives Himself to me."[2]

"But what of your promises, Lord?" I asked.

I looked back at the assurances held in the Twenty-Third Psalm: guidance, peace, restoration, provision. Yes, every one of his blessings had accompanied us throughout the recent years—in lavish measure.

What about the promise that had been blazoned across the star-studded night sky? "When all this is over, you're going to reap a harvest." It's only now, more than two decades later, that I realise how amazingly true that was. After John died, I returned to school for two years before taking early retirement. At the end of that time, as one door closed, not just one, but many doors of opportunity flew open: opportunities to minister, support, and encourage mission teams in Taiwan, Hong Kong, China, Singapore, South, North, and West Africa.

I girded my loins, sallied forth, and, with the words of Caleb in Joshua 14 on my lips, "full of zeal I went to take the hill country," claim the promises that God had given me, and start to reap the harvest.

---

2   Elisabeth Elliot, *These Strange Ashes*, (London: Hodder and Stoughton Limited, 1976), 108-109.

Lightning Source UK Ltd.
Milton Keynes UK
UKHW010629140622
404409UK00001B/249